STUDIES ON THE EARLY PAPACY

STUDIES ON THE RACE PLACE

STUDIES ON THE EARLY PAPACY

BY

DOM JOHN CHAPMAN

MONK OF DOWNSIDE ABBEY

KENNIKAT PRESS
Port Washington, N. Y./London

Nihil Obstat
D. Justin McCann, O.S.B.
Censor Congreg.

Imprimatur
W. E. Kelly, O.S.B.
Ab. Præses

Nihil Obstat
Georgius D. Smith, S.T.D., D.D.
Censor Deputatus.

Imprimatur
Edm. Can. Surmont,
Vic. Gen.

Westmonasterii, die 11° Junii, 1928.

STUDIES ON THE EARLY PAPACY

First published in 1928
Reissued in 1971 by Kennikat Press
Library of Congress Catalog Card No: 76-118517
ISBN 0-8046-1139-4

Manufactured by Taylor Publishing Company   Dallas, Texas

CONTENTS

ANALYTICAL SUMMARY

I. The Growth of Patriarchates

Catholic and Gallican views, p. 9. The papal letters, p. 10. Italy governed by the Popes as metropolitans, p. 10. The rest of Western Europe was governed by papal decretals, p. 11. Africa had its own canon law, under papal supervision, p. 12. Eastern Illyricum was administered according to Eastern usage and rite by a papal legate, p. 13. The council of Nicaea on the chief bishoprics, p. 14. Theodosius's decree of reunion with Rome in 380, p. 15. The dispositions approved by the council of Constantinople in 381, p. 17. Why St. Athanasius did not appeal to Rome after his condemnation at the council of Tyre, p. 21. The developments of patriarchates by the councils of Ephesus and Chalcedon, p. 23. Hormisdas accepts four œcumenical councils and five patriarchates, p. 24. The Byzantine theory of five patriarchs stereotyped by Justinian, p. 25.

II. St. Cyprian on the Church

Dr. Koch's book on St. Cyprian, p. 28. He makes St. Peter the first foundation-stone to be laid and not the Rock, p. 29. Or else a temporary Rock, p. 30. St. Peter's primacy according to Koch is priority of time, p. 32. The structure of the passage, *De unit.* 4, is in reality a statement, followed by objections, which are answered, p. 32. Koch's interpretation would be as true of sand as of rock p. 35 *note.* The alternative text of the passage (commonly called " the interpolations ") may well be by Cyprian, p. 36. What *primatus* means in Cyprian, p. 37 *note.* St. Cyprian's practical rather than dogmatic ideas of Church Government, p. 40. Firmilian is more an ecclesiastic, p. 41. Novatianism began as a question of rival Popes, not of heresy, p. 41 *note.* St. Cyprian or Marcianus of Arles, p. 43 *and note.* And on the Spanish appeal to Rome, p. 44. St. Cyprian's view of papal authority, p. 45. St. Jerome, St. Augustine and St. Vincent of Lerins on St. Cyprian, p. 48.

III. St. Athanasius and Pope Julius I

The results of the Nicene council, p. 51. The synods of Tyre and Jerusalem, p. 52. The Eusebians and St. Athanasius's councils both write to Rome, p. 54. The subsequent letter of the Eusebians to Pope Julius, p. 55. The reply of the Pope, p. 57. Socrates and Sozomen on this letter, p. 59. The council of Antioch, p. 60. The council of Sardica meets, p. 62. Its letter to the Pope, p. 63. The canons of Sardica about appeals, p. 65. Fr. Puller's view of them controverted, p. 67.

IV. St. Chrysostom on St. Peter

St. Peter's primacy does not imply that he ordered the apostles about, p. 72. The great volume of St. Chrysostom's writings makes his opinion of St. Peter's position easy to discover, p. 73. His reverence for St. Peter shown in the multiplication of epithets, p. 74. The promise to St. Peter in Matt. xvi, is explained by Chrysostom, p. 77. The commission given in John xxi, 15, is the primacy, not merely the apostleship, p. 79. Chrysostom's view of Luke xxii, 32, p. 84. Chrysostom thinks St. Peter had the right to appoint an apostle, p. 86. The apostolic council, Acts xv, p. 89. St. Peter and St. Paul compared, p. 90. The successors of Peter at Antioch and Rome, p. 95. Chrysostom and the schism between Meletius and Paulinus, *ibid.* St. Peter and Paul in Rome, p. 97. Pope Innocent and St. Chrysostom, p. 98.

V. St. Jerome and Rome

St. Jerome travestied as a Protestant, p. 99. The two passages alleged by anti-Catholic writers, p. 101. A head necessary against divisions, p. 103. St. Jerome on the pride of deacons, p. 106. St. Jerome distinguishes between equality of episcopal order and inequality of episcopal authority and jurisdiction, p. 109. His declarations as to papal authority in letters to Pope Damasus, p. 111. Rome is the Rock, p. 114, the centre of communion, p. 115, Roman faith, p. 116. Bishop Gore's view of Jerome's change of mind, p. 118. St. Jerome on Rome, p. 120. Against bishop John of Jerusalem, p. 122. Against Rufinus, p. 123. Disagreement with St. Augustine, p. 128. St. Marcella at Rome, p. 130. St. Jerome's last days, p. 131.

VI. The Condemnation of Pelagianism

The African Church and Rome, p. 133. Pelagius and Celestius teach heresy, p. 135. Opposed by Augustine and Jerome, p. 136. Pelagius tried at Jerusalem and acquitted at Diospolis, p. 138. Appeal to Pope Innocent by African Councils, p. 140. The replies of Innocent condemning the heresy, p. 146. The views of contemporaries as to Pope Innocent's action, p. 149. St. Augustine's satisfaction, p. 152. "The case is ended" p. 156. The personal guilt of Pelagius and Celestius tried by Pope Zosimus, p. 157. The submission of Celestius to his judgement, p. 159. The Pope defers his acquittal, p. 160. Zosimus is deceived, p. 162. The submission of Pelagius to the See of Peter, p. 164. An African council remonstrates with Zosimus, p. 165. The appeal to him by Paulinus of Milan, p. 166. Further letters of the Pope to Africa, p. 169. The *tractoria* of Zosimus condemning Pelagius in the whole world, p. 171. St. Augustine's account of it, p. 172. What Prosper, Mercator and Possidius say of it, p. 174. St. Augustine's letters to Sixtus and Pope Boniface, p. 178. St. Celestine I and the Semi-Pelagians, p. 182.

VII. Apiarius

Papal legislation and administration do not usually involve the question of papal infallibility in faith and morals, p. 184. The Protestant view of Apiarius, p. 185. His appeal to the Pope accepted because in Africa he had no appeal from his own bishop, p. 186. An African council in consequence grants a right of appeal for clerics to

neighbouring bishops and to African councils, p. 187. The legate
Faustinus sent to Carthage, p. 189. The canons of former African
councils reviewed by a council in his presence, p. 191. The letter of
this council to Pope Boniface, p. 195. Eastern bishops are asked for
authentic copies of the acts of Nicaea, p. 198. The letter of a subsequent council of Carthage to Pope Celestine, p. 200. The confession of
guilt by Apiarius, and the outrageous conduct of Faustinus, p. 202.
The Africans beg the Pope to hear no more appeals from Africa, even
from bishops, p. 203. Appeals of bishops had been common, and had
never been forbidden, p. 205. They occurred later as well, p. 208.

VIII. THE AGE OF JUSTINIAN

The empire at the accession of Justin I, p. 210. The Acacian schism,
p. 211. Justin and Justinian in 519 ask the Pope to send legates for
reunion with Rome, p. 213. The " formula of Hormisdas " sent for
signature by all bishops, *ibid*. No difficulty raised about its claims for
Roman infallibility, p. 216. John I sent to Constantinople, p. 217.
The character of Justinian, p. 218. A letter of John II becomes a
law in the code, p. 219. The emperor's plans for extending Christianity
by wars and persecutions, p. 221. Pope Agapetus visits Constantinople,
and Justinian has to sign the formula, p. 223. Theodora procures
the exile of Pope Silverius and the election of Vigilius, p. 224. Justinian
condemns Origen, and then the " Three Chapters," p. 228. Vigilius is
brought to Constantinople by force, p. 229. He twice changes his
mind, but the Patriarchs and bishops have to protest their submission,
p. 230. The fifth general council and Pope Vigilius, p. 233. Justinian
approves the Julianists, p. 237. His buildings, *ibid*.

PREFACE

THE papers included in this volume have nearly all been published before, but for the most part so long ago that they are out of print and forgotten. If they were ever useful, they can be useful now, as the subjects remain important, and have received scarcely any further elucidation by scholars. I have made alterations and additions here and there ; and a very few references to more recent studies, where it seemed really advisable, have been inserted. I have not omitted the replies to adversaries of a past generation, as they enliven the narrative and bring out important points. Occasionally I spoke sharply (at the end of the last century) against writers who had written violently or abusively. The late Dr. William Bright, Canon of Christ Church and Regius Professor of Ecclesiastical History, was a prominent example of anti-papal prejudice. But he was thoroughly well acquainted with the theology of the early centuries as to the Holy Trinity and the Incarnation, and entirely orthodox on these matters. At the present day few scholars are very anti-papal and few are orthodox ; and I look back with pleasure to the fact that Dr. Bright cared more for his orthodox beliefs than for his prejudices, and showed to me personally the same friendship as before, after I had replied to him in public with some plainness of speech.

The first number is developed out of a review [1] of Monseigneur Batiffol's admirable *Le Siège Apostolique*, of which an English translation by Father Vassall-Phillips has since been published. This book showed more clearly than ever before the varieties of the jurisdiction practised by the Popes in Western Christendom. I have used his results to bring out the evolution of the idea of the five Patriarchates. I have criticised some details in Mgr. Batiffol's work, so that I am anxious to express my indebtedness to it and my gratitude for such an important study of the subject.

[1] In the *Downside Review*, May 1925, vol. 43 (new series, vol. 24), p. 89.

7

"St. Cyprian on the Church" was originally entitled "Professor Hugo Koch on St. Cyprian,"[1] and was a criticism of that scholar's views. But he is typical of a certain cut-and-dried logic, which seems to me to misrepresent St. Cyprian, and the article expresses my own opinion as opposed to many Anglican writers, such as Benson, Puller, Denny, and to M. Saltet of Toulouse as well. In the original article I had quoted Dr. Koch in German, but it seemed more practical for this volume to render all these passages into English. A note has been added at the end.

The five articles which follow are all from the *Dublin Review*, 1897 to 1905.[2] Thanks are due to editors of the *Dublin Review*, *Revue Bénédictine* and *Downside Review* for their kind permission to reproduce the articles which appeared in them.

The last number, *The Age of Justinian*, has not been printed before ; it is a lecture which was delivered before the Society of St. John Chrysostom at St. Peter's Hall, Westminster, in February, 1928.

Though there is no organic connexion between the eight papers, yet they combine to illustrate the first of them by giving examples of papal procedure from the third to the sixth century in East and West. The fourth is an exception, as it deals only with St. Peter. On that subject it is sufficient ; as no other Father, except St. Augustine, is so voluminous as St. Chrysostom, and consequently none could give a better idea of the way St. Peter was spoken of in ancient times, whether in East or West.

But it should be noted that the subjects have not been chosen as being exceptionally difficult cases, still less as being exceptionally effective as proofs of Papal authority. The cases of Cyprian and of Apiarius are indeed well worn bits of controversy ; the remainder are average instances, where the historian has a fair amount of information at his disposal.

H. JOHN CHAPMAN.

DOWNSIDE ABBEY,
Ascension Day, 1928.

[1] In the *Revue Bénédictine* of Maredsous, October 1910, vol. 27, p. 447.
[2] These five articles appeared as follows : *St. Athanasius and Pope Julius*, July 1905, vol. 137, p. 29 ; *St. Chrysostom on St. Peter*, Jan. 1903, vol. 132, p. 73 ; *St. Jerome and Rome*, Jan. 1898, vol. 122, p. 42 ; *The Condemnation of Pelagianism* (original title : *The Holy See and Pelagianism*), Jan. and July 1897, vol. 120, p. 88 and vol. 121, p. 99 ; *Apiarius*, July 1901, vol. 129, p. 98.

I

THE GROWTH OF PATRIARCHATES

THERE is no reason why any Catholic writer should try to exaggerate the evidence for the high position of the Papacy in early days. We know that the discipline of the Church has developed and has altered, and dogmatic theology cannot attempt to lay down *a priori* the manner in which that development must have taken place. With regard to the influence and even the claims of the Bishops of Rome, we cannot tell how far they might in early times be merely in germ : partially misunderstood and hesitatingly claimed and vigorously protested against. It is for historians to elucidate this with such means as they find at their disposal.

The great Gallican historians approached the subject as partisans, and we are still suffering from the peculiarity of their doctrines. They wished to make it clear that the Papal power was of Divine Right and that the Roman prerogatives were in action from the beginning of the Church ; but they wrote in the royal interest, and were often unkind and unfair in their account of the Popes. It is true that these great men, especially the laborious, accurate and edifying Le Nain de Tillemont, have laid us under so great a debt that it is against the grain to find fault with their occasional failings.[1] But history has suffered rather seriously, and the full investigation remained to be carried out. Controversies with Protestants have tended rather to obscure than to elucidate such facts as we have to deal with.

Mgr. Duchesne's history, no doubt, outlines the story of the Papacy with knowledge and sympathy, but it is little more than a manual. Mgr. Batiffol at last has given us a sufficiently detailed yet readable and interesting study of the Papacy for

---

[1] Hefele's History of the Councils does not minimise or explain away the Papal prerogatives so much as it leaves them out of sight.

a single important century 359—451.[1]   It was wanted, and the work is admirably done with care and coolness.

During the period which Mgr. Batiffol has reached (for this volume is a continuation of his four admirable volumes, *L'Eglise Naissante, La Paix Constantinienne* and *Le Catholicisme de St. Augustin*) the evidence is fairly full, and of great interest. Earlier than this we know a good deal, yet the amount of our ignorance is often painful and even exasperating. We possess a great number of slight but important references for the second century ; we have a good deal of information between 200 and 260, including some brilliant flashes of light on a dim background. From about 260 to about 310—fifty years during which as much as usual was happening—we learn almost nothing. We know a good deal about the fourth century, yet we have no letter of Pope Melchiades, under whom the Church emerged from the catacombs and became imperial and established, not one of the famous Pope Silvester, only one (and it makes us wish for more) of Pope Julius. Of Liberius we have a few, and only a few out of the vast correspondence of Damasus. Consequently we have to induce large conclusions from but a few premises.

But from 385 the series of Popes is accompanied by a set of letters of first rate importance, if only a small survival out of a large number. Some were saved by Dionysius Exiguus in his collection of decretals ; but it is only a few specially famous Popes whose epistles have been preserved in large batches : Leo I, Gelasius, Hormisdas, Gregory, Nicholas the Great and John IX. The largest collection is, of course, that of St. Gregory, and these 850 are but a fragment of the original mass.

It is in consequence of this that various historians have oddly made the Papal power originate from St. Gregory or from St. Leo, both rightly called " the Great," having ignored the sparser evidence about their predecessors. But Mgr. Batiffol has passed over none of the facts, and shows that from Damasus to Leo we have enough details to give a sketch, if not a picture, of the Papacy in action.

He has rightly pointed out that we have to distinguish between questions of faith and questions of discipline. When

---

[1] *Le Siège apostolique*, 359—451, by Mgr. Pierre Batiffol. Paris, Gabalda, 1924. *Catholicisme et Papauté, les difficultés anglicanes et russes*, by Mgr. Pierre Batiffol. Paris, Gabalda.

the faith was concerned, it was always probable that the Pope would have to be invoked, or would himself take action, whatever part of the Catholic Church was involved, for the Catholic Faith is the same everywhere. Discipline, on the contrary, was not uniform ; " Canon Law " grew slowly, and custom having the force of law was in some cases universal, in some local. Mgr. Batiffol has therefore brought out very carefully the varying relations which the Popes had to different parts of the Church.

In the fourth century, the suburbicarian Churches were subject to the Pope in a peculiar way,[1] that is to say, Italy in the older sense (without Cisalpine Gaul) together with Sardinia, Corsica and Sicily. In this region, which possessed a very large number of small dioceses, every bishop was consecrated by the Pope or at least confirmed by him.[2] These bishops came in numbers to a Roman Council at least once a year on the anniversary of the Pope's consecration.

In this period Cisalpine Gaul, officially called " Italy," has Milan for its metropolis, while the Illyrian provinces eastwards (Dalmatia, Noricum, Pannonia), have Aquileia for their centre. Gaul was not centralised (except during an unfortunate and short-lived experiment by Pope Zosimus), and had several ecclesiastical provinces ; the same is true of Spain. Questions concerning the delimitation of the provinces come before the Popes, and are decided by them ; and they give or take away metropolitan power in the case of individuals.

---

[1] Later, after Chalcedon (451), and especially after Pope Hormisdas (519) the Easterns began to look upon the whole West as the Roman "Patriarchate." But in the fourth and fifth centuries the best parallel to the Alexandrian " Patriarchate " (as it came to be called) was rather the government by the Popes of the suburbicarian Churches. It would seem that in the third century North Italy and even Gaul were under this metropolitan jurisdiction of Rome. If so, it must have been a Papal act which put these provinces more " on their own."

[2] I am rather surprised that Mgr. Batiffol in his accurate account (pp. 34—6) of the sentiments of Ambrosiaster simply quotes, as proving that writer to be a Roman, the well-known words in *Comm. on* 1 *Tim.* iii, 14—15. " *Ut cum totus mundus Dei sit, Ecclesia domus eius dicatur, cuius hodie rector est Damasus.*" Ambst. does not say " here " or " at Rome." He constantly calls bishops " rulers " of a church, *rectores ;* but here he speaks of the ruler of the household of God ; he does not mean a local Church, but *totius mundi.* Consequently his words are the same as those of the famous decree of Valentinian twenty years later still : " *Tunc demum ecclesiarum pax ubique seruabitur, si* rectorem *suum agnoscat uniuersitas.*" (p. 459). I do not see how Ambst's words can be made to mean less than this. But I recognize that Mgr. Batiffol was loth to seem as if he were pressing them.

The metropolitans consecrate the bishops in their provinces, preside at local councils, and report when necessary to Rome, or send questions to be answered.

The Papal replies to these are " decretal letters," called *decretales*, but more often *constitutiones*, and have the force of law. Every bishop is bound to make himself acquainted with their contents. Thus Italy, Gaul, Western Illyricum and Spain gradually acquire a definite code of laws, consisting of a few Canons of Councils (especially Arles, Nicæa and Sardica) and an ever increasing number of Papal constitutions.

If we turn away from Europe, we find a slightly different state of things. Latin North Africa, from Numidia to the Pillars of Hercules, formed five ecclesiastical provinces, but had only a single metropolitan See. The senior bishop in each province was primate, except in Proconsular Africa, where Carthage was the metropolis of that province and of the whole of Africa. In no part of the Church—not even in Italy or in Asia Minor—were bishoprics so numerous and dioceses so small. Even in Cyprian's time there were more than a hundred sees, and six or seven hundred are enumerated for St. Augustine's days and later.[1] Provincial councils were regularly held, and a council representing all Africa took place at least once a year, under the presidency of the bishop of Carthage, though not necessarily in that city. In St. Cyprian's councils nobody ventured to dissent from the eloquent president, and in the time of Aurelius, who was so long St. Augustine's primate and friend, a similar unanimity seems to have prevailed.

So vast and so centralised a region, with an unrivalled number of prelates, illustrated by Cyprian, Lactantius and Arnobius, by Optatus and Victorinus and Augustine, might well have developed into a " Patriarchate," but for two causes. In the first place, the ecclesiastical importance of Africa was diminished by Donatism, which in the fourth century had in Africa more numerous, more powerful and more noisy adherents than had the Catholic Church. Secondly, it was close to Rome, materially and in affection, from the close of the second century when Tertullian wrote his *De praescriptionibus* until

---

[1] Dom Leclercq says Du Pin counted 690, F. Ferrère (1897) 632, Morcelli in his *Africa Christiana*, 720, and L. de Mas-Latrie, 768. But probably not all of these existed simultaneously. Some were villages, or even farms ; for the Donatist sects multiplied sees to gain importance against each other or against Catholics.

the Arian conquest (430), after which "Roman" and "Catholic" came to be synonymous in the mouths both of the African conquered and of the Vandal persecutors.

The Popes, however, respected this commonwealth of provinces under one presidency; while the Africans, who developed a code of canon law of their own, were anxious to conform in general to the customs and laws of the West. The Papal decretals were known there, and observed as far as seemed suitable. The Popes sometimes interfered. African bishops appealed to Rome. St. Augustine in a famous letter assumes that this was normal and correct, though it was against himself that a protégé of his had appealed. But when the hasty Pope Zosimus received the appeal of a priest (on the ground that the Africans had provided no proper court of appeal for priests) and sent a legate *a latere* to Africa, the African bishops were annoyed, and eventually (when the affair cropped up again) wrote to Pope Celestine that they hoped that no further legates would be sent, and that the Popes would refuse for the future to hear appeals, even of bishops.[1] It is surprising that this letter does not seem to have troubled the cordial relations which continued to reign between Rome and Africa.

But not only the Latin Churches in Europe and Africa were specially dependencies of the Popes, but so were the Greek-speaking provinces of Eastern Illyricum, that is to say, Greece itself, with Macedonia, Dacia, Dardania, Moesia, so that the Pope's special jurisdiction extended nearly to Constantinople. These Easterns had their own liturgies, and partially their own customs, so that they were exempt from some peculiarities of occidental canon law.[2] In order that they should not be Westernized, they were subjected to one of themselves : the bishop of Thessalonica was their head, not as a superior metropolitan but as Vicar of the Apostolic See.

These provinces were from other points of view a part of the Eastern half of the Catholic Church. For half a century— say from 330 to 380—the East was distracted by the Arian troubles, caused mainly by the ambition of Eusebius of Nicomedia, and carried on by Court bishops such as the Pannonian Ursacius and Valens.

[1] On this famous case of Apiarius, see pp. 184-209.
[2] Western canon law has never been applied to the East. The new " Codex " of Canon law is only for the Latin portion of the Church, and does not touch the Catholics of the many Oriental rites.

The successors of Eusebius had not his energy. Various bishops successively held the ear of Constans. But Eusebius's intention bore fruit, and grew into fact, that the bishop of New Rome must be the principal bishop of the East. Until Constantine two sees, Alexandria and Antioch, had overshadowed all others in the East. When Julius Africanus in 221 completed his ancient chronology with a short account of Christian times, he gave with the Emperors the lines of bishops of Rome, Alexandria and Antioch.[1] A hundred years later Eusebius of Cæsarea in his Chronicle took over Africanus's lists, and brought them up to date, adding the bishops of Jerusalem, which was in the province of which he was primate. What is more, in his History he uses these lists as the backbone of the whole.

Just when Eusebius was publishing his History the council of Nicæa made a canon concerning the rights of metropolitans, confirming the superior rights of Alexandria, and justifying them by those exercised in Italy by Rome ; it adds that Antioch is parallel—" and similarly with the other eparchies." Another canon confirms to Jerusalem an honorary primacy, though it remains under Cæsarea.

Thus Nicæa mentions by name only the sees of Rome, Alexandria, Antioch and Jerusalem, and all that we know of history between 221 and 325 confirms the idea that no other sees approached these in dignity and importance. Ephesus is less heard of in the third century than it had been in the second and the first. Ancyra was influential, Cæsarea of Cappadocia was more powerful still. But in the fourth century St. Basil's sway does not extend beyond his own provinces ; and though he is not subject to Antioch, he seems to look up to that see as a leader of unity for all Asia Minor as well as for *Oriens*.

When the semi-Arian vicissitudes under Constans, the pagan reaction due to Julian, and the short and sharp Arian persecution of Valens, had passed, Theodosius determined to unite the whole Church, not by the comprehensiveness which Constans had attempted (and which was to fail equally when Zeno and Anastasius attempted a similar policy) but by

[1] For Rome he had accurate dates ; for Alexandria (which he had visited) some were evidently guesses, systematized to fill a gap. For Antioch he apparently had a list without dates, and he simply synchronized the Antiochenes with the others. It is possible that he gave also the bishops of Jerusalem ; he had settled at Nicopolis, a Sabbath day's journey from Aelia.

reuniting the East to Rome. He was ecclesiastically a Western by birth and upbringing. As soon as possible after his accession, he issued the famous decree of February 28th, 380.[1] Mgr. Batiffol gives the decree in a note (p. 111), and summarises it partly as follows: *tous les peuples qui relèvent de Théodose se rallient à la foi de l'Eglise romaine et de l'Eglise d'Alexandrie.* This is a strange misinterpretation on the part of so careful a writer. Theodosius says that all his subjects are to hold *the religion which the Divine Apostle Peter delivered to the Romans, and which is recognized by his having preserved it there until the present day : in tali uolumus religione uersari quam diuinum Petrum Apostolum tradidisse Romanis religio usque ad nunc ab ipso insinuata declarat.* Not a word is said about the faith of the Alexandrian Church. Theodosius, like the Eusebians, holds Rome to have been a school of Apostles, and to have been the Mother-Church of the Faith from the beginning.[2] The *usque nunc ab ipso insinuata* is even more precise : it reminds us of the Council of Arles, about seventy years earlier, which speaks of Rome, "where the Apostles daily sit in judgment," and of Pope Julius's words to the Eusebians, preserved by Athanasius : "What we have received from Blessed Peter the Apostle, that I declare to you."[3] The new Emperor means that the religion taught at Rome by the Prince of the Apostles,[4] and preserved there by him, is to be the religion of the whole Empire of Rome.

The Emperor goes on : *quamque pontificem Damasum sequi claret et Petrum Alexandriae episcopum uirum apostolicae sanctitatis.* We may render thus : " And which is followed of course by the Pontiff Damasus, and by Peter, bishop of Alexandria, a man of Apostolic correctness of faith." *Sanctitas* cannot refer to moral qualities, which are not in question.[5]

---

[1] Mgr. Batiffol (p. 110) says Feb. 27th, but it was leap-year.

[2] See quotation on page 55.

[3] This is the first letter in which a Pope speaks as the mouthpiece of Peter, though this is common enough later ; but then we have no complete letters at all of any earlier Popes except one of St. Clement and a few of Pope Cornelius.

[4] So the Byzantine Sozomen paraphrases : " To have religion according as from the beginning Peter the Coryphaeus of the Apostles delivered to the Romans ; this was kept at the time by Damasus the bishop of Rome and by Peter of Alexandria."

[5] That the mention of Peter is a personal one and not principally on account of his see is also shown by the supplementary law of July 30, 381 (not preserved by Justinian, as it was *ad hoc*) where a further list of typical bishops who believe in the Trinity is given : not the great sees, but the new bishop of Constantinople Nectarius, Timothy

Damasus is mentioned, not because he is a good man, but because he is the Pontiff of the city already mentioned, where St. Peter has always " insinuated " his original teaching. The aged Peter of Alexandria is known to hold the same doctrine, and to be therefore a man of Apostolic (Petrine) sanctity, for he has been living for five years at Rome— *Claret* !

The essential part of the decree is especially to be noticed : the faith of St. Peter is not said to be the creed of Nicæa, nor the consubstantiality of the Son, but definitely the Roman faith, the faith of the West (which we find in Tertullian, Hippolytus, Novatian, Dionysius of Rome, but never explicitly in the East until " the theologian " *par excellence*, Gregory of Nazianzus) : " that is, that according to the discipline of the Apostles and the teaching of the Gospels we should believe *one Godhead of the Father and the Son and the Holy Ghost* in co-equal Majesty in one Trinity."

Theodosius concludes by assigning the name of " Catholic " to those who obey this law, and he brands all others " with the infamy of the name of heretic."

In a famous excursus in Harnack's History of Dogma, that great specialist in the early patristic time set out to prove that in the second century " Catholic " and " Roman " were the same. Theodosius was of that opinion, and Justinian made this identity the primary law of his Catholic and Roman Empire.

After so unfortunately misinterpreting this law of February, 380, Mgr. Batiffol (p. 113), says of the law of January 10th, 381 : *Etaient déclarés hérétiques tous ceux qui n'acceptaient pas la foi de Nicée. . . . Théodose ne parle plus de la foi de l'évêque d'Alexandrie, Théodose se réclame uniquement de la foi de Nicée. On a supposé avec vraisemblance que Théodose s'était convaincu, depuis qu'il était en Orient, que l'orthodoxie ne pouvait se rétablir en Orient que par l'action ' des forces orthodoxes ' de l'Orient lui-même*, referring to Harnack, *Dogmengesch.*, t. II⁴, p. 273. This suggests that Theodosius was annulling his former law and substituting an Eastern council for the faith of two bishops.

We have only to read the new law (which Justinian preserved as the second law in his codex) to see that it does not

the brother and successor of Peter, and famous men and defenders of Nicæa like Diodorus of Tarsus, Gregory of Nyssa, Amphilochius of Iconium.

define heretics as those who reject Nicæa. It opens with the words : *Nullus haereticis mysteriorum locus,* assuming that it is already known by the former law that heretics are all those who do not obey that law to hold the faith delivered by Peter to the Romans. These persons are to have no places of worship, and their meetings are to be broken up. Then only, comes the passage : " Perpetual observance is to be maintained of the Nicene faith, handed down by our forefathers and confirmed by the testimony and assertion of divine religion." The summing up of the Nicene faith is curious ; there is no mention of the consubstantiality of the Son, nor of the anathemas—the Holy Spirit is not to be denied, but " the undivided substance, (which is οὐσία in Greek) of an incorruptible Trinity," is to be believed. Those who do not accept this are not to take the name of true religion, but come under the laws against heretics, etc. It is evident that it must have been represented to Theodosius (by Acholius of Thessalonica, presumably) that he was seeming to ignore the Nicene council, and that many might pretend to be in agreement with Damasus or Peter, without explicitly accepting its decrees, which Damasus, and Liberius before him, had always insisted on as terms of communion. This law, therefore, does not supersede, but supplements, the former one. There is nothing Eastern about it ; Nicæa was presided over by Papal legates ; the Popes had stood up for it for fifty years, while the Easterns had either rejected or ignored it. Harnack's suggestion was not a happy one. Theodosius was a Western, of " Trinitarian " parents, and he was determined to bring the East into line with the West by strong measures. Thus the bishops who assembled at Constantinople soon after the decree could not merely pretend vaguely that they accepted the faith of Peter, but they were obliged to accept the creed of Nicæa. A venerable tradition, which persisted from the Council of Ephesus until the late Herr Loofs, declared that they did so, omitting the anathemas and adding what was necessary in the blank which the Nicene Fathers had left after " and the Holy Ghost."

I venture to think that Mgr. Batiffol makes rather too much of the second canon of the council of Constantinople in 381. He recurs many times to the subject (pp. 127, 140, 330, etc.) and sums up his view on p. 605 : *L'Orient est divisé désormais en cinq diocèses (on ne parlera de patriarcats qu'au VIe siècle), Thrace, Asie, Pont, Orient, Egypte, et chacun de ces diocèses, présidé par son métropolitain historique, est declaré autonome. Qui fera l'unité organique de ces cinq grands ressorts distincts ? Théodose peut-il assumer ce rôle ? Penserat-il le donner à l'évêque de Constantinople ? Cette double ambition, à Constantinople, est sûrement dans l'air.* Now the Easterns were already accustomed to model ecclesiastical divisions on those of the state. But they do not put these five secular dioceses on a par. This canon and the next may be rendered as follows :—

CANON 2. The bishops who are outside a diocese[1] are not to visit the Churches across the border nor to disturb the Churches ; but, according to the canons, the bishop of Alexandria shall administrate the affairs of Egypt only ; the bishops of Oriens shall look after the East alone (the prerogatives set down in the canons of Nicæa being preserved to the bishop of Antioch) ; the bishops of the diocese of Asia shall administrate only the affairs of Asia, the bishops of Pontus only the affairs of Pontus, and the bishops of Thrace only the affairs of Thrace. Bishops are not to go outside the diocese for ordinations unless invited, or for other ecclesiastical affairs. The above canon with regard to dioceses being observed, as a matter of course the council of the eparchy will administrate the affairs of each eparchy, according to the Nicene definitions. The Churches of God among the barbarian nations must be governed according to the custom which is in force from the Fathers.

CANON 3. The bishop of Constantinople, however, shall have the primacy of honour after the bishop of Rome, because that city is New Rome.

Egypt is not to be governed by its bishops, but by the Pope of Alexandria. The vast diocese of Oriens is to be governed by its bishops, but whatever powers Antioch exercises are to be preserved. So far it is certain that the intention is to prevent the great political power of Alexandria being exercised outside Egypt.[2] But it was also necessary

---

[1] Τοὺς ὑπὲρ διοίκησιν ἐπισκόπους can only mean " The neighbouring bishops across the border of a diocese." It cannot mean " who are set over a diocese," as ὑπὲρ has not that sense. Nor can it mean " who are all over (*i.e.* within) a diocese," as Mgr. Batiffol takes it. With the acc., ὑπὲρ regularly means *ultra*.

[2] The main efforts of the Court bishops under Constantine and Constantius had been to get rid of Athanasius, the most powerful ecclesiastical personage of the Eastern Empire. His successor Peter was attacked with equal violence from the moment of his appointment. Peter had been succeeded the year before by his brother Timothy, who at once tried to fill the see of Constantinople with a very orthodox

to prevent all the interference that had been disturbing the Churches for half a century. It would not be fair to confine all other bishops within their provinces, while under Antioch were so many provinces grouped together. Hence all the provinces of each diocese are allowed to act in common or take common counsel. But only Egypt has an overlord, only Oriens has a president ; Pontus, Asia and Thrace are acephalous groups.

And that only for emergencies. For the council adds that the ordinary government will be of provinces (ἐπαρχίαι) by the provincial bishops, as heretofore, and as the council of Nicæa had intended by its words " and similarly in the other eparchies." Thus the bishop of Cæsarea and the bishops of Cappadocia will manage that province, though in emergencies they may call in the aid of Pontus and Bithynia and Galatia,[3] all these being within the diocese of Pontus.

Hence the intention of the council is that the old groupings shall continue, but that larger occasional groupings, analogous to Oriens and Egypt, shall be encouraged for the other three dioceses. They add that they leave the barbarian nations to their own customs, and they do not mention Eastern Illyricum, which was under the Pope, although its ruler (Acholius of Thessalonica) was present as a member of the Eastern empire.[4] No organization is suggested. Thrace, Asia and Pontus remain without a central authority.

In fact the council, itself disorderly enough (according to St. Gregory), seems to intend decentralisation. These bishops had no idea of an " Eastern Church " over against the West, or even of a Church of the Eastern Empire, which was an entity of varying amount. Probably they would not have

but most unsuitable candidate of his own choosing, against whom the council strongly protested. In twenty years' time Theophilus of Alexandria was to behave as if he was lord of the whole Eastern Church, and especially of Constantinople. Duchesne says (vol. ii ch. 12, p. 438) : " *Pour qui sait lire, ces décisions conciliaires représentent autant d'actes d'hostilité contre l'église d'Alexandrie et ses prétentions à l'hégémonie. . . . Si la prééminence de Constantinople est relevée, sans que l'on conteste celle de Rome, c'est pour échapper à celle d'Alexandrie.*"

[3] The same will, no doubt, be the case with the provinces within the diocese of Oriens, in spite of the primacy of Antioch. But we are sure that in Egypt metropolitans and provincial councils will have little or no power, for Alexandria had almost absolute authority.

[4] He came late to the council, and was possibly its most influential member ; not only had he been the friend of Basil and of other great men, and was in constant communication with Rome as Papal Vicar, but he had the ear of the Emperor, whom he had just baptized.

considered the diocese of Egypt to form part of " the East " ;
it had always been more closely associated with Rome and the
West than with Antioch, with which it was always theologically
at variance.[1] The Eastern Empire is divided up into five
portions, according to the five civil dioceses, not in order that
each should be a self-governing entity, nor in order that the
five should have equal votes in a common assembly, but simply
in order to keep them apart, to prevent interference.

Each part would be the weaker for the resultant isolation.
So much the stronger would the West be over against them.
It is not possible that the council should have failed to perceive
this. They probably intended it. The canon, however,
remained almost a dead letter.

As for Constantinople, it apparently remains subject to
Heraclea, just as the Nicene canon had left Jerusalem subject
to Cæsarea of Palestine, while giving it high rank, next after
Antioch. It seems likely that this is an intentional humiliation
of Byzantium, which had been trying to get a primacy ever
since Eusebius. To give its bishop honour without power,
like that granted to Jerusalem, would flatter the Emperor,
would humiliate Alexandria, without exalting Byzantium
at the expense of any other Church. There is no proof that
the new bishop, Nectarius, had anything to do with the
canon, or that he was an ambitious man.[2]

---

[1] It is not clear that the bishops of Egypt were even summoned to
the council, which was assembled in order that the bishops might
accept the faith of St. Peter and the creed of Nicæa. Timothy of
Alexandria with some Egyptian bishops came, probably uninvited, to
superintend and interfere. No doubt he did not trust so many semi-
Arians and Homousians, even under the Emperor's supervision.

[2] This canon is obviously not directed against Rome. But did Rome
protest ? The question depends on the authenticity of the Gelasian
decree, which was attacked by E. von Dobschütz in 1912 (*Das decretum
gelasianum*, in *Texte und Untersuchungen*, 3rd Series, VIII, 3). Mgr.
Batiffol accepts his view. I published two papers against Dobschütz
in the *Revue bénédictine*, vol. 30 (April and July, 1913), and Professor
C. H. Turner read a paper on April 7, 1913, to the Historical Congress
in London similarly in favour of the authenticity both of the Gelasian
list of books recommended and banned, and of the fragment of a council
of Damasus which precedes it. Unfortunately Professor Turner's
paper has not yet been printed. His knowledge of the transmission
of ancient canon law is, of course, unrivalled, and he showed in his
paper that the *Praefatio Nicaena* (given by Dobschütz in part, pp.
88-9) is certainly an integral part of the " Isidorian " version of the
Nicene canons. Now the *Praefatio Nicaena* quotes that part of the
Decretum gelas. which is given as a council of Pope Damasus ; on the
other hand the Isidorian version was made soon after 418,—say forty
years after the supposed council of 381 or 382. This is in favour of
the genuineness of that council, and entirely precludes its being a

Apart from questions of faith, in which Rome was always concerned, it is clear that the greater bishops and metropolitans, and even simple bishops occasionally, could and did appeal to Rome against condemnations by higher bishops or local councils, small or great. One may doubt, it is true, whether any bishop subject to the severe rule of Alexandria ever managed to appeal to the Pope, up to the time of St. Athanasius. Of course, we have no information, and there may actually have been many such appeals; but *a priori* one is inclined to think no opportunity would be given. But the Popes of Alexandria—this was their special title—were quite certain that they were subject to the Pope of Rome. A famous case is that of St. Dionysius the Great in the very middle of the third century; it is reported for us in some detail by St. Athanasius. Still more famous is the case of St. Athanasius himself nearly a century later.[3]

It is curious at first sight that St. Athanasius had not appealed to Rome immediately after his condemnation by the council of Tyre. Mgr. Batiffol says elsewhere:

Mgr. Duchesne a écrit: "Athanase, déposé par le concile de Tyr, ne paraît pas avoir eu l'idée qu'un appel à Rome pourrait rétablir ses affaires." *Il est certain qu'Athanase à Tyr s'embarque, non pas pour Rome, mais pour Constantinople. Cette détermination s'explique par l'fait que, à pareille date, il n'y avait pas d'exemple[4] connu d'un recours porté à Rome par un évêque d'Orient condamné par un concile d'Orient.*[5]

forgery made between 492 and 518. The arguments in my own paper are of a different order. I still find them convincing, and I could add to them.

[3] The whole history is given on pp. 51-62. I am here merely explaining a point which is not made clear enough further on.

[4] We have no records of such appeals, but apparently Pope St. Julius had (*ap.* Athan. *Apol.* 35): " The judgment should have been according to the ecclesiastical canon, and not thus; it was necessary to write to all of us, in order that justice might be decreed by all . . . And why were we not written to about the Alexandrian Church especially? *Do you not know that this was the custom,* first to write to us and that from hence justice should be decreed?" Julius might mean here that no trial of an Alexandrian bishop should have been held, but that the case should have been brought in the first instance to Rome. But it is far more likely that he means that the condemnation by a council had to be submitted for confirmation. This is how Socrates understood: " μὴ δεῖν παρὰ τὴν γνώμην τοῦ ἐπισκόπου ' Ρώμης τὰς ἐκκλησίας κανονίζειν (Π 8).

Notice the words " to write to all of us "; this is what St. John Chrysostom did later—not to the Pope only.

[5] *Les recours à Rome,* in *Revue d'Hist. ecclés.* of Louvain, vol. 21, 1925, p. 7. Compare *Le Siège Apostolique,* p. 414.

I should have thought it obvious that, as St. Athanasius was accused to the Emperor of civil crimes, which Constantine (respecting the laws of exemption which he had made himself) refused to commit to the civil courts, but referred to the council of Tyre, he would naturally not await the infliction of punishment by the Emperor who would act on the council's report, but at once to fly to Constantinople, accost the Emperor and complain that the council had violated every law of justice. If Constantine could be persuaded that the council had not even heard the defence, there would be no reason to appeal to Rome. To make such an appeal from the council was to appeal in a criminal case from the Emperor to the Pope. This might be proper in the middle ages ; but the idea that a bishop could not be tried by secular judges was new to the law, and it was Constantine himself who had originally granted the privilege : he had now chosen this particular way of applying it to Athanasius. Had the latter been tried for ecclesiastical offences by an ecclesiastical court, his appeal would have been to Rome ; but he was tried for crimes by a court of bishops in council who represented the Emperor, and his appeal was to the Emperor, if he could get at him. The Pope could not reverse the Emperor's decision. Equally St. Eustathius of Antioch had had no chance of appeal ; he could not reach the Emperor who had condemned him, and it was no more useful to appeal to the Pope than it would have been for (say) St. Laurence to appeal to the Pope against the sentence of his judge, except in so far as the pious Constantine might have listened to the Pope's representations, if the latter thought justice had not been done. There is nothing in St. Julius's letter to suggest that St. Athanasius might have appealed to him ; nor that the Pope could have intervened to prevent his exile to Trèves. I do not suppose it entered St. Julius's head to remonstrate with the first Christian emperor, who had dealt with a bishop as a man either guilty of some of the crimes attributed to him or at least a cause of trouble and strife.

The council of Sardica (see pp. 62-71) extended appeals of bishops to Rome by arranging that the Pope should appoint judges on the spot or send legates, so that the appellants need not actually make a journey to Rome, which might be impossible. The cases to be tried would not be merely of faith, but of all such accusations of immoral or illegal practices as the Eusebians had been accustomed to put forward.

Questions of faith, or even of universal discipline such as the date of Easter, had, of course, always been referred to the Popes. The second century is particularly full of examples. The great councils of the fifth century and those of the seventh and eighth are outstanding and extraordinary instances of the joyful obedience of great bodies of Eastern bishops to Papal definitions.

Out of the fifth century councils arose a new development of the Patriarchates. At Ephesus and Chalcedon three points were settled : Cyprus obtained autonomy, and Jerusalem received a small Patriarchate, both at the expense of Antioch, and thirdly, Constantinople assumed Patriarchal jurisdiction as well as rank.

It is unnecessary to discuss here the famous twenty-eighth canon of Chalcedon. It was passed by a third only of the bishops, after the rest had departed. It decided for the first time that Constantinople should have jurisdiction over Thrace, and renewed the ordinance of 381, giving it precedence next after Rome. The bishops may even have intended that, as the Pope had power over all the other Patriarchs, so the bishop of Constantinople should have power over the three who ranked below him. The canon was anyhow interpreted in this sense by later Patriarchs. The reason given for the canon of 451, as for that of 381, is frankly Erastian. But it was a rule in the East, that is, for Asia Minor and for the diocese of Oriens subject to Antioch, that ecclesiastical provinces should follow the civil divisions ; and consequently it seemed to Orientals the proper thing for New Rome to rank immediately after Old Rome, and to have a Patriarchal jurisdiction.

But this rank and jurisdiction had been in fact exercised to some extent by the prelates of New Rome both before and after the council of 381, and they had extended their influence over a great part of Asia Minor. The bishops who crowded to the Imperial Court needed an introduction from the Court Patriarch ; and it was not to their interest to be chary of doing him honour. The canon of Chalcedon was intended to regularise the existing state of things. It was passed subject to the approval of St. Leo, and apparently Anatolius of Constantinople and his friends expected the Pope to make no objection.

But Leo the Great had not a high opinion of this Monophysite, so recently converted to please the new and orthodox

Emperor. He instantly annulled the canon, accusing Anatolius of ambition and usurpation. Anatolius humbly begged the Pope's forgiveness, and the Emperor Marcian disowned this unfortunate move. St. Leo did not see in it any infringement of Papal rights, but insisted that it was his duty to preserve the prerogatives of Alexandria and Antioch. Not the greatness of those cities, but their foundation by the Prince of the Apostles, gave them a right to the second and the third place after Rome.

But a few years later the Acacian schism was to divide the East from Rome for a generation ; and during this time Acacius and his successors at Byzantium consolidated their position, and used the twenty-eighth canon of Chalcedon as having force of law. The Popes protested. Especially in the last decade of the fifth century the letters of St. Gelasius I were characteristically vigorous and uncompromising : Byzantium is a mere bishopric subject to the metropolitan of Heraclea ; the first, second and third sees were instituted by St. Peter, and the rank and prerogatives claimed for New Rome are usurpations against justice and law.

But when reunion came under Justin I in 519 (see pp. 213-6) Pope Hormisdas drops this argument, and tacitly allows the importance and influence of the bishop of Constantinople. He takes care that this see should be absolutely obedient to Rome, and then even appoints its prelate as his representative for the East, to examine the question of omission or inclusion of deceased bishops in the diptychs. The successors of Hormisdas follow him in passing over the title of " œcumenical Patriarch," which St. Gregory the Great was later to misunderstand in so unfortunate a manner. Justinian makes laws about the five Patriarchs, and gives Constantinople the second place, thus enforcing the Chalcedonian law, regardless of the annulling by St. Leo and the indignation of his successors. The Popes are satisfied that Justinian makes them governors of the whole Church, and they make no protest against the tyrannical Emperor, whom it was dangerous to contradict.

For Egypt was wholly Monophysite, and the Catholic Patriarch of Alexandria had scarcely a flock. Antioch was sacked by the Persians, and rebuilt by Justinian ; it was in danger of the enemy, and riddled by heresy. Thus the two Petrine sees were too weak to demand anything but help from the Byzantine Emperor and Patriarch. The Pope was wise in ceasing to support their ancient position. They still ranked as Apostolic and Petrine sees; but their authority had decayed, and could not be revived.[1]

Hence from Justinian onwards the " Five Patriarchates " are a part of Eastern Canon law and of Roman civil law. This did not in reality correspond with facts. We have seen that the special jurisdiction of Rome was various in character, and included Greek-speaking countries. It was so vast, that it was far more than the four Eastern Patriarchates taken together. Alexandria and Jerusalem had a very small sphere. Antioch was more powerful for a time. Eventually all three were overwhelmed by the Mahometans. Byzantium then stood alone over against the Pope and the West.

The Eastern Emperors, even when orthodox, were inclined to increase the jurisdiction of their Court prelate. They helped him to usurp what he could of Macedonia and Greece and Illyricum, and even to assert his sway over the Greeks of Sicily and South Italy. In practice from the sixth century onwards, the Church was divided into East and West, not into five Patriarchates; and this was yet more strikingly true after the foundation of the Carolingian empire in 800.

But the Byzantines had become the chief representatives of the East, and they clung to old theories.

It was already assumed in the Fifth Council that the œcumenicity of a Council depended less on the number of bishops, or on the number of countries represented, than on the representation of the five Patriarchs, by their presence in person or through their legates. Byzantine canon law came to regard the Church as consisting essentially of five Patriarchates, and the theory lasted up to the canonists of the thirteenth century, and has endured through the Turkish conquests up to the present day. But since the schism under Michael Cerularius it has been held by the Byzantines that the Roman Patriarchate has fallen away into heresy, or even that

[1] A parallel to this silence of Hormisdas is found in his attitude towards the council of 381, which had until his time been regarded at Rome as an Eastern Council, whereas it was considered œcumenical by the Easterns, although no representatives of Rome and the West had been present. St. Hormisdas is satisfied to accept the Eastern view, and to reckon four œcumenical councils, instead of three. And henceforward East and West have the same count.

all Latin baptisms are invalid, and that the Westerns are not even Christians.

But in ancient times, and even up to the eleventh century, this theory of five Patriarchs did not militate against the reverence of the Easterns for the Apostolic See. The Pope was the chief Patriarch ; each Patriarch notified his election to the others, and the four Easterns sent a profession of faith to the Holy See. If the Pope approved, all was well. It happened fairly often that he could but refuse to approve, and deposed the unsatisfactory Patriarch. The Pope was more than the first Patriarch. He could and did interfere even over the heads of the Patriarchs. He could depose and he could appoint.

Beyond this, the Apostolic See was the depositary of the Faith of Peter. By civil law, every bishop was bound to hold the faith of Rome. If heretical Emperors arose, after the schism they had caused, reunion came again only by submission to Roman direction and acceptance of Roman faith.

From the fifth century onwards, appeals to Rome are not very frequent, because they are only as to the most important matters—usually questions of Faith. But the appeals are therefore vehement and heartfelt. They are from Saints and Confessors. It is to their words that we turn, to find the most eloquent and the most categorical descriptions of the Papal prerogatives—above all Patriarchs and Emperors, above General Councils, possessing the authority of Peter, the unvarying faith of Rome. Only the resounding epistles of some of the Popes can excel the words of Byzantine saints and Councils in explicitness.

The first five centuries of the Church show us a changeable East, wild for theological discussions, over against a more sober West. But from then onwards, the East means Byzantium.

Byzantine rigidity begins to set in. Theology and learning and literature are petrified. Original thought ceases. Ceremony and etiquette are all-important. It is by this peculiarity that the ancient doctrines and customs and liturgies and ceremonials have remained to the present day, unchanged but lifeless and mummified. The Eastern Church law, collected in the ninth century, has endured without alteration under Basileus and Sultan and Czar. The Byzantine Patriarch gained a new importance through his civil position at the head of his Christians under the Turk. The other Patriarchs became shadows. But the Patriarchates have been kept up by the heretics also; and the Catholics have them too—multiplied by the different rites, Latin, or Syriac or Coptic. The old theories are kept up in name. The Apostolic See alone remains with all its old prestige, its incomparable authority and unchangeable Faith.

II

ST. CYPRIAN ON THE CHURCH

FOR centuries it has been a commonplace in England to speak
of " the Cyprianic theory of the episcopate." From the time
of the Reformation Anglican episcopalians have appealed to
the great martyr of Carthage as a witness to their own theory
of government by bishops without a Pope. Cyprianic study
has been quite an Anglican speciality, from the great names of
Dodwell, Pearson and Fell to Archbishop Benson in our own
day, besides controversialists without number. In Germany,
on the other hand, the views of St. Cyprian have not had such
primary importance ascribed to them by Protestants, for
Lutherans have not been so anxious to claim the third century
on their side, nor was St. Cyprian of the least use to them in
any case. Consequently a number of German Protestant
authorities have taken much the same estimate of his opinions
as Catholics have done. It is to be noted that many Catholics
have exaggerated in claiming St. Cyprian as a witness to
" Ultramontane " doctrines which he does not teach, and
that they may be to some extent answerable for the reaction
on Dr. Koch's part which has led him to publish a study of
St. Cyprian in German which reproduces the main arguments
which have been all along so familiar in England and so little
heeded in Germany.[1] Professor Koch has written tem-
perately and carefully, and has studied his subject. I do not
find that he has said anything very new. But he is rather
more rigid and thorough-going in his theory than most
Anglicans have ventured to be.

Prof. Koch begins by giving an interpretation of the famous
fourth chapter of the *De unitate*, with which I cannot alto-

[1] *Cyprian und der Römische Primat, eine kirchen- und dogmenge-
schichtliche Studie*, von Hugo Koch. Leipzig, 1910. (In *Texte und
Untersuchungen*, 3rd series, V, 1).

gether agree.[1]   He cites Fr. Poschmann's explanation, and
comments thus (p. 13) :

" This is so far true, that Cyprian does distinguish between
the building of the Church on Peter and *the commission of the
power of the keys ;* and he reserves the one to Peter, and lets
the other be received by the other Apostles as well. Correct
likewise is the comparison : *super unum aedificat ecclesiam—
unitatis originem ab uno incipientem sua auctoritate disposuit—
exordium ab unitate proficiscitur.* But precisely this comparison
shows how Cyprian understands *super unum aedificat ecclesiam.*
This clause finds its interpretation in the other two clauses,
and simply means : *the building of the Church begins with one
(mit einem)."*

Not *mit* but *auf,* and that makes all the difference : *upon
one,* not *with one.* Cyprian never thought of Peter as the
first to be laid of the foundation stones, but as the Rock on
which the foundations are laid.   You cannot begin to build
with a rock ; you begin to build *upon* a rock ! Firmilian
understood the passage rightly, when he said :[2] *super quem
fundamenta ecclesiae collocata sunt,* " upon whom the foundations of the Church were laid."   Koch continues (p. 13) :

" The Lord could have delivered the power of the keys to
all the Apostles at once.   But he gave the full powers first to
Peter, and only later to the rest of the Apostles, in order that
He might show clearly that His Church should be one."
And p. 14 : " As a distinction for Peter there remains only

---

[1] I subjoin the passage for reference.   *De catholicae ecclesiae unitate,*
c. 4, pp. 212-3 : " *Quae si quis consideret et examinet, tractatu longo
adque argumentis opus non est ; probatio est ad fidem facilis compendio
ueritatis.   Loquitur Dominus ad Petrum : ' Ego dico tibi,' inquit, ' quia
tu es Petrus, et super istam petram aedificabo ecclesiam meam, et portae
inferorum non uincent eam.   Dabo tibi claues regni caelorum : et quae
ligaueris super terram erunt ligata et in caelis, et quaecunque solueris super
terram erunt soluta et in caelis '* (Matt. xvi. 18, 19).   *Super unum
aedificat ecclesiam ; et quamuis apostolis omnibus post resurrectionem
suam parem potestatem tribuat, et dicat : ' Sicut misit me Pater, et ego
mitto uos ; accipite Spiritum sanctum : si cuius remiseritis peccata,
remittentur illi : si cuius tenueritis, tenebuntur '* (John xx. 21-3), *tamen
ut unitatem manifestaret, unitatis eiusdem originem, ab uno incipientem,
sua auctoritate disposuit.   Hoc erant utique et ceteri apostoli quod fuit
Petrus, pari consortio praediti et honoris et potestatis ; sed exordium ab
unitate proficiscitur, ut ecclesia Christi una monstretur.   Quam unam
ecclesiam etiam in Cantico Canticorum Spiritus sanctus ex persona
Domini designat,"* etc.   In quoting St. Cyprian the pages given are
those of Hartel in the Vienna Corpus (1868).
[2] Cypr. *Ep.* 75, 17, p. 821.

the *priority of time* of his investiture with the power of the keys, the remembrance of the short-lived numerical unity of the apostolic authority, and the exemplification, which was thereby created for all time, of the moral unity of the Church. In this sense Peter is for all time ' the foundation of the Church,' the man *super quem aedificauit Dominus ecclesiam.* ' "

St. Cyprian does not explicitly say this. Did he mean it ? There are good reasons, I think, for doubt.[1] *A priori* we may argue that it is a very far-fetched explanation of " the rock on which the Church is built " to say that it signifies a man who for a short time, while our Lord was still on earth, possessed nominally (but without exercising it) the supreme government of the Church.[2]   I do not think I should feel comfortable in a house built on a temporary rock.

I quite admit that to Cyprian Matt. xvi. 18 is " not a promissory bill for a future time, but an actual making over of authority."   But from this passage we could not have gathered so much : it is from *Ep.* 73 that we learn this directly :   Cyprian is not speaking there of the unity of the

---

[1] He certainly does not call Peter ' the foundation of the Church,' but says ' the Church was *built* upon him ' (*Epp.* 71, p. 773 ;   59, 7, p. 674 ;   66, 8, p. 732°; 73, 7, p. 783) or ' was *founded* upon him ' (*Epp.* 43, p. 594 ;   70, p. 769 ;   73, 11, p. 786 ;   *De hab. virg*, 10, p. 194 ;   *Ad Fortun*, 11, p. 338).   We see that *aedificare* and *fundare* are equivalent as to Peter.   On the other hand, the ground on which a building is founded is sometimes improperly called its ' foundation.'   We may say of a house whose foundation is on the sand or on gravel, ' its foundation is sand ' or ' is gravel.'   In this extended sense later Fathers speak of Peter, the Rock, as the *fundamentum* or θεμέλιος of the Church. The name *Petrus* (though already used as a Christian name) was strange to Latin ears, and it always suggests *Petra* to Cyprian.   But to the German Koch it is too familiar, and he thinks of Peter as a foundation stone, a ' first stone,' an idea which never entered Cyprian's head.

[2] Even this is saying too much, for the Church could scarcely be said yet fully to exist, and her divine Head was there.   If we are to get any sense out of such a proposition, we must, I think, reduce it to the ordinary Anglican view of Cyprian's meaning—that he re-garded our Lord's words to Peter not as giving him any real power, but as allegorical and as saying to him alone what He intended later to say to all.   This is very nearly Koch's view, only a little more sensible, for it does not oblige us to think of Peter as possessing alone for a time a power which was not to be exercised until the day when it was given to all.   But Benson was right in considering the argument a poor one, though he persisted that Cyprian meant nothing more. Further, both Koch and the Anglicans attribute to Cyprian an argu-ment from a purely allegorical interpretation, of a kind which cannot be paralleled elsewhere in his writings, and they suppose him to have been unnecessarily stupid.

Church, nor of the episcopate, but of the power of bishops alone to forgive sins :

Nam Petro primum Dominus, super quem aedificauit ecclesiam et unde unitatis originem instituit et ostendit, potestatem istam dedit ut id solueretur quod ille soluisset.   Et post resurrectionem quoque ad Apostolos loquitur dicens : sicut misit, etc.[1]

But surely we must presume that in Cyprian's idea Matt. xvi 18 " gave a power " which was not to be exercised as yet, whereas John xx. 21, was a real investiture ; for he was not ignorant of Matt. xviii. 18, where before the resurrection the Lord says to all the Apostles not equivalent words merely but the same which he had recently addressed to Peter.[2]   Consequently we must suppose that he prefers to quote John xx. 21 because that solemn occasion was a real investiture of the Apostles with an actual power, not a merely future power. It is inconceivable that he should have regarded Peter as the sole possessor of the power of binding and loosing from the promise or gift at Caesarea Philippi until after the resurrection, as though the text Matt. xviii. 18 were non-existent ! I venture to suggest that it is a pity Koch did not treat Cyprian's view of Peter chronologically, and that he would have done well to consider *Ep.* 33 before coming to the *De unitate.*   In that letter, which Koch has frequently cited but never discussed, there is no question of the unity of the Church, but only of the authority of the bishop, which had been attacked by the issue of an " indulgence " as though in the name of the Church, without Cyprian's knowledge.   He is indignant at being thus ignored :

Dominus noster, cuius praecepta metuere et seruare debemus, episcopi honorem et ecclesiae suae rationem disponens in euangelio loquitur et dicit Petro : " Ego dico tibi . . . etc. . . . et in caelis."   Inde per temporum et successionum uices episcoporum ordinatio et ecclesiae ratio decurrit ut ecclesia super episcopos constituatur et omnis actus ecclesiae per eosdem praepositos

---

[1] *Ep.* 73, 7, p. 783.
[2] St. Cyprian does not actually quote Matt. xviii, 18, but he *twice* quotes the preceding verse (*Ep.* 59, 20, p. 690, and *Ep.* 69, 1, p. 750) and *three times* the following verse (*Testim.* iii, 3, p. 115 ; *De unitate*, 12, p. 220 ; *Ep.* xi, 3, p. 497).   It is especially noticeable that verses 20 and 19 are quoted in the *De unitate*, and the latter is commented upon.   It can hardly have been quoted by heart, and it agrees with *Test.* iii, 3.

gubernetur. Cum hoc ita diuina lege fundatum sit, miror quosdam audaci temeritate, etc. (p. 566).

Here there is nothing about *post resurrectionem ;* the text Matt. xviii. 18 is the charter of monepiscopacy entirely apart from any consideration of Peter possessing his powers alone for a certain period. The power given to Peter of binding and loosing is the episcopal power. What is more important is that the founding of the Church upon Peter is identified with the founding of the Church upon bishops : ut ecclesia *super episcopos* constituatur," and the meaning of " being founded on " is explained as " being governed by." Bishops are successors of the Apostles[1] ; but so far as the monarchical character of the episcopate is concerned, they are rather for Cyprian the successors to Peter's unique position as rock on which the Church is built, which he has not in common with the other Apostles, as Koch has allowed. But is it consistent with this to say : " As a distinction for Peter there remains only the priority of time of his investiture"? If Peter is the foundation only in the sense that he was for a time alone the holder of episcopal powers, how can the Church be " founded upon bishops " ? Surely bishops have not *zeitliche Priorität* ! It is no good for Koch to explain that Peter receiving alone the episcopal powers is the type of the bishop—everyone can see that, and no one denies it—but Koch has explained that " to be a foundation " means to be first in order of time, and is equivalent to *unitatis originem ab uno incipientem* understood of time, in a transient sense, and to *exordium ab unitate* in the same transient sense. Apply this to bishops, and we get the sense " Bishops are the foundation of the Church as having authority first in order of time " ! If Cyprian really meant priority of time by foundation, he could never have thought of saying that the Church was founded upon bishops.

Again, the treatise *De habitu uirginum* is doubtless earlier than *De unitate.* Here Cyprian has *Petrus etiam, cui oues suas Dominus pascendas tuendasque commendat, super quem posuit et fundauit ecclesiam.*[2] Now Cyprian habitually says that Christ founded the Church on Peter, when he mentions that Apostle, and it is certain that he regarded this as a special prerogative of Peter. Here he apparently names the charge to feed the sheep as a similarly honourable distinction belong-

[1] *Ep.* 3, 3 ; *Ep.* 45, 3, etc.
[2] C. 10, p. 194.

ing to Peter alone. He undoubtedly thought this charge to Peter was addressed to bishops in his person, for it is impossible to consider all his expressions about bishops as shepherds of a flock to be derived solely from John x ; rather the application to bishops is from ch. xxi, the unity of the flock from ch. x. Can we suppose him unaware that the charge to Peter alone in ch. xxi was subsequent to the investiture of all the Apostles in ch. xx ? This would be even more violent than to suppose he always forgot Matt. xviii. 18 !

Very shortly before the *De unitate*, Cyprian wrote *Ep.* 43, which was in reality the basis of that book. Here we find :

Deus unus est et Christus unus et una ecclesia et cathedra una super Petrum Domini uoce fundata. Aliud altare constitui aut sacerdotium nouum fieri praeter unum altare et unum sacerdotium non potest. Quisque alibi collegerit spargit.[1]

Here we are told, as if the argument needed no development, that one Church and one chair (i.e. the monarchical character of the episcopate) were founded upon Peter. Again—as in *Ep.* 33—not a word about priority of time. The founding upon Peter is held to prove in the same way both the unity of the Church and the monarchy of the bishop. What is that way ? It seems to me clear enough that Cyprian means that Peter just as much as the bishop is a permanent not a transient guarantee of the unity of the edifice which rises upon a single rock.

Next in order we come back to *De unitate* 4. The structure of the passage is easy enough to analyse :

1. Introduction : *Tractatu longo atque argumentis opus non est...*
2. Argument : *Loquitur Dominus ad Petrum : " Ego dico tibi . . . et in caelis."* SVPER VNVM AEDIFICAT ECCLESIAM.
3. Objection : *Quamuis apostolis omnibus parem potestatem tribuat... tenebuntur.*
4. Reply : *tamen ut unitatem manifestaret, unitatis eiusdem originem ab uno incipientem sua auctoritate disposuit.*
5. Objection repeated : *Hoc erant utique et ceteri apostoli quod fuit Petrus, pari consortio praediti et honoris et potestatis.*
6. Repeated reply : *Sed exordium ab unitate proficiscitur...*

---

[1] (C. 5, p. 594).

Now Koch makes the objection an integral part of the argument : " that Peter alone was at first what the other Apostles only became later on " (p. 15, note). But that does not suit the structure of the sentence, and the earlier passages have taught us that the whole argument is contained in Matt. xvi. 18-19. It is summed up in the four words SUPER VNVM AEDIFICAT ECCLESIAM. The objection is not intended to make the argument clearer. On the contrary, it is an objection which has presented itself (or very likely was urged by Felicissimus or the five rebel priests) and must be met somehow. The replies are really nothing else but reiterations of SUPER VNVM AEDIFICAT ECCLESIAM in ponderous and pompous language. If Cyprian had wanted to reply : " At any rate Peter was the first to be given the power, and that is what I mean by his having the Church built upon him," he could have said so plainly, though it would have been a complete change from his view in *Epp.* 33 and 43. But his words are far from having such a meaning on the surface. Take the solemn metrical close *sua auctoritate disposuit* : Are we to understand : " He made by His authority the disposition that Peter should be the first in order of time " ? Surely it is odd to invoke " authoritative disposition" for a merely typical and allegorical precedence ! And *exordium ab unitate proficiscitur*—can we construe : *Exordium*—the first giving of the power, *proficiscitur*—takes its start, *ab unitate*—from a single individual ? Is not this too far-fetched ? Surely *ab uno* means " from Peter considered as the one rock," and *ab unitate* means " from the unity of the one man who is the rock." I should paraphrase the two replies somewhat as follows : " That He might make unity manifest, BY HIS AUTHORITY HE ORDAINED for this same unity an origin beginning from one, *i.e.* He built His one Church upon one " and " but the beginning of the Church takes its start from the unity of the one rock." I don't think Cyprian meant any more than this. *Zeitliche Priorität* never entered into his head ; he merely repeats that there were indeed many Apostles with co-ordinate jurisdiction, but only one rock : *super unum aedificat ecclesiam.*

In what does this prerogative of Peter consist ? " Nothing remains," says Koch, " but priority of time." I have given enough reasons to show that priority of time does not remain. What remains is obviously the metaphor used by our Lord, the name He gave to Peter—this alone is sufficient to prove[1] the unity of the building erected upon him, *without defining precisely what it implies.* The objection is not really gone into, it is thrust aside : " Yes, I know they all had the same power, but the Church is built upon one." I think it is useless to interrogate the passage further, for Cyprian never saw very far, though he was always quite clear and logical as far as he saw. Koch's fault, and a pardonable one, is that he has tried to make a complete theory out of what is incomplete. Now I do not want to fall into the same mistake (I find myself constantly on the verge or over the verge as I write), and therefore I will not draw any conclusion from this passage as to the position of Peter as centre of the Church's unity ; I only observe that there is something substantial and permanent about a rock-foundation.[2]

But I think one may say that Cyprian was not satisfied with the passage, and for this reason re-wrote it. Koch, indeed, does not accept the proofs I gave in 1902-3[3] that the so-called

---

[1] Koch appeals to *manifestaret* and *monstretur* to show that a type, a picture, an allegory is intended, and nothing more, and he wishes to make out that Poschmann could not deny this (p. 17). For my part I believe that *manifestaret* means " *make plain to the meanest understanding,*" that *monstretur* means " demonstrate," and that both of them are simply taking up *probatio* at the beginning of the chapter. In fact this seems to me so obvious, that I imagine it has only to be pointed out in order to be accepted. But I admit that unless it has been seen, Koch's misunderstanding looks very plausible !

[2] Let me repeat Koch's view so that there may be no mistake: *Petrus ist nicht Realgrund, nicht Ursache und Mittelpunkt, sondern nur der zeitliche Ausgangspunkt und der Erkenntnissgrund der kirchlichen Einheit (p. 43).* " Peter is not the principle, not the cause and centre, but merely the *starting-point in time* and the *means of recognition* of Church unity " ; as if we should say " the Rock is not the principle nor the cause nor the stabilising, but merely the *starting-point in time* and *means of recognition* of the building raised upon it." This resembles the interpretation of Cyprian by English scholars, from Dodwell and Fell to Benson and Puller and Denny. It is obvious that the Rock must be previous in time to the House built upon it. The conjecture is interesting that St. Cyprian had remarked this practical truth, which is verified equally in the case of sand. If this is the inner meaning of the surname " Peter," it follows that " Sandy " would have been equally to the point. In fact it would have been better ; for it would have suggested cracks in the walls, followed by splits and by ruin in accordance with the views of these critics about Church history. But it would not agree with St. Cyprian's argument for monepiscopacy ; and the subsequent words about " the Gates of Hell " not prevailing would need some conjectural modification. Still the obvious and familiar unreliability of sand is at least less alarming than the mysterious and incalculable terrors of the temporary rock.

[3] In the *Revue Bénédictine* of Maredsous, July and October, 1902, and January, 1903.

"interpolation," or alternative form of this chapter, was really written by Cyprian. I will not swear to it. But I simply cannot discover any other explanation of the phenomena. The objections raised by Koch are not very important, and like Dr. Watson and Mgr. Batiffol, he has entirely neglected a point which has always seemed to me of the very first importance, the variety of reading in ch. 19.[1] Hartel's text of that chapter makes the *lapsi* " here " and the schismatics " there "; in the MSS. which have the "interpolations " we find all the successive *hics* and *illics* interchanged ; the schismatics are " here " and the lapsed are removed to " there." This seems to imply adaptation to a schism which was not at Carthage, but at a time when the Carthaginian lapsed were still bewailing their errors ; it must therefore (so far as I can see) be a contemporary change, and a change made by the composer of the alternative version of Ch. 4, since it is witnessed to by the same codices. Further, both alterations seem to be intended against Novatianism.

Another argument has more force than Koch has perceived. I gave so many parallels from St. Cyprian, with the intention of showing how the alternative version is saturated with Cyprianic expressions, that the result was rather confusing.[2] I will here give parallels carefully chosen, omitting the hundred and one distantly similar passages ; I give every word of the alternative passage in capitals, the parallels also in capitals :

1. ET EIDEM POST RESVRRECTIONEM DICIT PASCE OVES MEAS.
   Petrus etiam cui OVES SVAS Dominus PASCENDAS tuendasque COMMENDAT. *De hab. uirg.* 10, p. 194.
2. VNAM TAMEN CATHEDRAM CONSTITVIT.
   Una ecclesia et CATHEDRA VNA super Petrum Domini uoce fundata. Ep. 43, 5, p. 594.
3. (*unitatis originem*) ATQVE RATIONEM.[3]

---

[1] Koch has repeated (p. 159) a mistake of Batiffol (*L'Eglise naissante*, 3rd ed., p. 440, note) who supposed that Watson accepted my view. On the contrary his note in the *Journal of Theol. Studies* (April, 1904, p. 432) is directed against it. I replied *ibid.*, p. 634.

[2] Even to myself, for in my reply to Watson (mentioned in the preceding note) I spoke too doubtfully of these parallels, as if they were an argument from style appealing to individual taste.

[3] Koch says *ratio* means *Erkenntnissgrund ;*—if so, there is no " Romanizing " about the interpolation of the word here ! Of course it really means *character, constitution*, i.e. monepiscopal character, there is no mystery or difficulty about the meaning, especially in 33, 1.

Una ecclesia . . . super Petrum *origine unitatis* ET RATIONE fundata. Ep. 70, 3, p. 769.

4. SED PRIMATVS PETRO DATVR.

Nec Petrus . . . adsumpsit, ut diceret se PRIMATVM tenere.[1] Ep. 71, 3, p. 773.

5. ET CATHEDRA VNA, as above, n° 2.

6. ET PASTORES SVNT OMNES SED GREX VNVS OSTENDITVR.

Et si PASTORES *multi* sumus, VNVM tamen GREGEM PASCIMVS Ep. 68, 4, p. 747.

7. QVI AB APOSTOLIS OMNIBVS VNANIMI CONSENSIONE PASCATUR Haec VNANIMITAS sub APOSTOLIS olim fuit. *De Vnit.* 25, p. 232. Coepiscoporum . . . quorum numerus . . . concordi VNANIMITATE CONSENSIT. Ep. 55, 8. p. 629.

8. QVI CATHEDRAM PETRI . . . DESERIT.

Ad PETRI CATHEDRAM atque ad ecclesiam principalem, *unde unitas sacerdotalis exorta* est, . . . Ep. 59, 14, p. 683.

9. PETRI . . . SUPER QVEM FVNDATA ECCLESIA EST.

SVPER QVEM posuit et FVNDAVIT ECCLESIAM. *De hab. uirg*, 10, p. 194, and often elsewhere.

Now the doctrine of this interpolation is so " moderate,"

---

[1] Koch takes this passage to mean that primacy of time gives no real superiority (pp. 45-7). But *primatum teneo* does not mean " I was the first to be appointed." I understand Cyprian to mean : " Even the most dignified and authoritative persons ought to listen to reason when their inferiors remonstrate with them ; Peter gave an excellent example of this : he listened to Paul, he did not say to him : ' I am the Prince of the Apostles, I was an Apostle long before you—why, you were a persecutor ! ' " The argument implies at least that Peter was not a persecutor, that he was an apostle before Paul, and that he had the primacy (whether of honour or of jurisdiction is not said). I may notice here that Koch (p. 50) makes *primatum assumere* (of Novatian *Ep.* 69, 8, p. 757) not " assumed the rank of primate," but merely " claimed the *cathedra* of bishop." I am glad to see him willing to admit that *primatus* may be used by Cyprian of firstness not in time or even honour, but in actual jurisdiction : " The ' Primacy ' in this place consists precisely in the possession of the ' Cathedra ' and in the plenitude of power of baptizing and sacrificing, that is to say, in official authority and directorship in the Church—the office of bishop." But though I am delighted that he makes so large an admission, yet I cannot agree with him. Rome is the *ecclesia principalis*, and when Novatian makes himself bishop of Rome he is naturally said *primatum assumere*. There is no instance in Cyprian (or in any other writer, so far as I know) of episcopal power being referred to absolutely and without explanation as *primatus*. I daresay Cyprian might have enumerated Novatian's claims in a more logical order, but his meaning is plain : " he ' set up a chair ' (made himself bishop), what is more, he assumed the primacy— the chief of chairs—he even claimed to exercise his office by baptizing and offering the holy Sacrifice—a fearful sacrilege." But Koch ought to have rendered " he assumed the rank of priority of time," to be consistent.

if we compare it with, say, St. Optatus and St. Augustine, that it is early ; and it is surely against Novatian rather than against the Donatists. No one supporting Roman claims even in Stephen's day but would have been tempted to say more. It is not a pro-Roman forgery.

But it is impossible to deny that every expression is Cyprianic (I am not speaking of the doctrine), and must have been written by someone who was saturated with the Cyprianic style. Would this be characteristic of Cyprian's own disciples ? It is not true of Pontius, at least ! Would it be true of a later student of Cyprian ? I doubt it.

Is it a clever forger with whom we are dealing ? This seems far more impossible. The passages imitated are in all parts of Cyprian's writings. A forger or imitator *must* have consulted at least all the following documents :

> *De habitu uirginum* for 1. (No other passage is parallel).
> *Epist.* 43, 5, for 2 and 5. (No other passage is parallel).
> *Epist.* 70 for 3.
> *Epist.* 59, 14 for 8 (the only parallel).

Probably also *Ep.* 71 ; and he must have carefully noted how fond Cyprian is of *unanimis* and *consensio*, and how he repeatedly speaks of the *unanimitas* of apostolic times. The documents are by no means found together in the MSS. *De hab. uirg.* belongs to the group of treatises and letters mentioned by Pontius ; *Ep.* 43 belongs to the group which I have called Dg. ;[1] *Epp.* 70, 71 to the baptismal group Cg ; *Ep.* 59 to the Cornelius group Bg. These are not among the rarer groups, it is true, but only a large and comprehensive codex would contain them all. The second of these groups is, for example, wanting in the Cheltenham list (4th century, it seems) ; the first is wanting in the famous MSS. L and N ; they were not all in the archetype of M Q ; not all are in *h*, and so forth. Still it is by no means improbable that comprehensive MSS. of the type of T, or at least MSS. containing all may have existed at an early date. The impossibility lies in the idea that the imitator or forger should have combined passages from distant parts of an MS. or from different MSS.

---

[1] I refer to my article " The order of the treatises and letters in the MSS. of St. Cyprian," in *Journal of Theol. Studies*, IV, p. 103 (October, 1902). The groups are easily found in the tables to Hans von Soden's *Cyprianische Briefsammlung*.

with such simplicity and success, without introducing an un-Cyprianic word. He has produced a perfectly logical and harmonious whole. He has even carefully observed the metrical cadences of his finals, as to which Cyprian was so particular ; this has lately been pointed out by Fr. L. Laurand S. J. in the *Berliner Philologische Wochenschrift* (1909, August 7th, p. 1016).

Now I am much impressed by the way in which all the *data* of the evidence are accounted for by the hypothesis that St. Cyprian himself composed the alternative passage. This supposition explains the alteration of ch. 19, the early date according to the MS. evidence (I do not expect many people to follow this) the early quotations and (above all) the language, for Cyprian had the habit of repeating himself, and is sure to have the same phrase again when he returns to the same idea. This hypothesis does not seem to leave any serious difficulty, and I have been quite unable to invent any alternative theory. Neither of my courteous critics, Dr. Watson and Prof. Koch, has suggested any explanation. Until another theory is propounded, I imagine mine holds the field. But it depends entirely on circumstantial evidence, and is therefore liable to be dethroned if a better or equally satisfactory hypothesis is suggested.[1]

---

[1] I am not at all convinced by Mgr. Batiffol's arguments that the " Roman form " (or " interpolation ") is what St. Cyprian originally wrote, and that the " pure text " is a correction by the author " *peut-être pour enlever à son argument ce qu'il y avait de trop spécial au cas de Novatien, pour en rendre par là la portée plus universelle* " (*L'église naissante*, 3rd ed., p. 447). I regard as impossible that the *De unitate* should have composed against Novatian ; it is not directed against an episcopal schism, but against the party of Felicissimus, a deacon. Further the history of the council of 251 leaves no room for the composition of the book after the tidings of Novatian's consecration had arrived (I think Batiffol has followed Harnack's incorrect chronology, *Chronol.* II, pp. 349-53 ; for the correct sequence see my article, *Rev. Bénéd.* 1903, p. 28). I acknowledge that I was wrong in thinking that the two books *De lapsis* and *De unitate* were taken to Rome with *Ep.* 54 (Batiffol, p. 445 ; Koch, p. 167) ; they were certainly taken with *Epp.* 45, 46, 47 by the sub-deacon Mettius ; this mistake was pointed out first by M. Callewaert soon after my articles had appeared. I think my view that the " Roman " form of *De unit.* 4 was introduced by Cyprian for the benefit of Maximus and Nicostratus is confirmed by what I have said above as to the unsatisfactory character of the original form : Cyprian makes the argument more precise, introduces the charge to Peter *after the resurrection* (which weakens the objection which had been drawn from the same chapter of St. John), and he correspondingly makes a third statement of the objection in a new form " *et pastores sunt omnes.*" But his third reply makes it evident

So far I have been speaking merely about matters of scholarship, which scarcely affect the question of Cyprian's opinion about the Roman primacy. But this last is what mainly interests Koch. I must say I do not think it is a very important question. There is indeed plenty of room for difference of opinion as to details. But the main point is clear—on an important matter Cyprian refused to accept the judgment of the Pope, and enuntiated the absurd doctrine that bishops must agree to differ on all points where the faith does not come in. This is at least what his words come to, if we turn them into a theory of Church government. But I have always held that such a treatment of Cyprian is unjustifiable. He was a practical man, without philosophy or theology. His generalisations are working rules for the moment, and do not apply beyond the circumstances with regard to which he framed them. His outlook was extremely narrow, and his logic was very short-sighted. In his passionate anger at Pope Stephen's unreasonableness (as he thought it), he argues as though the Roman tradition were heresy of the most absurd and blasphemous character, but he adds that every bishop is free to hold it if he pleases—the Roman view cuts at the root of Church unity, and thus at the ground of all truth and of all authority, but it would be wrong to break with a bishop who holds it—baptism by heretics defiles instead of cleansing, yet the bishop is to rebaptize or not as he thinks fit ! The measures he took in the case of the lapsed are based on propriety, prudence and kindliness, rather than upon theological principles. Not that he cannot argue from principle ; on the contrary, he lays down the law and deduces the conclusion, without seeing how far it may lead him. He never perceives that his theory of the independence of bishops leads to anarchy, and could not be acted upon for a single year. He does not realise that his doctrine of church unity has led him into heresy and into schism. When tradition is quoted against him, his answer is ready : So much the worse for tradition ! What would Irenaeus, what would Tertullian have said to such a doctrine ?

that he is not trying to prove Peter's authority, for he merely says " Sed grex unus ostenditur qui ab apostolis omnibus unanimi consensione pascatur." How any one can regard this as a wicked Roman forgery passes my understanding ! I do not see any " Romanizing " in the " Roman " form, except the " qui Cathedram Petri . . . deserit," which (pace Koch p. 166, 6, citing Turmel) seems an especially suitable turn of phrase to apply to the Roman confessors.

The contrast with Firmilian is amusing. The Cappadocian does not run down tradition, he meets the Roman tradition with an Asiatic tradition—this is to argue like a Churchman. He accepts Cyprian's arguments against Stephen, but he rationally concludes : " Thou art worse than all the heretics ! " At the threat of excommunication Cyprian apparently determined not to break with Rome, even if Rome broke with him ; but Firmilian has no such scruples, Stephen has excommunicated himself, he is a schismatic as well as a heretic—here again we hear an ecclesiastic speaking. In contrast to this great Eastern bishop, the martyr of Carthage is a recent convert who has mastered but few Church principles and has exaggerated those few. He knows that he is supreme in his diocese as bishop, and his autocratic ways arouse a fierce opposition, in spite of his holiness, his eloquence and the generosity with which he distributes his wealth. Opposition makes him cling the more to his authority, he makes the unity of the diocese and the monarchy of the bishop the same as the unity of the whole Church, and contempt of the bishop's power is the root of all heresy and schism ! Novatianism throws the Church into a turmoil, and this confirms his theory, for at its rise the Novatian schism was simply a question of rival popes, not of rival views about penance.[1] He had

---

[1] Koch points out that Novatianism was not a mere question of rival bishops, it was a question of dogma : " In the Novatianist schism [sic] one concept of the Church stood over against another ; hence its rapid and wide-spread diffusion not only in the West but more especially in the East " (p. 91). The first clause is quite true of the Novatian heresy in general ; it was not much a question of rival popes after the beginning. But in its beginning, *just when it raised such commotion throughout East and West*, it seems to have been almost entirely a " schism " as to the true bishop of Rome. When Dionysius of Alexandria (Euseb. vii, 5) speaks of all the Eastern churches, which had been at variance (αἱ πρότερον διεσχισμέναι), having been reunited, there is no reason to think that the question of the lapsed was at all prominent. What remains to us of the letter of Cornelius to Fabius of Antioch (*ibid.* vi, 43) is concerned with the bad life of Novatian, not with his teaching. The letter of Dionysius to Novatian (*ibid.* 45) reproves him for making a schism and bids him resign his pretensions, but says nothing about false doctrine. Similarly in Cyprian's first letters on the subject (44, 45, 46, 47, 48, 51) there is not a word about any heresy of Novatian, (for in *Ep.* 51 *schismatico immo haeretico furore* and *fallacia et perfidia* evidently refer to the wickedness of opposing the true bishop). The same is true of *haereticae prauitatis nocens factio* in *Ep.* 52. In *Ep.* 54, we find Cyprian has sent his *De lapsis* to Rome, but *Ep.* 55 is the earliest in which the " Novatian heresy " is argued against. The letters of Cornelius (49-50) and of the Roman confessors (53) do not speak of it, though Cornelius speaks of Novatian vaguely as a schismatic and heretic. It is indeed impossible to suppose that in the East any

defended himself against the encroachments of the confessors, of the five opposing priests, of the deacon Felicissimus, and of the rival bishop Fortunatus, when he was yet more rudely disturbed by the edict of Stephen. It is another attack on his rights as a bishop—that is all he sees. His main argument is that Stephen is illogical, and wrong, but he adds that the very idea of uniformity in such a matter is shocking, for it interferes with episcopal rights !

This is very remarkable. We know from Cyprian that Stephen issued an edict which ordered obedience under pain of excommunication. We learn from Firmilian that Stephen based his edict on an appeal to his succession from Peter. As to both these points Firmilian has, of course, an answer ready : the excommunication recoils upon Stephen, and his edict shows him to be no true successor of Peter. But Cyprian has nothing to say on either point. He is angry at the threat, but remains passive ; it never strikes him that he is in the same case as Privatus of Lambese when branded by the letters of Donatus of Carthage and Fabian of Rome,[2] or as Marcianus of

more than in the West, the question could arise " Do you prefer Cornelius's doctrine or that of Novatian ? " If Novatian were ever so orthodox, the first question was whether his ordination was legitimate or not. Consequently his letters sent throughout the church consisted mainly of calumnies against Cornelius, to prove that his consecration was null : so Cornelius says : " *quod per omnes ecclesias litterae calumniis et maledictis plenae eorum nomine frequentes missae fuissent et paene omnes ecclesias perturbassent* " (*Ep.* 49), and so does Cyprian (*Ep.* 44), and he thought Novatian's letter too disgraceful to be read to the council (*Ep.* 45, 2). I have written this long note because it is very important to our knowledge of the third century to make no mistake about this witness of the first month of the Novatian difficulty to the tremendous position of Rome in the Church. It is the more curious that Koch should have spoken of Novatianism as a doctrinal question (as in fact it was, after the very first) in that he has most clearly explained St. Cyprian's view, p. 6 : " The same Cyprian, who is so passionate against the rigorist theory and practice of the schismatic Novatian, informs us that at an earlier date in his own province various bishops had denied penance and absolution to adulterers, and he declines to condemn them, on the ground that they had not abandoned the fellowship of their colleagues who acted otherwise, and had not broken the unity of the Church (Ep. 55, 21). But in the case of Novatian one need not search for any heresy. In the fact that he stands outside the Church, all is said ; and together with his separation from brotherly charity and Church unity, he has besides lost what he was before." This is well said. But he is outside the Church because he claims to be bishop of Rome, when there is already a legitimate bishop, and so are all his followers who have brotherly charity and unity with him instead of with the true Pope Cornelius. To Cyprian it was not a question of " *Kirchenbegriff.*"

[2] *Ep.* 59, 10, p. 677.

Arles when denounced to Stephen by Cyprian himself ! And
he does not deal with the Pope's claim to give a binding
decision ; his reply is simply that no one can interfere—he
never adds, " not even the successor of Peter." This omission
is so very astonishing that I always understand it to mean
that Cyprian never quite took in the situation ; he never
realized, as Firmilian realized at once, that here was a command from one who meant to be obeyed, or he would have
denied his credentials. I think he is quite convinced that the
Pope has some undefined sphere of authority, but he must
not interfere with the rights of bishops as exercised at Carthage !

But it is a practical matter, based on no large theory ; for he
holds that, though a large number of bishops agreed with
Novatian about the penance of the lapsed, they have no right
to their view, they are heretics ! If the bishops of Southern
Gaul cannot get rid of their colleague at Arles, the bishop of
Rome is the person to notify them of their duty.[1] Why

[1] With regard to this famous case of Marcianus of Arles, Koch says :
" In the whole of Ep. 68, as in Ep. 67, Stephen comes into consideration
neither as Pope nor even as ' Western Patriarch,' but merely as the
occupant of the Roman Chair, so highly esteemed morally " (p. 199).
It is a great deal to admit this " moral " eminence of the Roman See!
But how are we to distinguish in the third century, before almost any
canon law, or (still more) in Cyprian who denies all canon law, between
moral and juridical eminence ? However this may be, the " moral "
eminence implied in the letter is very remarkable. Faustinus of
Lyons and his colleagues are powerless against the Novatian bishop ;
Cyprian's influence is insufficient ; and Marcianus still " appears not
to have been yet excommunicated by us." But a letter from the Pope
will be enough to depose him and ensure a new bishop ! *Quapropter
facere te oportet plenissimas litteras ad coepiscopos nostros in Gallia
constitutos, ne ultra Marcianum peruicacem et superbum et diuinae
pietatis ac fraternae salutis inimicum collegio nostro insultare patiantur,
quod necdum a nobis uideatur abstentus . . . Dirigantur in prouinciam
et ad plebem Arelate consistentem a te litterae quibus abstento Marciano
alius in loco eius substituatur. Significa plane nobis quis in locum
Marciani Arelate fuerit substitutus.* Koch naturally asks : *Warum soll
Stephan den Africanern den Namen des neuen Bischofs von Arles mitteilen ?*
But from his point of view he can give no answer ! He holds that recognition of the new bishop by the Pope was not necessary, and also assumes
(as I have done till lately) that the new bishop is to be elected by the
clergy and people of Arles and confirmed by his comprovincials. But
I am afraid this is wrong, however much our modern notions may be
disturbed by the literal translation of *literae quibus alius in loco eius
substituatur.* I now believe that Stephen is not only considered to be
the right person to excommunicate Marcianus, and (in this case) the
only person who can do so effectively, but that he is to *appoint* a sub-
stitute. For this is what Cornelius did in the case of two of the bishops
who consecrated Novatian; he says so in his letter to Fabius ; Καὶ τῶν

should not Marcianus of Arles be as free as Faustinus of Lyons to act as he pleased about the lapsed ? There is no answer, except that Cyprian happened to agree with Stephen about the lapsed and to disagree with him about rebaptism. In the case of the Spanish bishops who were said to have lapsed, both sides tried to get the countenance of the Pope—I do not see that we shall be saying too much if we call this appealing to Rome.

Cyprian must, I think, have been at the moment blinded by rage against Stephen, for he heard only one side, and yet declared that Stephen had been basely deceived ! He sees that Stephen gave a formal sentence ; but he never denies his right to do so. Yet his decision is that the judgment is incorrect, and therefore need not be attended to ; the rights of the other side remain what they were. This is bad law.

As councils have no compelling force, as the Pope need not be obeyed, unless one happens to agree with him, there is no remedy left for disorder. Yet Cyprian has complete confidence in the divine ordination of Church unity, and in the moral unanimity of bishops " glued together." [2] I fear it was the shortness of his experience which made it possible to put forward a theory which no one has ever held before or since. This is why I think " St. Cyprian's theory of the episcopate " is of no importance except for his own biography. No one

λοιπῶν δὲ ἐπισκόπων διαδόχους εἰς τοὺς τόπους ἐν οἷς ἦσαν χειροτονήσαντες ἀπεστάλκαμεν (Euseb. vi. 43, 10). In this case the bishops were actually chosen and consecrated at Rome. Novatian had been doing the same thing on a larger scale : *cumque iam pridem* per omnes prouincias et per urbes singulas *ordinati sint episcopi in aetate antiqui, in fide integri, in pressura probati, in persecutione proscripti, ille super eos creare alios pseudoepiscopos audeat, quasi possit aut totum orbem noui conatus obstinatione peragrare aut ecclesiastici corporis compaginem discordiae suae seminatione rescindere* (*Ep.* 55, 24, p. 642). Here Cyprian does not say that schismatics in every city clung to Novatian and set up pseudo-bishops ; he says that Novatian set them up, and that is his point. Koch gets out of this by saying (p. 50 note) that Novatian is not here characterized as Antipope but as Antichrist who " sends his new Apostles to many cities." Yes, but I am not appealing to Cyprian's argument—it is quite true that he is speaking of Novatian as Antichrist (but how Antichrist unless because Antipope ?)—but to the historical facts he is relating. I do not see how to avoid the inference that Novatian and Cornelius themselves appointed the substituted bishops, and that Cyprian in *Ep.* 68 enjoined on Stephen to do the same at Arles. It is useless to reply : " But Cyprian admitted no authority in the Pope." I am convinced that he had no consistent theory on the subject, but he was acquainted with the customary procedure and found it convenient in this case.

[1] *De unit.* 23, p. 231 ; *Ep.* 66, 8, p. 733 ; *Ep.* 68, 3, p. 746.

else has ever held it, and Cyprian himself held it only as a practical determination : " I will be master in my own diocese," and did not push it to its ultimate results ; he did not see where it must lead and he did not apply it to other bishops.[1]

It is just when we realize how strongly Cyprian felt about this authority of bishops that we see how important are his admissions and his silences on the subject of Rome. Here we have not his own theorizing but current ecclesiastical views which he could not avoid assimilating.[2] The chief text is *Ep.* 59, 14, p. 683 : *Post ista adhuc pseudoepiscopo sibi ab haereticis constituto nauigare audent, et ad Petri Cathedram adque ad ecclesiam principalem unde unitas sacerdotalis exorta est ab schismaticis et profanis litteras ferre, nec cogitare eos esse Romanos, quorum fides Apostolo praedicante laudata est, ad quos perfidia habere non possit accessum.* Koch is obliged to admit that Cyprian sees in Rome a peculiar dignity, though no authority ; but he thinks that Cyprian's language is elsewhere so distinct in denying all authority above that of bishops, that he must regard Rome as having only a moral supremacy, an honourable fame. Quite true, if we are to take his occasional protests about the independence of bishops as a complete, logical (and absurd) theory. But even so, what a place this single passage assigns to Rome ! Koch's attempt to harmonize it with Cyprian's supposed theory is not very successful. Look at the contrast between the " schismatics and profane persons " and the immaculate faith of the Romans, which the Apostle had praised two hundred years before, and of which it was still possible to predicate that

[1] Koch says : " The loss of Cyprian from tradition tears a hole in it which can never be filled up again. In such a case one swallow makes a whole summer. For the point is not simply that Cyprian does not bear witness to the Primacy, but he is an outspoken adversary of every claim, every exercise of Primacy."(p. 144). This is quite unfair ! If we explain away with Koch all Cyprian's witness to Roman primacy, and base our view of his " theory " on a few selected passages about the independence of bishops, we are bound to be consistent, and not conclude merely that Cyprian rejects all primatial right, but that he rejects all conciliar authority, all possible canon law, all uniformity of practice ! Either he is answerable for the whole of this anarchical theory or for none of it, for the proofs of the whole are the same.

[2] Batiffol well says (p. 457, quoted by Koch 118, note) : *Ce que nous oserions appeler l'ultramontanisme de Faustinus, de Basilide, et même de malheureux Félicissimus, est le catholicisme traditionel bien plus authentiquement que le provincialisme inquiet et inconséquent des Africains.*

where it reigns unfaith has no access.[1] And why has it this prerogative ?   It is the Chair of Peter, on whom the Church was built, it is thus the " primatial Church," from which the unity of the episcopate had its rise.   Is it not cutting it rather fine to say this means only that Peter received his apostolic powers as a type of unity before the other apostles received theirs, consequently the Church where he settled later on is said to be " the place whence unity had its rise " ? [2]   I do not think I could believe this, however much I tried.   I do not attempt to define exactly how much St. Cyprian meant, but he meant a good deal more than that.

I may seem to have been speaking most disrespectfully of an illustrious saint.   On the contrary I have been defending him.   He was not so far-sighted or consistent as Koch thinks, but he had far more common sense, and his devotion to the unity of the Church atones, as St. Augustine saw, for his over-vehemence and exaggerations.   I studied St. Cyprian before I became a Catholic.   I was first introduced to him in a theological college, where I was told to understand him much as Koch does.   But I was chiefly impressed by his arguments about unity.   I think them now after twenty years what I thought them then—unanswerable arguments for the truth of the Catholic Church.[3]   I was not and am not concerned

---

[1] Of course, *perfidia* means ' unfaith,' ' heresy,' not simply ' deceit,' in early ecclesiastical Latin.

[2] It may seem hardly credible that Koch means this, so I give his own words : The Roman Church is the *ecclesia principalis* because the *princeps* Peter is its first bishop.   But the Apostle Peter according to Cyprian, is only *princeps* in the chronological sense, without any primatial rank.   *As Peter is chronologically the oldest apostle, so Rome is for Cyprian ideally the oldest ' cathedra ' and ' ecclesia ' with which the sacerdotal unity began.*"   The italics are Koch's.   But *unde* is not " with which," but " out of which."   To infer the meaning of *principalis* from Cyprian's use of *princeps* is odd, for he never uses the word *princeps* of St. Peter !

[3] I cannot sum up my view better than by quoting some words I wrote a few years ago ;   I chose my words with some care :
" There was not even a beginning of canon law in the Western Church of the third century.   In Cyprian's view each bishop is answerable to God alone for his action, though he ought to take counsel of the clergy and of the laity in all important matters.   The bishop of Carthage had a great position as honorary chief of all the bishops in the provinces of Proconsular Africa, Numidia and Mauretania, who were about a hundred in number ;   but he had no actual jurisdiction over them.   They seem to have met in some numbers at Carthage every spring, but their conciliar decisions had no real binding force.   If a bishop should apostatize or become a heretic or fall into scandalous sin, he might be deposed by his comprovincials or by the Pope.   Cyprian probably

with his opposition to the Pope—" *quae in Stephanum irritatus effudit* "—for the Church has decided against him ; Optatus is a complete antidote ; Augustine holds his view to be heresy and his conduct reprehensible, though his martyrdom atoned ; St. Jerome speaks yet more clearly ; St. Vincent of Lerins says that Stephen behaved just as befitted the high place he held. The good Anglicans in appealing to Cyprian neglect his main doctrine, the necessity of one Church, and appeal to his error with the Donatists and the Luciferians.

Prof. Koch is a very good-natured controversialist ; he is accurate and never does wilful violence to the texts he interprets, though I cannot always think he has got hold of the right interpretation. Still I often agree with him. His fault is his attempt to systematize what is unsystematic. He has studied the ultimate results of a few expressions, and uses them as a norm, explaining away whatever is out of harmony with them. In much the same way some Catholic controversialists have been so impressed by a few texts of Cyprian about Rome that they have understood other passages without sufficient warrant in a similar sense, and have glossed over some difficulties. This is equally mistaken in method, but it is at least kinder to the Saint !

And after all, how slight his errors are ! He resists the Pope on a point which he is sure does not touch the faith, and wherein consequently the Pope might be in the wrong. He wishes for more elasticity in discipline than experience has found practical. He is a little irreverent to tradition, but not to tradition about the faith. His chief error—one day to be called heresy—was caused by his very hatred of heresy and his

thought that questions of heresy would always be too obvious to need much discussion. It is certain that where internal discipline was concerned he considered that Rome should not interfere, and that uniformity was not desirable—a most unpractical notion. We have always to remember that his experience as a Christian was of short duration, and that he became a bishop soon after he was converted, and that he had no Christian writings besides Holy Scripture to study but those of Tertullian. He evidently knew no Greek, and probably was not acquainted with the translation of St. Irenaeus. Rome is to him the centre of the Church's unity ; it was inaccessible to heresy, which had been knocking at its doors for a century in vain. It was the See of Peter, who was the type of the bishop, the first of the Apostles. Difference of opinion between bishops as to the right occupant of the Sees of Arles or Emerita would not involve breach of communion, but rival bishops at Rome would divide the Church, and to communicate with the wrong one would be schism." (*Catholic Encyclopaedia*, art. " Cyprian," Vol. IV, p. 588).

devotion to unity. Contrast the errors, some monstrous, some childish, of Clement of Alexandria, of Tertullian, of Hippolytus, of Origen. No one wishes to appeal to the mistakes of these great men as witnesses to ancient tradition, because they are for the most part views which no one wants to hold to-day. In comparison with them, the great episcopate of Cyprian (marred only by a few not ignoble errors of judgment) and his immaculate faith shine with redoubled lustre, nay outshine even the glory of his martyrdom.

*   *   *

St. Jerome (*c. Lucif.* 23) tells us : " Bl. Cyprian attempted to avoid heresy, and therefore rejecting the baptism conferred by heretics, sent [the acts of] an African Council on this matter to Stephen, who was then bishop of the city of Rome, and twenty-second from St. Peter ; but his attempt was in vain. Eventually those very bishops, who had decreed with him that heretics were to be rebaptized, returned to the ancient custom, and published a new decree." This event is not otherwise testified. In fact, we do not know what happened after St. Cyprian's last letter to Pope Stephen. We cannot guess what was St. Jerome's authority. It is fairly clear that St. Cyprian was not cut off from communion with Rome under Dionysius and Xystus. It is inconceivable that Stephen withdrew his decision ; it is almost as unlikely that Dionysius or Xystus dropped it. On the other hand, St. Cyprian's extreme anger, shown in his letter to Pompeius, is likely to have passed, as anger does. He had previously admitted the ancient custom, for bishops who preferred it. It is not very probable that his hundred bishops should have continued to support him against Rome. Did he make some explanations or concessions ? The Donatists knew no more than St. Augustine knew. St. Optatus assumes that peace was never broken. Indeed, had Cyprian and all Africa been cut off from Rome by a minor excommunication (as we might gather from Firmilian's letter) the event would have been tremendous in import and notoriety. St. Augustine must be right that peace was somehow patched up without any weakening on the part of Rome.

St. Augustine was at one time doubtful whether St. Cyprian's letters on this matter were genuine *c. Cresc.* I 32 (38), II 31 (39), though he preferred simply to say that they are not canonical Scripture, and that he does not follow them (*ibid.*). But elsewhere he admits that the style is Cyprian's *Ep.* 93, 10 (35), remarking that, though we do not know whether he changed his mind, " it is not incongruous to suppose that so

great a man did correct his view " ; at any rate, *si quid in
eo fuerat emendandum, purgauit Pater falce passionis* (compare
De bapt. I xviii. 28, *in catholica unitate permansit, et charitatis
ubertate compensatum est, et passionis falce purgatum.*)

The question whether Cyprian was likely to give in depends
on the other question, which view did he hold more strongly :
the one, that nothing can justify the breaking of unity ; the
other, that it was permissible for some bishops to teach that
heretics could only baptize into the devil, whereas others might
justly hold their baptism to be valid, according to a mistaken
tradition. It is natural that Anglicans should assume that
Cyprian must have adhered loyally and generously to the
comprehensiveness which includes contradictory theories and
acts, whereas he would willingly give up (for the sake of the
view that black is white) his former declarations that it is
necessary to be inside the Church. St. Augustine judges
contrariwise that the martyr was not at heart a latitudinarian,
but was above all a lover of unity. Perhaps the fourth and
fifth centuries were nearer in sympathy to Cyprian than were
the seventeenth or the nineteenth.

" *What he poured forth against Stephen in his irritation
I will not discuss over again,*" says Augustine (*De bapt.* V
xxv. 36). He believes that " *uicit tamen pax Christi in cordibus
eorum.*" But only Donatists could think Cyprian was in
the right, and not the Pope. Puller takes the Donatist side,
and parodies St. Augustine's words about Cyprian. He
doubts whether Stephen was a martyr (and the fact is
doubtful), adding :

" If he [Stephen] did so die, we may hope that he purged away in that second baptism whatever was amiss in his life " (*Prim. Saints*, 3rd ed., p. 70).	" He [Cyprian] merited to attain the crown of martyrdom ; so that any cloud which had obscured the brightness of his mind was driven away by the brilliant sunshine of his glorious blood " (*De bapt.* I xviii. 28).

St. Vincent of Lerins takes the orthodox view : " The
custom has ever flourished in the Church, that the more
religious a man is the more he opposes novel inventions.
Examples are very numerous. But to be brief, let us take
but one, and that one especially *from the Apostolic See ;* that
all may see more clearly than daylight with what power,
with what energy, with what perseverance *the integrity of the*

Religion once received has always been defended by the blessed succession of the Blessed Apostles."

" Once upon a time, Agrippinus of venerable memory, bishop of Carthage, first of all men, against the divine Canon of Scripture, against the rule of the universal Church . . . thought rebaptism ought to be practised. . . . Then *Pope Stephen of blessed memory, Prelate of the Apostolic See, together with his colleagues, indeed, but yet beyond the others, resisted ; thinking it fit, I deem, that he should surpass all others as much by the devotion of his faith as by the authority of his rank. . . .* What was the end ? What force was there in the African council ? By God's gift, none at all. All, as a dream or a tale, was abolished, forgotten."

" *Et, o rerum mira conuersio ! Auctores eiusdem opinionis catholici, consectatores haeretici iudicantur ; absoluuntur magistri, condemnantur discipuli ; conscriptores librorum filii regni erunt, adsertores uero gehenna suscipiet ?"* "For who is so mad as to doubt that blessed Cyprian, that light of all saints and martyrs, with his colleagues shall reign for eternity with Christ ? Or who, on the contrary, so sacrilegious as to deny that the Donatists and the other plagues, who boast that it is by the authority of that Council that they rebaptize, shall burn with the devil for ever ? " (*Commonitorium* I 6.)

In the East there were others in the fourth century besides St. Basil who thought it might be well sometimes to rebaptize heretics ; but such peculiarities were apparently only put in practice in rare cases. It was certainly not the custom anywhere to rebaptize Arians or Semi-Arians. From the fifth century onwards the East is absolutely in line with the West, and St. Basil's theoretical opinion remains a dead letter. All St. Cyprian's torrents of argument, eloquence, invective against the teaching of Rome were in vain.

ST. ATHANASIUS AND POPE JULIUS I

It is quite common to find well-read Englishmen speaking as though the history of Arianism was a difficulty in the way of the defenders of the Roman Primacy. They talk as if Rome had but an unimportant share in the troubles of the fourth century, and as if no testimony to the authority of the Papacy could be drawn from the relations between the East and West during the controversy.

This curious notion has its root, of course, in the Anglican manuals of history, in which the action of the Papacy is either ignored, or where this is impossible, minimised. In the following paper it will not be possible to go through the whole period of the Arian distress. I shall confine myself, therefore, to the time which elapsed between the Council of Nicaea in 325 and the Council of Sardica in 343 or 344. During these years the West was at peace, and all the troubles were caused by the Arianizing court party in the East.

The first Œcumenical Council seems to have been Constantine's own idea, and he expected peace to follow the condemnation of Arius by so large a body of bishops as that which met at Nicaea. The heresiarch himself was exiled, as were also the two bishops who alone had refused to sign at the Council. Soon afterwards the famous bishop Eusebius of Nicomedia and Theognis, bishop of Nicaea, who repented the signature they had made through fear of the Emperor, were also exiled. In 328 St. Athanasius became Bishop of Alexandria.

It was not long, however, before the exiles were recalled, through the influence, it is said, of Constantine's sister Constantia, the widow of the Emperor Licinius. In 330 the party of Eusebius was able to procure the deposition, on false charges, of the orthodox St. Eustathius of Antioch by a Council held in that city. Various attempts were made to discredit Athanasius, whose See was yet more powerful and who was also the bishop of the Alexandrian priest Arius, whom he steadfastly refused to receive back to communion. At length Constantine was persuaded that peace should precede the solemn opening of the great church he was building at Jerusalem, and he consented to the summoning of a council at Tyre in 335, at which the accusations against the Patriarch of Alexandria were heard. Athanasius attended, accompanied by forty-nine of his suffragans, but when he saw he could expect no justice, he retired with them and was condemned in his absence.[1]

At a synod of the same bishops at Jerusalem immediately afterwards, Marcellus of Ancyra, whose views may have been really heretical, was deposed also, while Arius and his followers were received back into communion. Athanasius went to Constantinople and appealed to the Emperor for protection from his enemies. Constantine ordered the bishops who had been at Tyre to come to Constantinople. The more orthodox bishops were kept away by intimidation, and the Eusebians alone answered the summons. Athanasius was exiled to Trèves, where he was well received by the Emperor's son, afterwards Constantine II. Arius was to have been solemnly received back into the Church at Constantinople, but this was prevented by his sudden death, which was looked upon as a miracle. The aged bishop of that city having died, his orthodox successor, Paul, was banished, by the intrigues of Eusebius of Nicomedia. It was apparently Eusebius who baptized Constantine on his death-bed at Nicomedia in 337.

Thus the work of the Council of Nicaea was being insidiously destroyed in the East. Eusebius and his followers were not professed Arians, though they showed no horror at his doctrines and tried to steer a middle course between Arianism and orthodoxy. It must be remembered that up to this time they were in full Catholic communion, and were accused of heresy only by the victims of their unscrupulous intrigues. To Athanasius, conscious of their determined enmity, it was clear that the Eusebian party was aiming at the subversion of the Nicene faith by gradually depriving it of its main supports. By absurd and incredible charges they had emptied the most powerful sees of the East—Alexandria, Antioch and Constantinople, and had exiled the champions of the truth.   Probably the vast number of Eastern bishops

[1] It is unnecessary to relate here the well-known accusations and the triumphant disproofs of them.

held the doctrine which was taught at Nicaea. But they understood as little as Constantine the real views and intentions of Eusebius and his friends. They did not know the truth concerning the accusations brought against Athanasius, Eustathius and Paul, or against Asclepas of Gaza or Marcellus of Ancyra. Plenty of mud was thrown and some of it stuck. Besides, the Council of Nicaea was not to the men of those days, as it is to us, the first and most venerable of a long series of Œcumenical Councils received by the whole Church. It was to them simply a particularly large and representative assembly recently held at the Emperor's wish in order to pacify the Church by the condemnation of Arius. The Council might well have been imprudent, some thought, in employing the word ὁμοούσιος, for this expression was said to have been disapproved by the Council of Antioch which condemned Paul of Samosata in 269. The Arianizing faction was thus able to pose as orthodox, and it was said that Arius himself had made a sufficient recantation.

After the death of Constantine all the banished Bishops were permitted to return ; yet this was the beginning of a worse period for the East. The sons of Constantine divided the empire, the semi-Arian Constantius became Emperor of the East, while the West was at peace under Constantine II and Constans. Bishop Paul of Constantinople was soon sent again into exile, and Eusebius of Nicomedia obtained possession of the See of the imperial city. In 339 his party was bold enough to set up an excommunicated priest, one of the original followers of Arius, called Pistus, as Bishop of Alexandria, on the ground that Athanasius had been deposed at Tyre ; and they sent an embassy to Rome to Pope Julius to give an account of the accusations against Athanasius and to ask that the communion of Rome should be given to Pistus.

Up to this point the troubles had been only in the East. It is to be noticed that no ecclesiastical law yet existed with regard to the trial of Bishops. A synod like that of Tyre had no jurisdiction over a Patriarch of Alexandria ; it was, from the Church's point of view, a purely moral force. But the Emperor had looked upon synods as ecclesiastical juries, and had punished with the secular arm the secular offences of which the deposed Bishops were unrighteously convicted. The Eusebian party further used the imperial power to thrust Arian Bishops into the Sees which they had made vacant. But they were well aware they were not *en règle*. It is for this reason that we find them the first to appeal to the Pope. If they could persuade Julius and the Western Church to believe the charges brought against the victims of their slanders they would have right as well as might on their side.

" But they could not deceive that See," as St. Augustine said on another occasion. Pope Julius acted with a due sense of justice. To the disgust of the Eusebians, he at once sent to St. Athanasius the alleged proofs of his guilt, which had been forwarded to Rome, and which the accused himself had not been allowed to see. Athanasius assembled in consequence a great Council at Alexandria of more than eighty Bishops, which addressed to Julius and to all Bishops a lengthy defence.[1] This letter was taken to Rome by the envoys of Athanasius. When their arrival became known to Macarius (the priest who had brought the letter of Eusebius) he left hurriedly in the night. His companions, two deacons, were unable to reply to the statements of the Egyptians, so they demanded a synod, and requested the Pope himself to be judge.[2]

Julius made no objection to this, and at once wrote both to the Bishop of Alexandria and to his accusers summoning them to a synod, the time and place of which they themselves could decide.

---

[1] Ath. *Apol.* 3-19.

[2] It is best to give the words of the authorities : (Athanasius, *Apol. c. Arian.* 20) : " The Eusebians (or Eusebius) also wrote to Julius, and thinking to frighten us, they asked for a Council to be called, and that JULIUS HIMSELF, IF HE WISHED, SHOULD BE JUDGE." Socrates, *H. E.* ii. II : Eusebius having accomplished what he desired, sent an embassy to Julius, Bishop of Rome, calling upon him TO BE THE JUDGE of the charges against Athanasius, and TO SUMMON THE CASE TO HIMSELF." Sozomen, *H. E.* iii. 7. : " Eusebius . . . wrote to Julius that he SHOULD BE JUDGE OF WHAT HAD BEEN DECREED AT TYRE." Here Sozomen copies Socrates, who has himself misunderstood the passage of Athanasius. This last must be interpreted by another passage of the same Saint. *Hist. Arian, ad mon.* 9 : " The priests sent by them also asked for the same thing (viz. a synod) when they saw that they were refuted." So the letter of St. Julius (Ap. Athan. *Apol. c. Arian.* 22) : " Those who were sent by you Eusebians with letters (I mean the priest Macarius, and the deacons Martyrius and Hesychius) when they were here, not being able to reply to the priests of Athanasius who had come, but being confuted and convicted in all points, thereupon asked us that a synod might be convoked, and to write to Alexandria to Bishop Athanasius and to the Eusebians that the just judgement might be arrived at in the presence of all." From this it is clear that the letter of Eusebius had not asked for a synod or for the Pope as judge. This was only an insincere pretext of the envoys used to avoid an immediate condemnation.

Meanwhile the Emperor Constantius had intruded another Bishop at Alexandria, Gregory the Cappadocian, with the greatest violence. Athanasius escaped and obeyed the summons of the Pope,[1] arriving at Rome just after Easter, 399.[2]

The accused having presented himself, but his accusers, whose representatives had demanded the Council, not having put in an appearance, St. Julius sent them another summons, fixing the end of the year as the limit of his patience. The Eusebians retained the legates until the term was passed and only allowed them to return in the January following (340), bearing a letter from their meeting at Antioch, the tenor of which has been preserved by Sozomen.[3]

" Having assembled at Antioch, they wrote to Julius an answer elaborately worded and rhetorically composed, full of irony and containing terrible threats. For in their letter they admitted that Rome was always honoured as the school of the Apostles and the metropolis of the Faith from the beginning, although the teachers had settled in it from the East.[4] But they did not think they ought to take a secondary place because they had less great and populous Churches, since they were superior in virtue and intention. They reproached Julius with having communicated with Athanasius, and complained that their synod was ' insulted and their contrary decision made null,' and they accused this as unjust

---

[1] Athan. *Apol. c. Arian.* 20, and *Hist. Arian.* 11 ; St. Julius (ap. Athan. *Apol. c. Arian.* 29) : " For he did not come of himself,.but was summoned by letters from us, as we wrote to you." Theodoret *H. E.* ii. 3. " Athanasius, knowing their plot, retired, and betook himself to the West. For to the Bishop of Rome (Julius was then the Shepherd of that Church) the Eusebians had sent the false accusations which they had put together against Athanasius. And he, *following the laws of the Church*, both ordered them to repair to Rome, and also summoned the divine Athanasius to judgement. And he, for his part, started at once on receiving the call ; but they who had made up the story did not go to Rome, knowing that it would be easy to see through their falsehood." Sozomen. iii. 10 : " Julius learning that it was not safe for Athanasius to remain in Egypt then, sent for him to Rome."

[2] So Gwatkin, *Studies in Arianism,* 116. Hefele (Eng. tr. ii, 88) gives 340, and shifts all the events in the same way up to the Council of Sardica.

[3] III, 8, Socrates merely has : " They complain with great acerbity to Julius, declaring that he must make no decrees if they wished to expel some from their Churches, for they did not contradict him when (the Romans) drove Novatus from the Church," ii, 15.   Both historians mistakenly place this letter after an imaginary restoration of Athanasius and others to their Sees by the Pope.

[4] viz. Peter and Paul. Compare the inscription of St. Damasus *ad Catacumbas :* " Discipulos Oriens misit, quod sponte fatemur."

and contrary to ecclesiastical law. Having thus reproached
Julius and complained of his ill-usage, they promised, if he
would accept the deposition of those whom they had deposed
and the appointment of those whom they had ordained, to
give him peace and communion ; but if he withstood their
decrees, they would refuse this. For they stated that the
earlier Eastern Bishops had made no objection when Novatian
was driven out of the Roman Church. But they wrote
nothing to Julius concerning their acts contrary to the decisions of the Nicene Council, saying that they had many necessary reasons to give in excuse, but that it was superfluous
to make any defence against a vague and general suspicion
of wrong-doings."

Eusebius of Nicomedia seems to have been dead when this
letter was written. In the autumn of 340 the Council was at
length assembled at Rome, and met in the church of the
priest Vito, who had been Papal Legate at Nicaea. Not only
Athanasius, Patriarch of Alexandria, and Marcellus, bishop
of Ancyra in Galatia, were present, but also many bishops
from Thrace, Coelesyria, Phoenicia and Palestine, who had
taken refuge in Rome. Besides, deputies came from Alexandria and elsewhere, complaining of the continued acts of
violence and barbarity perpetrated in the name of the Eusebian party. Priests from Egypt and Alexandria deplored
that many Bishops were prevented from coming, and some,
even confessors, were beaten and imprisoned, while the
Catholic people were oppressed and persecuted. Bishops had
been exiled for not communicating with the Arians. Similar
outrages had occurred at Ancyra in Galatia.

The council gave peace and communion to Athanasius and
Marcellus, the orthodoxy of the latter being warmly upheld by
Athanasius and Julius. At the instance of the bishops, the
Pope at length replied, in the name of all, to the unseemly
letter of the Eusebians. His lengthy and important epistle
is preserved complete in St. Athanasius' apology.[1]

[1] Tillemont says of this letter : " *St. Athanase nous l'a conservée
toute entière ; et on peut dire sans flatterie, que c'est un des plus beaux
monumens de l'antiquité. On y voit un génie grand et élevé ; et qui a
en même temps beaucoup de solidité, d'adresse, et d'agrément. La vérité
y est défendue avec une vigueur digne du chef des Evesques, et le vice repré-
senté dans toute sa difformité. Mais l'aigreur de ses répréhensions y est
tellement modérée par la charité qui y paroist partout, que bien que la
force et la générosité épiscopale domine dans cette lettre, on voit néanmoins
que c'est un père qui corrige, non un ennemi qui veut blesser." Vol.
vii. p. 278. (St. Jules, art. 8).*

The letter from the Easterns, says St. Julius, was improper and proud, in answer to his own letter, which was full of love ; even their apparent flattery was ironical. Out of charity Julius had not published their letter for a long time, until he was forced to give up all hope that any of them would attend the Council. Their studied eloquence was of no value. They ought to have been glad of a synod, even had it not been attended by their own envoys. The Council of Nicaea had set the example of revising the decision of former synods. " If you say that every Council is unalterable, who is it, pray, who sets Councils at naught ? The Arians were expelled by that of Nicaea, and yet they are said to be received by you. They are condemned by all, while Athanasius and Marcellus have many defenders. In fact, Athanasius was not convicted of anything at Tyre, and the acts in the Mareotis were invalid, being drawn up by one party only." The Pope then speaks of affairs at Alexandria, of envoys sent to Rome by the usurp- ing Gregory, and of the intruded bishop Pistus. The Euseb- ians asserted that the Western condemnation of Novatian, and the Eastern condemnation of Paul of Samosata, had been respected by all, and subject to no revision. Why, then, did they not similarly respect the Council of Nicaea ? They had violated that Council also by frequent translations of Bishops from see to see. Bishops, they said, were not measured by the greatness of their cities ; why, then, were the Eastern bishops not content with a small city ? (This refers, above all, to Eusebius, who from being bishop of Berytus had changed to the city of Nicomedia, where the Court frequently was,[1] and then had usurped the see of Constantinople, the newly-founded capital.) They complained that the time appointed was too short, but they kept the legates till January. This letter, like the former one, was in the name of all ; but the former was addressed only to those who had written to Rome. " Our admission of Athanasius and Marcellus to communion was not rash. We had the former letter of Eusebius, and now this letter of yours, and the letter of the bishops of Egypt and of others in favour of Athanasius. Your first and second letters did not agree ; the Egyptian bishops were on the spot. Arsenius is still alive, and the evidence from the Mareotis is a mere party statement. Athanasius waited here a year and a half, and his mere presence puts his accusers to shame, since

[1] Libanius tells us that Nicomedia yielded to no city in beauty and to four only of the world in size.

he showed his confidence by obeying our summons. Is it we
or you who act against the canons, when you ordained a
bishop at Antioch, thirty-six stages distant, and sent him
with soldiers to Alexandria ?   If Athanasius had been really
convicted at Tyre, you should have made another bishop
years ago, when he was exiled in Gaul."

"When we had sent to summon a Council you could not
prejudge the matter. The violence exercised at Alexandria
is terrible, and you call it peace ! As for Marcellus, he denied
your charges ; his confession was approved by the priests Vito
and Vincentius (the Papal representatives at Nicaea) ; Eastern
as well as Western bishops were at the Council, and deputies
from the East, complaining of violence and that bishops were
prevented from coming by force or banishment. We hear
that only a few are the causes of this schism. If you really
believe that anything can be proved against Marcellus and
Athanasius, let any come to accuse who wish to do so, and
we will have a fresh trial."   The next sentence I will give in
full :

"For if really, as you say, they did some wrong, the judgement ought to have been given according to the ecclesiastical
canon and not thus.   You should have written to all of us,
so that justice might have been decreed by all.   For it was
Bishops who were the sufferers ;   and it was not obscure
Churches which have suffered, but Churches which Apostles
in person ruled. With regard to the Church of Alexandria
in particular, why were we not consulted ?   Do you not know
that this has been the custom, first to write to us, and thus for
what is just to be defined from hence ?   If, therefore, a suspicion of this sort fell upon the bishop of that place, it was
necessary to write to the Church here.   But now, though you
gave us no information, but have done as you pleased, you
ask us to give our agreement, though we have not ourselves
condemned.   These are not the statutes of Paul, these are
not the traditions of the Fathers ; this is another rule, a new
custom. I beseech you to bear willingly what I say, for I
write for the common welfare, and *what we have received from
Blessed Peter the Apostle, that I declare to you.*"

This famous passage plainly declares that " the Church
here " (not the Church of the West, but obviously, the Church
of Rome), and no other, was able to judge the bishop of
Alexandria, who ranked in order next after the Pope. St.

Julius solemnly states that he is giving the tradition handed down from Peter, as the successor of whom he speaks. But the first part of the quotation is more general ; it says that, " according to the ecclesiastical canon," in a case of deposition of bishops on such a large scale, the whole West—" all of us " —should have been consulted.

It is extremely interesting to see how this sentence was understood a century later by two Eastern historians. Socrates thus commences his summary of this famous letter :

" Julius, writing back to those who were assembled at Antioch, reproved them, first, for the bitterness of their letter, then for acting contrary to the canons, because they had not invited him to the synod, since the ecclesiastical canon orders that the Churches shall not make canons against the judgement (παρὰ γνώμην) of the bishop of Rome " (ii. 17).

Sozomen has evidently copied him :

" He wrote blaming them for making stealthy innovations in the Nicene dogma, and for not inviting him to the synod, contrary to the laws of the Church, saying that it was a sacerdotal law that what was done against the will of the Roman bishop was null and void " (iii. 10).

The statement that Julius complained of not being invited to their Council is a mistake. The famous assertions that the ecclesiastical law invalidated any canons disapproved by the bishops of Rome is doubtless implied in his letter, but it is not stated. It is remarkable that the two Greek historians of the following century read into the letter of the Pope the claim which they thought it natural he should make. They also state that Julius, by letter, restored other Eastern bishops to their Sees, " by reason of the prerogative possessed by the Roman Church," " on the ground that the care of all belonged to him, on account of the dignity of his See," but these letters are lost,[1] and there may be some confusion of date.

---

[1] Socrates ii. 15 "ἄτε προνόμια τῆς ἐν 'Ρώμῃ 'Εκκλησίας ἐχούσης. Sozomen iii. 8. " οἷα δὲ τῆς πάντων κηδεμονίας αὐτῷ προσηκούσης διὰ τὴν ἀξίαν τοῦ θρόνου."
The ἄτε and οἷα give the reason alleged by Julius in his letters. Dr. Bright, Bishop Gore, and others have actually asserted that we should understand Socrates and Sozomen to reject the claims he made. Of course there is no trace of any such intention on their

Meanwhile the famous synod *in Encæniis* met at Antioch.
It consisted of a large number of Bishops (Prof. Gwatkin
thinks about ninety) who were for the most part conservative
and orthodox. They drew up twenty-five canons, and
anathematized Marcellus and anyone who should hold with
him,[2] and had no idea that the condemnation of Athanasius
at Tyre could have been unjust. They also signed three
creeds : the first a vague one, evidently proposed by the
Eusebian party, and considered insufficient by the rest ; the
other two being in parts perfectly explicit, but in other parts
less satisfactory, and of course avoiding the Nicene ὁμοούσιος,
which many of the most orthodox believed to be ambiguous
and unserviceable. It seemed to the Easterns that Arianism
had been condemned once for all at Nicaea, while Arius
himself was said to have submitted and to have been reconciled.
The Eusebians did not teach the doctrines of Arius, but
promoted a moderate and undefined medium between the
Nicene dogma and pure Arianism. The Eastern bishops
seem to have had a very uncertain grasp of the theological
question. While Alexandria and Rome possessed a perfectly
definite tradition with regard to the Three Persons and One
God, the Easterns seem to have had no such knowledge.
They appear to have inherited a theological position similar
to that of some of the second century apologists, or of the
author of the *Philosophumena*, and many others, which made
the Word of God His image and divine, and yet not one with
Him, while their doctrine of the Holy Spirit was quite undefined. The Monarchian controversies of the third century
had been caused by a revulsion from this attitude of many
within the Church. The *Philosophumena* describes Pope
Callistus as a kind of Monarchian, evidently because in condemning Monarchianism he had asserted the unity of the

part. Dr. Bright had conveniently forgotten the similar passage
of Socrates ii. 8 : " Nor was Julius present (at the Council of Antioch)
the Bishop of great Rome, nor had he sent anyone in his place ; *although
the ecclesiastical canon orders that the Churches may make no decisions*
(i.e., binding oecumenically) *without the approval of the Bishop of Rome.*"
(καίτοι κανόνος ἐκκλησιαστικοῦ κελεύοντος, μὴ δεῖν παρὰ τὴν γνώμην
τοῦ ἐπισκόπου 'Ρώμης τὰς ἐκκλησίας κανονίζειν.) This is a perfectly
clear statement of the Church's law as it was understood at Constantinople at the beginning of the fifth century, a hundred years after
Nicaea. Socrates is here not quoting any other writer, but stating
a fact as he knew it to be. This makes it entirely indubitable that his
own view coincides with the opinion he attributes to St. Julius in ii.
15 and ii. 17, quoted above.
    [2] Probably they had not received the letter of Julius and his Council.

Father and Son as one God.   Similarly the Eusebians
denounced the chief upholders of the Nicene doctrine as
followers of the Monarchianism of Sabellius, who made no
real distinction between the Divine Persons for fear of injury
to the perfection of the unity of God.   The large number of
Eastern bishops who were deceived by this are called " con-
servatives " by Professor Gwatkin, but it was a conservatism
based upon ignorance, and scarcely consistent with Mono-
theism.   At Alexandria the predecessors of Athanasius,
Alexander and Peter, had taught as he did, and he has proved
the same of the great Dionysius in the middle of the third
century, and of his namesake at Rome.   The teaching of the
Nicene faith was clearly conservatism in the West and in
Egypt.   Arianism was the exaggerated expression of tendencies which had long been latent in the Antiochian provinces and Asia Minor, and the revulsion against it in those
provinces was but slight, except when presented in the
blasphemous form given to it by Arius before Nicaea, and
later by the Anomoeans.   With these the bulk of the Eastern
bishops never communicated ; but the Eusebians, the original
court party, and their successors in court favour, the Homoe-
ans, found these well-meaning prelates an easy prey.   They
were assured that the real danger was not Arius, who had
repented, but the criminal Athanasius, and the Sabellian
Marcellus.   The doctrine of the latter was possibly incorrect ;
it was not Sabellian.   Thus, though the great synod *in
Encaeniis* was dominated by the Eusebians, and though its
creeds fall short of the Nicene standard, yet the Bishops who
composed it were not heretics in intention, and St. Hilary
calls it an assembly of Saints.

In spite of the statements of Socrates and Sozomen, it
seems most unlikely that any of the dispossessed bishops
could have been actually restored to their Sees after the
Roman Council, for Constantius was wholly given over to the
Arianizing party ; though the historians may be right in
stating that the Pope gave them letters which authorised
their restoration.   St. Athanasius, at all events, remained in
Rome for more than three years altogether, and he apparently
superintended there the writing of a Bible for the Emperor
Constans.   Some modern scholars have suggested that this book
is to be identified with the most famous of all biblical manuscripts, the *Codex Vaticanus*, B.[1]   In the fourth year of his

[1] Athanasius. *Apol. ad Const.* 4.   So Rahlfs. Zahn and others.

exile he was summoned to the Emperor at Milan, who had decided to follow the suggestion of Pope Julius, Hosius of Cordova, and other Bishops, and write to his brother Constantius the Emperor of the East, in order to arrange for the meeting of a great synod of East and West, in which all difficulties could be smoothed away. Constantius agreed, and Sardica, on the borders of the two empires, was appointed for the place of meeting.

The Council apparently met in the summer of 343.[1] Sardica was just within the dominions of Constans, though only some fifty miles from Constantinople. This was disastrous for the Eusebians, the Court party, who could do nothing without a " Count," St. Athanasius says, to control the proceedings in their favour. The Easterns, who numbered seventy-six, shut themselves up in a palace and demanded that the deposition of Athanasius and Marcellus should be received without discussion, repeating their complaint that one Council had no right to revise the acts of another. This amounted to a denial of the right of the Pope and his Roman Council to try the case once decided at Tyre. It did not admit the right of a bishop to any appeal from his first condemnation, and left St. Athanasius at the mercy of his shameless accusers. The majority of bishops, probably about ninety-four or ninety-six, refused to agree, and the Easterns retired in a body on the plea that the development of the Persian war of Constantius rendered it impossible for them to be away from their flocks. They stopped, however, just within the border of the Eastern Empire at Philippopolis and composed an encyclical letter, which was written after the Western decisions,[2] so that their haste was evidently a mere pretence. This letter informs us that the Council was summoned by the wish of Julius of Rome, Maximus of Trèves, and Hosius of Cordova. These the heretical assembly proposed to condemn, and especially Julius as the *princeps et dux malorum*.[3]

Meanwhile the orthodox Bishops had acquitted Athanasius and Marcellus, judging that the latter had been misrepresented. They wrote to the Church of Alexandria informing them of the acquittal of their bishop, and to the bishops of

---

[1] So Gwatkin, p. 124. Hefele shifts it to the following year (ii. pp. 86-9). I have repeated a few sentences from the account of the Council which follows, in *Bishop Gore and the Catholic Claims*. ch. vi.

[2] Hefele thinks not.

[3] Mansi. iii. 126. Hil. *Frag*. 3.

Egypt and Libya and to all bishops of the world, and also a special letter to St. Julius. The contrast with the heretics is striking. These had excommunicated the Pope, and addressed their conciliar epistle to the pseudo-Bishop Gregory of Alexandria, who had been intruded by the secular power, and actually to the Donatist bishop of Carthage—so far had they receded from all decency. The orthodox bishops, on the other hand, in communion with the great Athanasius, and presided over by the venerable Hosius, together with two priests as papal legates, wrote a special report of their proceedings to the Pope. They excommunicated eight of the chiefs of the Eusebian party, and the intruded bishops of Alexandria, Gaza and Ancyra, and invited all bishops to sign their encyclical. To the Pope they wrote :

" What we have always believed, that we now experience ; for experience proves and confirms what each has heard ; true is that which the most blessed teacher of the Gentiles, Paul the Apostle, said of himself : ' Do you seek a proof of Christ who speaketh in me ? ' Though of a surety, since the Lord Christ dwelt in him it cannot be doubted but that the Holy Spirit spoke by his mouth, and was heard through the instrumentality of his body. And you likewise, beloved brother, though separated in body, were present in mind and agreement and will, and your excuse for absence was good and unavoidable, that the schismatic wolves might not steal and rob by stealth, nor the heretic dogs bark madly in the excitement of their wild fury, or even the crawling devil pour forth the poison of blasphemy. For this will seem to be most good and very proper, *if to the head, that is to the See of Peter the Apostle, the bishops of the Lord shall refer from all provinces.*[1] Since therefore all that has been transacted and decided is contained in the documents, and can be truly and faithfully explained by word of mouth by our beloved brothers and fellow-priests, Archidamus and Philoxenus, and our dear son, the deacon Leo, it seems almost superfluous to write it here."

[1] It has been suggested by several writers that this clause should be omitted as an interruption of the sense, and therefore an interpolation! This, however arbitrary, would be convenient for some people's views. But the connection is not difficult to see : Julius was right to be unwilling to leave Rome, for there would have been no head there who could keep in order from thence the schismatic wolves and heretic dogs and hear appeals. But it should be noted how the authority of the Roman See is connected here as always with St. Peter.

Then follows an account of the doings of the Council somewhat shorter than in the other letters. The Pope is asked to
publish the decrees in Italy, Sicily, and Sardinia. In each
letter the refusal of the Eusebians to obey the summons to
Rome is emphasized.[1]

A number of canons was drawn up [2] concerning discipline,
the most important of which are those which deal with the
question of appeals of bishops. Apart from the Council of
Arles there was practically no canon law in the West, except
those decrees of custom vaguely referred to as " the ecclesiastical canon." In practice it is probable that all the more
serious matters came before the Pope, and the evolution of a
system of Metropolitans was only just beginning in the
Western Church. In the East several Councils had published
canons, and the Council of the Dedication at Antioch had
just drawn up twenty-five, one of which appeared to be aimed
at Athanasius. It had attributed considerable power to the
Metropolitans, and had allowed to a bishop an appeal to the
neighbouring bishops from a condemnation by his comprovincials, if their verdict was not unanimous; but if unanimous, it was irreversible.

It was natural that a larger right of appeal should be
desired by the orthodox at Sardica, and that they should
keep in view the present situation. The hope of orthodoxy
was in the West, where the bishops, almost without exception,
adhered to the Nicene settlement, where the Emperor supported them, and where the admittedly indefectible faith of
the Roman Church formed a rallying point. Every heresy
had beaten against that Church, but in vain. And now its
bishop had exercised his prerogative in annulling the decisions
of the Council of Tyre, in summoning both the Patriarch of
Alexandria and the Eusebians to Rome, and in restoring the
ejected bishops to their sees, even though he could not,

___

[1] In the letter to Julius : sed et conuenti per presbyteros tuos et per
epistolam ad synodum quae futura erat in urbe Roma, uenire noluerunt.
  To the Church of Alexandria : καὶ διὰ γραμμάτων καὶ διὰ ἀγράφων
ἐντολῶν ὑπεμνήσθησαν οἱ τῆς ἑώας, καὶ ἐκλήθησαν παρεῖναι. And to
all Bishops : καὶ εἰ τὰ μάλιστα ἐκ τοῦ κληθέντας αὐτοὺς παρὰ τοῦ
ἀγαπητοῦ ἡμῶν καὶ συλλειτουργοῦ ᾿Ιουλίου μὴ ἀπαντῆσαι. καὶ ἐκ τῶν
γραφέντων παρὰ τοῦ αὐτοῦ ᾿Ιουλίου, φανερὰ τούτων ἡ συκοφαντία πέφηνεν.
ἦλθον γὰρ ἄν, εἴπερ ἐθάρρουν οἷς ἔπραξαν καὶ πεποιήκασι κατὰ τῶν
συλλειτουργῶν ἡμῶν.
  [2] Their genuineness was recently shown in the J.T.S. (April 1902)
by Mr. C. H. Turner against a Tendenzschrift by Dr. Friedrich.

owing to the Emperor's opposition, give effect to this latter decision. The Council had met at his desire, and it is highly probable that the canons proposed to the Council by Hosius had been previously drawn up in Rome, under the direction of Pope Julius. The first canon of all has verbal reminiscences of his letter to the Eusebians. It re-asserts the fifteenth canon of Nicaea, which forbade the translation of bishops, and Hosius adds, like Julius, that such translations always come from the desire to be bishop of a greater city. At Nicaea such translations were simply declared null ; at Sardica even lay communion is refused to a bishop who has been translated. There can be no doubt that the canon was aimed directly at the late leader of the Court party, Eusebius. The canon may be presumed to have been contemplated and drafted before the death of Eusebius, more than a year previously, and it was founded upon the letter of Julius himself.

The laws for appeals have been much discussed, but the meaning is undoubtedly as follows :

CANON III.—If a bishop has been condemned, and he thinks he has a good cause, let his judges, or (if they will not) the bishops of the neighbouring province, write to the Roman bishop, who will either confirm the first decision or order a new trial, appointing the judges himself. (On the motion of Gaudentius, bishop of Naissus in Dacia, it was added that when any bishop had appealed to Rome, no successor should be appointed until the matter had been determined by the bishop of Rome.)

CANON VII (V).—Further, if, after condemnation by the bishops of the region, a bishop should himself appeal and take refuge with the bishop of Rome, let the latter deign to write to the bishops of the neighbouring province to examine and decide the matter. And if the condemned bishop desires the Pope to send a priest *a latere*, this may be done. And if the Pope shall decide to send judges to sit with the bishops, having authority from him who sent them, it shall be as he wills.[1] But if he thinks the bishops alone suffice, it shall be as his wisdom shall think fit.

Fr. Puller's comment is : " It seems most strange that

---

[1] *Si decreverit mittendos esse qui praesentes cum episcopis judicent habentes auctoritatem a quo destinati sunt, erit in suo arbitrio.* So Mr. Turner reads. All editions have " *ejus auctoritatem.*" (Canon vii. al. 5).

Roman Catholics should refer with any pleasure to these canons of Sardica." The reasons he gives are not new. They were repeated *ad nauseam* by the obsolete Gallican school,[1] and have been retailed by Anglicans, *e.g.* the late Dr. Bright and Bishop Gore.

To begin with, Fr. Puller misunderstands the Catholic view. He says :

" According to the view laid down by the Vatican Council, the supremacy of the Pope belongs to him *jure divino*, and as a consequence of that supremacy every member of the Church, whether he belongs to the clergy or to the laity, has an inherent right of appealing to his judgement in any matter appertaining to the jurisdiction of the Church " (p. 143).

The logic of this is deplorable. How can the fact that the Pope's supremacy belongs to him *jure divino* give to every member of the Church an inherent right of appeal to him ? The conclusion Fr. Puller could have drawn was that the Pope must have an inherent right to hear appeals if he chooses. The manner in which he exercises this right and the classes of persons whose appeal he will consent to hear are questions to be settled by canon law. In the present case Pope Julius left it to the Council ; though I believe the form of the canons had been previously prepared by himself, no doubt in consultation with neighbouring bishops and with St. Athanasius and the other exiles who were so nearly concerned. Fr. Puller continues :

" But here we have the Fathers of the Council of Sardica carrying a resolution, so to speak, in favour of the Roman See, and determining that, in honour of the memory of St. Peter, they will in certain rare cases give the Pope a very restricted right of determining whether there shall be a re-hearing, and of appointing bishops who shall form the court of appeal, and of deputing one or more legates to sit with them in that court. And all this is proposed by Bishop Hosius tentatively —'*si vobis placet*,' 'if it please you.' On the papalist theory, the whole proceeding must appear insufferably impertinent."

[1] Fr. Puller quotes (p. 4, note 2) : " The words of the canon prove that the institution of this right was *new*. ' If it please you ' says Hosius of Cordova, the President of the Council, ' let us honour the memory of Peter the Apostle,' " as from " Archbishop de Marca of Paris." This is unfair, for the famous " Concordia " was written by De Marca when a layman. Before obtaining the bulls for his first bishopric he was obliged to disown the Erastianism of his lawyer days,

There are two points here to be answered. The first is that the right granted is a " very restricted right " ; the second is that even this right is granted as a favour.

A " very restricted right " it seems to Fr. Puller, because there was no thought of giving to the Pope any right of evoking the case to Rome, for which statement he produces the authority of Hefele. It is certainly true that the Council had no intention of doing anything so " impertinent." They did not mention this right in the canon, but they assumed it in other documents, and their whole case against their opponents depended upon it. It is a pity that Fr. Puller has not better understood the position of affairs. The Easterns had claimed the Councils of Tyre and of Jerusalem to have been plenary Councils, well able to depose the Patriarch of Alexandria. They had tried to get their decisions recognized in the West by getting the Pope to grant his communion to the intruded bishop of that city. The Pope, on the other hand, had declared, as we have seen, that the decisions of a Council in which he had no share could not be final. He summoned St. Athanasius to Rome, and that Saint obeyed him. The envoys of Eusebius, however insincerely, even asked the Pope to be judge. Julius offered the Easterns a new Council, at which he would be represented. But they replied that their Council could not be revised by another. They implied— though they did not venture to say it—that the Pope himself could not revise it. Julius then, to avoid all tergiversation, decided upon the date of the Council, and ordered that it should meet in Rome. It does not appear that they absolutely refused to obey the summons ; but they made excuses, and none of them appeared.

There was no doubt, therefore, in the minds of the orthodox party at Sardica *that the Pope could summon a Patriarch of Alexandria to Rome, could order a Council to be held, could restore bishops by the prerogative of his See, and could quash the proceedings of any Council, however large, if he had sufficient reason.* But the canons are intended to go further. It was easy for the Easterns to avoid coming to Rome when summoned. It was a long journey, communication was slow, and delays and excuses were not hard to make. On the other hand, it meant voluntary exile to an orthodox bishop who undertook the journey, for his see would be filled up in his absence, and the Emperor would not permit his return. At Sardica a new system was devised. After a bishop had been condemned, and had complained of injustice, it was to be allowed for his judges, or the bishops of a neighbouring province, or the accused himselr, to appeal to the bishop of Rome to order a fresh trial by neighbouring bishops, with or without the assistance of a papal envoy or plenipotentiary. The enquiry would thus be held on the spot, or nearly so, and there would be no possibility of evasion. The new judges need not be more numerous than the former, and there would be no reason to demand an impossible general Council, or to apply to the Emperor for protection. It was an attempt to make the Pope's influence more felt in the East, now that the two greatest sees, Alexandria and Antioch, were filled by Arians of the worst reputation. It was well planned, but the court party would hardly have accepted the innovation. As it happened, the breathing space for the orthodox marked by the Council of Sardica did not last. The death of Constans in 351 brought the violence of imperial semi-Arianism upon the West. When the death of Valens at length brought permanent peace, the canons of Sardica were no longer wanted ; though in the fifth century the Popes appealed occasionally to the principles contained in the canons, under the mistaken belief that they were Nicene.

The "restricted right " is thus seen to be a proposal for the attribution to the Pope of most extraordinary powers (leaving the choice among them to him) over and above his admitted right of hearing appeals at Rome in a Council called by himself. The Pope is to decide whether he chooses to confirm the first decision or to appoint a commission to try the case again, and he is left absolutely free to appoint judges, or the bishops of a neighbouring province to sit, with or without a legate, " at his own most wise discretion." It seems to me perfectly inconceivable that such immense and undefined authority could have been given to a mere honorary primate, in whom no superior jurisdiction was recognized. On the other hand, when we remember that the Council already admitted the Pope's right to summon the case to his own court, if he thought justice was not being done, the extension of this principle by the new canons is comprehensible and natural. It is quite clear that the Pope was looked upon as having a duty of general guardianship over the whole Church. But in the very lowest view, we must conclude nobody to have been surprised that the Pope should intervene where justice needed to be enacted, and it was for the most

part considered to be his duty. The very highest view, on
the other hand, would not be so ridiculous as to suppose the
Pope to be infallible in any act of jurisdiction ; it might be
right to disagree with him, or even to avoid his judgment
when it seemed to be prejudiced. This was the view taken by
the not unorthodox bishops at the Council of the Dedication
of Antioch. They believed the Pope and the Westerns to
have been circumvented by Athanasius and Marcellus ; they
ignored the former, and excommunicated the latter with all
his adherents, among whom they did not, of course, count all
the bishops of the Roman Council.

In this fashion the whole history is clear. On Fr. Puller's
supposition that the Pope was a dignitary of great influence
but no real superiority, the whole becomes incomprehensible.
On what ground, if we admit this, could Julius summon the
Patriarch of Alexandria to Rome ?   On what ground could he
summon Eusebius and his friends ?   How had he the right to
insist upon a Council, and then upon a particular time and
place for that Council ?   What right had he to review the
decisions of Tyre and Jerusalem ?   Why did nobody protest
against his claim to restore bishops ?   If St. Athanasius did
not believe the Pope to be a general overseer of the Church,
was it not unworthy of him to utilize the pretensions of Julius
for his own purposes ?   If Hosius and the leaders of orthodoxy
at Sardica, the men to whom Christendom owed the preservation of the Nicene faith, thought Julius's claim pre-
posterous, is it conceivable that they would have given him
the enormous powers he was intended to wield under the new
canons ?

Such questions might be multiplied. Let us turn to the
second point we had to answer : the " very restricted right "
was granted to Julius as a favour. Part of the third canon
runs thus :[1]

" Hosius, the bishop, said. . . . If any bishop shall have
been condemned in any matter, and thinks that he has right
on his side, so that a new trial should be made, if it please you,
let us honour the memory of St. Peter the Apostle, and let the
Bishops who have judged the case, or those who dwell in the
neighbouring province, write to [Julius] the Roman bishop ;
and if he shall determine in favour of a new trial," etc.

[1] Best text given by Turner, *J.T.S.* April, 1902, p. 396.

In former times it has been argued that the grant was to
Julius personally, not to the bishop of Rome. But the word
" Julius " is absent from all MSS., except those representing
the collection of Dionysius Exiguus.[1] It is therefore a mere
explanatory addition, of which we need take no account.
Si uobis placet implies that the Council is asked to approve,
modify or reject the proposal. Why not ? Even in the
extreme case of rejection there could be no " impertinence."
As for the famous words " *sanctissimi Petri Apostoli memoriam
honoremus,*" " let us honour the memory of St. Peter the
Apostle," I have no objection whatever to their being taken
to imply that the right is new, and the brothers Ballerini
admitted this interpretation. But I cannot see that they do
naturally imply that a new right is given, and not a new way
of putting an old right in practice.[2] Anyhow, they mean one
thing which Fr. Puller must not pass over so lightly—that the
powers given to the Pope in the canons are not given to the
bishop of the imperial city, but to the successor of the Prince
of the Apostles, who was the Foundation of the Church and
the Shepherd of all Christ's sheep. Fr. Puller has no right to
blink the plain meaning of the words, by which a duty is laid
upon the successor of St. Peter of exerting a superiority
which is acknowledged in the coryphaeus of the apostolic
choir.

It seems most strange that Fr. Puller should " refer with
any pleasure to the canons of Sardica."

The Council was not œcumenical, for it was not concerned
with the Faith. The retirement of the Eusebian party had
left it with less than a hundred members, mainly Western.
But it was of a broadly representative character. The most
eminent Bishop of the day, Hosius of Cordova, was its president. St. Julius was represented. St. Athanasius voted in
it, and stood for the united voice of the ninety Bishops of
Egypt who were his suffragans, and held his views. In the
letter of the Council to Alexandria, preserved by the Saint,

---

[1] So Turner, l. c., p. 376.

[2] The wording of the canons seems to me to imply that the bishops
are speaking of the action of a superior: " Let the Pope deign " ;
" If the Pope shall decide to . . . it shall be as he wills " ; " But if he
thinks . . . it shall be as his wisdom shall think fit." The bishops do
not prescribe an invariable procedure, but suggest various methods,
which the Pope can choose from, according to circumstances. Surely
this is because they cannot legislate for the Pope, but only for the
appealing bishops.

it describes itself as composed of Bishops from Rome, Spain, Gaul, Italy, Africa, Sardinia, Pannonia, Mysia, Dacia, Noricum. Tuscany, Dardania, the second Dacia, Macedonia, Thessaly, Achaia, Epirus, Thrace, Rhodope, Palestine, Arabia, Crete and Egypt.

IV

ST. CHRYSOSTOM ON ST. PETER

I

THERE is one difficulty in proving the primacy of St. Peter from the Fathers. Most Anglicans of any intelligence or reading are willing to admit that the Fathers with one voice proclaim him to be the " first of the Apostles " ; and indeed the evidence for this is so obvious and so inevitable that they cannot well ignore it. But one thing they refuse to grant, and that is that he had a real primacy, a primacy of jurisdiction over the whole church, extending over the apostles themselves.

Now it is here that the difficulty comes in. The apostles were all inspired and led by the Holy Ghost. There was no necessity to order them about, or to keep them in strict discipline, still less to judge between them or to punish them ; hence we see St. Peter's jurisdiction in Holy Scripture principally in the form of leadership. I do not think that any unbiased person could carefully study the place of St. Peter in the Bible without coming to the conclusion that he was really set over the whole Church by Our Lord, and that he actually exercised a real primacy of jurisdiction. Even to the casual reader there are few doctrines that lie so patently upon the surface of the sacred writings. And, I think, few people could read Mr. Allies' admirable digest of Passaglia, *St. Peter, His Name and Office*, without acknowledging the proofs to be overwhelming. But then, Protestants do *not* study the place of St. Peter in the Bible, they pass it over. They do *not* read Mr. Allies' excellent book : they either have never heard of it, or they avoid it. " If," asks a recent writer, " as de Maistre thought, ' the supremacy of the Pope is the capital dogma without which Christianity cannot subsist,' why is there nothing about it in the Scriptures of Truth ? " If I admitted the supposition, I should merely reply that ' the Bible ' is not an exhaustive and elaborate

manual of theology, like Hurter's ' Compendium ' and that
the Church's teaching is quite sufficient proof of the dogma.
But, of course, I do not admit it ; I urge on the contrary, ' If
the primacy of St. Peter is so unimportant a fact—if it gave
him no prerogatives, no duties, no successors—why on earth
is it so extraordinarily prominent in Holy Writ ? '

Outside the Bible the question is less easy to solve, for many
of the Fathers have left but few writings, and say little about
St. Peter. It is true that they seldom forget, when they do
mention him, to call him the first, the prince, the coryphaeus,
the leader, of the apostles ; but it is, of course, not so natural
to them to exhibit him as exercising a coercive jurisdiction
over his colleagues. There are numbers of well-known
passages which in their obvious meaning suggest a real
primacy, but which may easily be " explained away " by
ingenious persons, whose theological training has largely
consisted in learning the art of explaining away the Thirty-nine
Articles and the Prayer Book.

St. Chrysostom has left us a huge mass of writings, chiefly
sermons. His references to St. Peter are exceedingly
numerous, lengthy and explicit. His name has been in the
forefront of the controversy as to St. Peter's prerogatives,
especially in a contest between the late Dr. Rivington on the
one side and Dr. Gore and Fr. Puller on the other.[1] It has
seemed to me that the only way to settle a discussion of this
sort is to examine the question exhaustively. I have been
at pains to find and read whatever St. Chrysostom has said
about St. Peter, and I have found more than ninety passages
to copy out and set together, having reference either to the
primacy of St. Peter or to his relations with the other apostles.
The conclusion at which I have arrived, and at which I expect
the reader to arrive, is that St. John Chrysostom, at once
the most voluminous and the most popular [2] of the Greek
Fathers, believed and taught, and was ever anxious and
careful to teach, that St. Peter was really the chief ruler of
the Church.

The importance of this conclusion is that it leads us
naturally to interpret in the same sense the expressions,
similar to those of Chrysostom, which we find in other Greek

---

[1] Puller. *Primitive Saints and the See of Rome.* 3rd. ed. p. 116.

[2] I mean popular in ancient times. The amount of spurious sermons
attributed to him surpasses in bulk the genuine works of any other
Greek Father.

Fathers who have bequeathed us a less amount of material.
St. Chrysostom, priest of Antioch and bishop of Constantinople, is a central and typical figure.   If the evidence from
his writings is found to be clear and unmistakable, it will
hardly be necessary to interrogate the rest of the Eastern
Church in detail.   It will be amply sufficient to examine (and
verify [1]) the copious quotations to be found in such meritorious
and useful collections as Mr. Allnatt's " Cathedra Petri " and
Waterworth's " Faith of Catholics."

In the first place, let us note St. Chrysostom's habit of
showing his extraordinary reverence for St. Peter, by habitually adding to his name a whole list of titles, for instance :

" Peter, that head of the Apostles, the first in the Church,
the friend of Christ, who received the revelation not from man
but from the Father . . . this Peter, and when I say Peter,
I mean the unbroken Rock, the unshaken foundation, the
great apostle, the first of the disciples, the first called, the
first to obey." [2]

Or again :

" Peter the coryphæus of the choir of apostles, the mouth of
the disciples, the foundation of the faith, the base of the
confession, the fisherman of the world, who brought back
our race from the depth of error to heaven, he who is everywhere fervent and full of boldness, or rather of love than of
boldness."[3]

" The first of the apostles, the foundation of the Church, the
coryphæus of the choir of the disciples."[4]

" The foundation of the Church, the vehement lover of
Christ, at once unlearned in speech, and the vanquisher of

---

[1] I add " verify " for the reader is at liberty to dissent from these
writers on minor points ; and it is best to be severe in keeping a rule
of *never* trusting anyone's quotations without verifying them.   To make
this easier, I will try to make my references as accurate as I can.   I
use Migne's edition, giving his volumes and pages, adding in brackets
the pages of Dom Montfaucon's edition (the vols. have the same numbers) which Migne reprinted entire, except vol. VII, which contains the
homilies on St. Matthew ; this he gives from Field's edition.   The
number therefore which I give in brackets, when I quote this volume,
refers to Field and not to Montfaucon.
   [2] (*De eleemos* III. 4, vol. II, p. 298 [300]).
   [3] (*Hom. de decem mille talentis*, 3, vol. III, p. 20 [4]).
   [4] (*Ad eos qui scandalizati sunt*, 17, vol. III, p. 517 [504]).

orators, the man without education who closed the mouth of philosophers, who destroyed the philosophy of the Greeks as though it were a spider's web, he who ran throughout the world, he who cast his net into the sea, and fished the whole world."[1]

" Peter, the base, the pillar."[2]

" This holy coryphæus of the blessed choir, the lover of Christ, the ardent disciple, who was entrusted with the keys of heaven, he who received the spiritual revelation."[3]

We shall meet presently with many more passages of the same kind.[4] The commonest title of all is *coryphaeus*, the head-man, or (of a chorus) leader, conductor. The word of itself implies no idea of jurisdiction. It is used in the singular by St. Chrysostom of St. Peter only, so far as I can discover, but he calls Peter, James and John together, " the coryphaei,"[5] and similarly with Andrew they are "two pairs of coryphaei,"[6]

---

[1] *In illud, Vidi dominum*, 3, vol. VI, p. 123 [124].

[2] Hom. *Quod frequenta conueniendum sit*, 5, vol. xii, p. 466 [328].

[3] *In Acta Apost.* VI, 1. [chap. 2, verse 22] vol. IX, 56 [48].

[4] In the doubtfully genuine homily on SS. Peter and Elias (vol. II, p. 727 [731]) we find : " Peter was to be entrusted with the keys of the church, or, rather, he was entrusted with the keys of heaven, and he was to be entrusted with the multitude of the people. . . . That Peter the head of the apostles, the unshaken foundation, the unbroken rock, the first in the Church, the unconquerable port, the unshaken tower . . . he who was to be entrusted with the Church, the pillar of the Church, the port of the faith, Peter, the teacher of the whole world. . . . Peter, that column, that bulwark." I quote nothing in this article from the certainly spurious sermon on SS. Peter and Paul, (vol. VIII, p. 491) though it is interesting, as showing the views of some later and second-rate imitator of the golden-mouthed preacher.

[5] *Hom.* 56 (57) *in Matt.*, vol. VII., p. 550 (566) : " He took the coryphaei and led them up into a high mountain apart. . . . Why does he take these three alone ? Because they excelled the others (ὑπερέχοντες). Peter showed his excellence by his great love of Him, John by being greatly loved, James by the answer . . . ' We are able to drink the chalice.' " So also *Hom.* 26, *in Act.*, vol. IX, p. 198 (208) and compare *ibid* p. 199 (209) : " Do you not see that the headship (κεφάλαιον) was in the hands of these three, especially of Peter and James ? This was the chief cause of their condemnation (by Herod)." And compare *Hom.* 46 (47) *in Matt.* 3, vol. VII, p. 480 (485) : " He said not to Peter, ' If thou lovest Me, do miracles,' but, ' Feed My sheep ' ; and everywhere giving him more honour than the rest, with James and John, wherefore, tell me, did he prefer him?" Also *Hom.* 70 (69) *in Joann.* 2, vol. VIII, p. 383 (415) : " It seems to me that He washed the feet of the traitor first. . . . Though Peter was the first, it is probable that the traitor being impudent, reclined even above the Coryphaeus."

[6] *Hom.* 37 (38) *in Matt.* vol. VII, p. 424 (420).

or James and John, or Peter and John, are " the two coryphaei,"¹ and so especially are St. Peter and Paul.² Still " the
coryphaeus " *par excellence* is Peter.³ It is best to give St.
Chrysostom's own explanation.

" In the Kingdom, therefore, the honours were not equal,
nor were all the disciples equal, but the three were above the
rest ; and among these three again there was a great difference, for God is exact to the last degree ; ' for one star differeth
from another star in glory.' And yet all were apostles, all will
sit upon the twelve thrones, and all left their possessions,
and all were with Christ. And yet he selected these three.
And, again, among the three, He said that some must yield
or excel. For, ' to sit on My right hand and on My left,'
he said, ' is not Mine to give, but to them for whom it is
prepared.' And He set Peter before them saying : ' Lovest
thou Me more than these ? ' And John loved Him more than
the rest. For of all there will be an exact examination ; and
if you excel your neighbour ever so little, God will not overlook it."⁴

¹ *Hom.* 32 (33) *in Matt.* vol. VII, p. 380 (368) and *Hom.* 10 *in Acta*,
vol. IX, p. 85 (80).
² *Contra ludos et theatra*, 1, vol. VI, p. 265 (273) : " The coryphaei,
Peter the foundation of the faith, Paul the vessel of election." *Hom.
quod frequenter conveniendum sit*, 5, vol. XII, p. 466 (328) : " The
coryphaei, and heads and towers and bulwarks, and the principal
persons of those in the N.T." Compare also the doubtfully genuine
De precatione, vol. II, 784 (788) : " Columns of the Church, coryphaei
of the apostles, renowned in heaven, the wall of the world, the common
bulwark of all sea and land."
³ To the dozens of instances which occur in the course of the article,
I add : *In inscript. Act.* ii, 4, vol. III, p. 83 (66) ; *Hom.* 54 (55) *in
Matt.* 4, vol. VII, p. 536 (550) ; *Hom.* 33 (32) *in Joann*, 3, vol. VIII,
p. 191 (193) ; *ibid. Hom.* 72 (71), 1, p. 390 (423) and *Hom.* 73 (72),
1, p. 396 (430) ; *Hom.* 22 *in Acta.* 1, vol. IX, p. 171 (177) ; *Hom. in
1 Cor.*, 4, vol. X, p. 36 (29), etc. So when the saint compares the
Apostles with the philosophers, he contrasts Peter with Plato, " the
Coryphaeus of philosophers " (*Hom.* 4, *in Acta*, 4, vol. IX, p. 48 [39]).
St. Jerome has the same idea. " As Plato was prince of philosophers,
so is Peter of the apostles, upon whom the Church is founded in massive
solidity, which is shaken by no surge of floods nor any storm " (*Dial.
c. Pelag.* 1, 14, p. 506 [707]). The homilies on the Acts were preached
at Constantinople about the year 400 ; St. Jerome wrote his dialogue
in 415, so he may have borrowed from Chrysostom, who had been dead
eight years. This is worth noticing, in view of the fact that the Homilies
on Acts were considered spurious by Erasmus (though his opinion has
not been followed), whilst the first certain reference to them is said to
be in Cassiodorus.
⁴ *Hom.* 31, *in Rom.* 4, vol. IX, p. 672 [750].

But the holy Doctor does not mean merely that certain disciples (and especially Peter) were honoured by their Master because of their greater love. He adds, further, that Peter had a rank, a precedence, accorded to him by the other apostles. Before the Passion they disputed who should be the greatest, and Our Lord told them that their chief (whoever he should be) must not lord it over them after the fashion of a Gentile king, but that he must be the servant of all. Clearly it was not mere precedence and rank that the chief of the apostles was to receive by Christ's institution, but higher duties and work more strenuous than the rest. So thought St. Chrysostom: " See the unanimity of the apostles," he says, on *Acts* ii, 4 : " they give up to Peter the office of preaching, for it would not do for all to preach." " Hear how this same John, who now comes forward (to ask for a seat at Christ's right hand) in the Acts of the Apostles, always gives up the first place to Peter both in preaching and in working miracles. Afterwards James and John were not thus. Everywhere they gave up the first place to Peter, and in preaching they set him first, though he seemed of rougher manners than the others." Again, he remarks how St. Paul " gives up to Peter the first place."[1]

This certainly resembles less the primacy of the Duke of Norfolk among English peers (to which the primacy of Peter has been likened) [2] than it does the position of leader of the House.

II

In examining the interpretation of certain Petrine passages by this greatest of commentators, we naturally begin with the promise to Peter in the sixteenth chapter of St. Matthew. The rock on which the Church is to be built is regularly taken by St. Chrysostom to be the confession of Peter, or the faith which prompted this confession. It is well known that this oblique interpretation—" on the faith of Peter " for " on Peter because of his faith "—was invented as a useful weapon against Arianism : " It is upon Peter's confession of Christ as

---

[1] *Hom.* 4, *in Acta.* 3, vol. IX, p. 46 (37) ; *Hom.* 65 (66) *in Matt.* 4, vol. VII, p. 622 (648) ; *ibid. Hom.* 50 (51), p. 506 (515) ; *Hom.* 35 *in* I *Cor.* 5, vol. X, p. 303 (329) ; *Hom.* 8, *in Acta.*, 1, vol. IX, pp. 71-72 (64-65).
[2] Puller, p. 489.

the true Son of God that the Church is immovably built." [1]
This does not prevent Chrysostom from enunciating with
equal emphasis the direct form : " He was made the foundation
of the Church " [2] and continually he entitles Peter ὁ θεμέλιος,
ἡ κρῆπις, τὸ στερέωμα, " The Foundation of the Faith " or
even " of the confession." Some instances have been quoted,
some will appear as we proceed.

It is in the fifty-fourth homily on St. Matthew that we find
a complete commentary on the passage :

" [When Christ has asked : ' Whom say ye that I am ?]
What, then, does the mouth of the apostles, Peter, everywhere
fervent, the Coryphæus of the choir of the apostles ? All are
asked, and he replies. When Christ asked what were the
opinions of the people, all answered ; but when He asked for
their own, Peter leaps forward, and is the first to speak :
' Thou art the Christ.' And what does Christ answer ?
' Blessed art thou,' etc. . . . Why, then, said Christ :
' Thou art Simon, son of Jona, thou shalt be called Cephas '
(John i. 42) ? Because thou hast proclaimed My Father,
I name thy father, as though I said : 'As thou art son of Jona,
so am I son of My Father. . . . And I say to thee : Thou art
Peter, and upon this rock I will build My Church, *that is upon
the faith of this confession.*' Hence He shows that many will
believe, and raises his thoughts higher, and *makes him Shepherd.*
'And the gates of hell shall not prevail against it.' If they
prevail not against it, much less against Me : so be not terrified
when thou shalt hear ' I shall be betrayed and crucified.'
And then he speaks of another honour : 'And I will give thee
the keys of the kingdom of heaven.' What is this : 'And I
will give thee ' ? 'As the Father hath given thee to know Me,

---

[1] " He who built the Church upon his confession " (*Hom.* 82 (83)
in Matt. 3, vol. VII, p. 741 ([786]) ; the same in *Hom.* 21 (20) *in Joann.* 1,
vol. VIII, p. 128 (120). Otherwise on chap. 2 of *Galat.* 4, vol. X,
p. 640 (686) " He received his name for the unchangeableness and
immobility of his faith ; and when all were asked in common, he says,
leaping forth before the others : ' Thou art the Christ,' etc., when he
was entrusted with the keys of the kingdom of heaven." So also
Hom. 2 *in Inscr. Act.* 6, vol. III, p. 86 (70) ; and compare *Hom.* 19
(18) *in Joann.* vol. VIII, p. 121 (111-112).

In a spurious sermon we find : " He said not ἐπὶ τῷ Πέτρῳ, for it
was not upon the man, but upon the faith that he built His Church " ;
and then, oddly, we are told by the author that Christ called His Church
the " Petra " (*Hom. spur. in Pentec.* 1, vol. III, p. 806 [790]). Cp.
also Palladius. *Dial. de vita Chrys.* (in vol. 1), p. 68 : " Upon
this rock, that is, upon this confession."

[2] *Hom.* 3, *in Matt.* 5, vol. VII, p. 38 (42).

so will I give thee ' . . . Give what ? The keys of heaven, in order that whatsoever thou shalt bind on earth may be bound in heaven, and whatsoever thou shalt loose on earth may be loosed in heaven.' Now, then, is it not His to give to sit upon His right hand and on his left, since He says : ' I will give thee ' ? Do you see how He Himself leads Peter to a high consideration of Himself, and reveals Himself and shows Himself to be the Son of God by these two promises ? For what is proper to God alone, that is, to forgive sins, and to make the Church immovable in so great an onset of waves, and *to cause a fisherman to be stronger than any rock, when the whole world wars against him,* this He Himself promises to give ; as the Father said, speaking to Jeremias, that He would set him as a column of brass and as a wall ; but *Jeremias to a single nation, Peter to the whole world.*

" I would willingly ask those who wish to lessen the dignity of the Son : Which are the greater gifts, those which the Father gave to Peter, or those which the Son gave him ? The Father gave to Peter the revelation of the Son, but the Son gave to him to spread that of the Father and of Himself throughout the world, and to a mortal man He entrusted the power over all that is in heaven, in giving the keys to *him who extended the Church throughout the world, and showed it stronger than the world.*"[1]

I think this passage alone would have made it clear that the Rock is Peter, in St. Chrysostom's view, as well as, and because of, the firmness of his confession. He has no idea of the two notions, " Peter is the Rock " and " his faith is the Rock " being mutually exclusive, as, in fact, they are not. It is equally clear that the promise is understood as granting him an oecumenical jurisdiction in a way which is not given to the other apostles.

III

The charge to St. Peter " feed my sheep " is referred to very often by St. John Chrysostom. Father Puller says : "According to St. Chrysostom's view, the *Pasce oves* restored to St. Peter the apostolical office, which had been suspended, so far as he was concerned, in consequence of his denial of Our Lord." [2]

---

[1] *Hom.* 54 [55] *in Matt.* VII, p. 531 [546] seqq.
[2] *Primitive Saints*, p. 126.

I have been quite unable to find in the thirteen volumes of the Saint's works anything which supports this statement of Fr. Puller's.[1] There is only one place in which any " suspension " of office or of honour is suggested, and there, as everywhere else, St. Chrysostom uses words which show that he considered that something special, not given to the rest was conferred upon St. Peter. He says : " After that grave fall (for there is no sin equal to denial) after so great a sin, He brought him back *to his former honour* and entrusted him with the headship (ἐπιστασία) *of the universal church*, and, what is more than all, He showed us that he had a greater love for his master than any of the apostles, for saith he : ' Peter, lovest thou Me more than these ? ' " [2]

Of course if we urge that all the apostles had the headship of the universal Church committed to them (which is in a sense quite true) we may understand the " former honour " to be the apostleship. But it seems obvious that if St. Chrysostom meant this, he would have said : " he entrusted to him in union with the other apostles," or something to that effect, and would not have joined the mention of a participated headship in jurisdiction over the faithful, with the mention of a singular primacy over the apostles in love.

But Father Puller urges the passage : " Since they—Peter and John—were to receive the care (τὴν ἐπιτροπήν) of the world, they must no longer be joined together, else a great loss would have happened to the world."[3] This shows, of course, that all the apostles together had the care of the world, but it certainly does not show that St. Peter had not a real primacy over the apostles themselves, nor is it easy to see how Father Puller managed to conclude that it does. We must take next St. Chrysostom's commentary on the text in question :

" He saith to him, ' Feed My sheep.' Why does He *pass over the others and speak of the sheep to Peter* ? He was the chosen one of the apostles, the mouth of the disciples, and the head of the choir ; for this reason Paul went up to see him rather than the others. And also to show him that he must have confidence now, since his denial had been purged

---

[1] I will remind the reader of the passage already quoted, " And He sets Peter before them, 'lovest thou Me more than these,'" where this text is cited by Chrysostom as the most obvious proof of St. Peter being set above the others.

[2] *Hom.* 5, *de Poen.* 2, vol. II, p. 308 (311).

[3] *Hom.* 88 [87] *in Joann.* 1, vol. VIII, p. 480 (528).

away, *He entrusts him with the rule* (προστασία) *over the brethren;* and the fervent love which thou hast shown throughout, and in which thou didst boast, show now ; and the life which thou saidst thou wouldst lay down for Me, give for My sheep."[1]

As if St. Chrysostom was prescient of some future critic who would wish to explain that any of the apostles might be said to preside over the brethren, and that what is said to Peter as head of the choir is meant for all, he adds further on : " If anyone should say ' Why then was it James who received the See of Jerusalem ? ' I should reply that He made Peter the teacher not of that See but of the world." It would be difficult to imply more clearly that the προστασία was given to Peter alone, than by this anticipating surprise at his not at once assuming the episcopal throne on the spot where the Holy Ghost was given.[2] " He so wiped away the denial that he even *became* the first of the apostles, and was entrusted with the whole world "[3] that is, " to be first " and " to be entrusted with the world," were two things (or rather one) granted to Peter, after his denial, by the commission " Feed My sheep." And so he acts upon the commission : " In those days Peter stood up in the midst of the disciples and said : ' as being fervent, *and as having the flock entrusted to his care,*

[1] Hom. 88 [87] *in Joann*, 1, vol. VIII, p. 477-9 (525-6).

[2] The passage continues : " Peter, therefore, turning seeth the disciple whom Jesus loved, who also reclined on His breast at supper, following, and saith : ' Lord, what shall this man do ? ' (2) Why did he mention the reclining ? Not without reason or by chance, but to show what confidence Peter had after his fall. For he who then had not dared to ask a question, but committed it to another, was given the *presidency over the brethren.* And he not only commits his own case to another, but even himself puts a question to the Master about another, and John this time is silent, while it is Peter who speaks . . . Peter loved John greatly. . . . Since then He foretold great things for Peter, *and entrusted him with the world*, and predicted his martyrdom and testified that his love was greater than that of the others, Peter wishing to receive John as his fellow, saith : And what of this man ? Shall he not go the same way ? "

Obviously St. John is here said to have understood that to Peter, not to himself, was entrusted the world.

As to the meaning of προίστασο τῶν ἀδελφῶν, if we translate : " Be the first among the brethren," then " the brethren " will be the Apostles. If we translate " Rule over the brethren " (so Puller) then it is doubtful whether the apostles are meant, or the faithful, or the faithful including the apostles. It will be safest to take " the brethren " to be the faithful, and we shall see presently that the apostles are included among them.

[3] *Adv. Judaeos*, 8, 3, vol. i, p. 931 (677).

and as the first of the choir (or, as preferred in honour) he is always the first to begin to speak."[1]

I must give another passage on which Father Puller has relied, from the treatise *De sacerdotio*. The saint is proving to his friend Basil that he must not complain of being made a bishop, since there is no way so perfect of showing love to Christ as to feed His sheep.[2]

"Addressing the coryphæus of the apostles, he says : ' Peter, lovest thou Me ? ' and on his declaration that he does, He adds : ' If thou lovest Me, feed My sheep.' The Master asks the disciple if He is loved by him, not that He may learn (how should He, who searches the hearts of all ?), but that He may teach us *how much at heart He has the headship* (ἐπιστασία) *over these sheep.* Since that is plain, it will also be evident that a great and unspeakable reward will be laid up for one who has laboured at a work so greatly honoured by Christ." . . .

Thus far it is clear that the charge to Peter is taken as the type of the commission given to all pastors of souls. Father Puller's quotation begins after this point :

" It was not Christ's intention to show how much Peter loved Him, because this already appeared in many ways, but how much He himself loves His Church ; and He desired that Peter and we all should learn it, that we may also be very zealous in the same work. For why did God not spare His Son and only-begotten, but gave Him up, though He was

---

[1] *Hom.* 3, *in Acta* (i, 15), vol. ix, p. 33 (23), cp. *Hom.* 4, 3, p. 46 (36) : " He was the mouth of all."

[2] The same doctrine is found elsewhere, with the same proof from the charge to St. Peter. *Hom.* 29 *in Rom.* c. 15, vol. IX, p. 660 (737) " For this reason *to him*, who was the coryphaeus of the apostles, and who loved Him more than the rest, *He entrusted this* (to feed His flock) having first asked him if he loved Him, that you may know that He sets this above all else as a testimony of love towards Himself, for it needs a noble soul." Again *In illud, scitote quod in noviss. diebus,* 4, vol. VI, p. 275 (282-3) : " Peter, the coryphaeus of the choir, the mouth of all the apostles, the head of that company, *the ruler* (προστάτης) *of the whole world,* the foundation of the Church, the fervent lover of Christ (for He said : ' Peter, lovest thou Me more than these ? ') I speak his praises, that you may learn that he truly loves Christ, for the care of Christ's servants is the greatest proof of devotion to Him ;—and it is not I who say this, but the beloved Master : ' If thou lovest Me,' saith He, 'Feed My sheep.' Let us see whether he has truly the primacy (προστασία) of a shepherd, whether he really cares for and truly loves the sheep and is a lover of the flock, that we may know he also loves the Shepherd."

His only One.   That He might reconcile to Himself those who were His enemies, and make them a people for Himself. Why did He also pour forth His blood ?   To purchase those sheep whom He committed to Peter and his successors."

Here Father Puller stops, remarking correctly that " his successors " does not mean the Popes, but all bishops.   But how this citation assists his theory I utterly fail to discover. St. Peter is very commonly said by the Fathers to be the type of monepiscopacy,[1] precisely because of his unique position above the other apostles.   If Father Puller is anxious to emphasize here the *episcopal* office of St. Peter over the flock, he should recollect that this office is essentially both singular and authoritative.   It is not, however, necessary to dig more out of the passage than the perfectly plain argument, " Since St. Peter is set above the rest of the apostles by being given the supreme headship of the flock because his love was greater than that of the rest it is to be understood that the pastoral office involves the highest act of love."   If, on the other hand, we are to suppose that what is given to St. Peter is simply what all the apostles had received, the edifice of St. Chrysostom's reasoning falls to the ground.[2]

[1] I quoted some rather out-of-the-way examples of this doctrine in the *Revue Bénédictine*, Jan., 1903, in a third article on the Cyprianic interpolations, p. 29 note.   The argument is this : as Peter had power over the others, so have bishops in their own sphere.   Peter was to the ancients the type of centralised power.

[2] The saint continues (and Fr. Puller has not, I suppose, seen any importance in the passage, or he would have quoted it all) : " Rightly therefore, did Christ say, ' Who is that faithful servant and prudent, whom the Lord will set over His house ? '   The words are again as of one who knows not ; but He Who spoke them did not speak in ignorance.   But, as when He asked Peter whether he loved Him, He questioned His disciple's love, not because He did not know it, but because He desired to show the excess of His own love, so now when He says : ' Who is that faithful servant and prudent ? ' He says it not because He knew not that faithful and prudent servant, but because He wished to show the rarity of the thing and the greatness of the rule (ἀρχή). See how great is the reward : ' I will set him,' saith He, ' over all My goods.'   Will you, then, still complain that I have deceived you, when you are to be set over all the goods of God, and when you are doing those things in doing which Christ said that Peter would be able to surpass (ὑπερακοντίσαι) the other apostles ?   For He said : ' Peter, lovest thou Me more than these ?   Feed My sheep.' " (*De Sacerdotio*, 2, i, p. 632 [371-2]).

It would seem from the words, " He says it, not because He knew not that faithful and prudent servant," that St. Chrysostom takes our Lord's words (from Matt. xxiv. 45-7) as designating St. Peter, and as applying in a general way to bishops.

IV

It was to prepare Peter for a unique position that he was allowed to sin beyond the rest : " He allowed the coryphaeus to fall, to make him more self-restrained, and to anoint him for yet greater love.[1]

This training of St. Peter is to be understood in another famous text, where Peter is told to " strengthen his brethren " (Luke xxii. 32). It is curious that St. John Chrysostom habitually quotes the text incorrectly : " Satan hath desired to have *thee* that he may sift *thee* as wheat " ; whereas in St. Luke all manuscripts give " To have *you*," and " may sift *you*," meaning all the apostles. The holy doctor necessarily loses the contrast between Satan's lying in wait for all, and Our Lord's prayer for one, who is to strengthen the rest. Yet he understands the passage rightly in spite of this. It is true that in his commentary on St. Matthew xxvi he explains simply that Our Lord prays for Peter, because his fall was to be the gravest.[2]

But elsewhere he says :

" Again, that coryphæus Peter, after a thousand wonders and signs and so much warning and counsel, did He not rebuke him when he had fallen this grave fall ? Nay, He passed it over, and *appointed him first of the apostles. Wherefore He said :* ' Simon, Simon, behold Satan hath desired to sift thee as wheat, and I have prayed for thee that thy faith fail not '."[3]

And yet more plainly :

" God allowed him to fall, *because He meant to make him ruler of the whole world,* ἄρχοντα τῆς οἰκουμένης ἁπάσης, that, remembering his own fall, he might forgive those who

---

[1] *Hom.* 82 (83) *in Matt.* 4, vol. vii, p. 743 (787). Immediately there follows a celebrated and exquisite passage on Holy Communion.

[2] *Hom.* 82 (83) *in Matt.* 3, vol. 7, p. 741 (785). He next asks, why did Our Lord *pray* ? " For He Who built the Church upon his confession, and so fortified it that ten thousand dangers and deaths should not prevail against it, He Who gave him the keys of heaven, and made him lord (possessor) of so much authority, and Who needed not prayer for this (for He said not ' I have prayed ' but with authority ' I will build ' and ' I will give '), how did He need prayer that He might save the soul of one man ? " The answer is, to give confidence to the disciples, whose faith was weak.

[3] *In Psalm* cxxix, 2, vol. v, p. 375 (369).

should slip in the future. *And that what I have said is no guess,* listen to Christ Himself saying : ' Simon, Simon, how often hath Satan desired to sift thee as wheat, but I have prayed for thee that thy strength fail not, and when thou art converted, strengthen thy brethren '."[1]

Another quotation to the same effect will be given when we come to the election of St. Matthias. The same intention is attributed to our Lord when He rebukes Peter's boasting by prophesying his fall :

" When he is told, ' Thou canst not follow Me now,' he says, ' Though all should deny Thee, yet will not I deny.' Because, then, it appeared likely he would be puffed up even to madness, since he practised contradicting, He warns him not to rebel. This is what Luke refers to when he says that Christ said : ' And *I have prayed for thee that thy faith fail not,* viz. that it may not be lost to the end, throughout teaching him humility, and proving that human nature is nothing by itself. For since his great love made him contradictory, He moderates him, that *he might not in the future have the same fault, when he should receive the government of the world, but that remembering his fault he might know himself.*"[2]

St. Chrysostom also calls attention to the episode of the tribute money (Matt. xvii 23). Christ, he says, had to pay the didrachma as being a first-born son, " and as Peter seemed to be the first of the disciples," the collectors came to him for information. When Our Lord by a miracle pays for Peter as well as Himself, " Do you see " cries the commentator " the excellence of the honour ? See also the philosophy of Peter's disposition : Mark, his disciple, did not write down this incident. . . . ' In that hour the disciples of Jesus came to Him, saying : Which is the greatest in the kingdom of heaven ? ' The apostles felt a human passion, wherefore the evangelist notes it, saying, ' in that hour,' when Christ honoured Peter above the rest. For either James or John was a first-born, yet He did nothing of the sort for them. Then being ashamed to acknowledge their feeling, they say not openly : ' Why hast thou honoured Peter more than us ? ' and ' Is he greater than we ? ' for they were ashamed. But they inquire vaguely : ' Who is greater ? ' For when they saw the three preferred they did not mind, but when the honour

---

[1] *Hom. quod frequenter conveniendum sit,* 5, vol. xii, p. 466 (329).
[2] *Hom.* 73 (72) *in Joann.* i. vol. viii, p. 395 (429).

was given to one instead, they were distressed. And not only at this, but putting many things together, they were angry. For He had said to Peter : ' I will give thee the keys,' and ' Blessed art thou, Simon Barjona ' and now ' give to them for Me and thee ' : and seeing his great boldness besides, they were irritated."[1]

V

It is in the Acts of the Apostles that the primacy of St. Peter is seen in exercise. St. Chrysostom's commentary on the first chapter is very remarkable. I give his words according to the Oxford translation, which renders the " short text " from good manuscripts :

" 'And in those days,' it says, ' Peter stood up in the midst of the disciples and said : *Both as being ardent, and as having been put in trust by Christ of the flock, and as having precedence of honour,*[2] *he always begins the discourse.* (The number of names together were about a hundred and twenty.) ' Men and brethren,' he says, ' this Scripture must have been fulfilled, which the Holy Ghost spake before.[3] [etc.] *Why did he not ask Christ to give him some one in the room of Judas ?*

[1] *Hom.* 58 (59) *in Matt.* 1-2, vol. vii, pp. 566-9 (584-7), Chrysostom is apparently imitating Origen *in loco.* See also *Hom.* 38 *in* 1 *Cor.* 3, vol. x, p. 326 (354) : " ' he was seen of Cephas.' He mentions at once the most worthy of credit." *Ibid.*, p. 326 (355) : " Among men He was seen by him first who most desired to see Him." *Ib.*, p. 327 (355) : " It was not because Paul was the least that He was seen by him after the others, since though He called him last, he appeared more illustrious than many who were before him, or rather than all." *Ib.*, p. 327 (356) : " The first who was thought worthy to see Him, needed much faith. . . . Therefore He appears first to Peter. For the first who confessed Him to be Christ, was rightly thought worthy to be the first to see His resurrection. But not only for this does He appear first to him, but since he had denied Him, consoling him abundantly, and showing that he has not been reprobated, He both vouchsafed to him this sight before the others, and gave to him first the sheep." This is a good instance of the way St. Chrysostom gives many reasons for one event—and also different reasons in different places.

[2] Montfaucon reads " as the first of the choir " with the " long text," which is said to be a remodelling of the original " short text." Both seem to be simply shorthand notes of Chrysostom's sermons. "προτιμότερος B, C, προτιμώμενος A and Catena ; τοῦ χοροῦ πρῶτος E, D, F " *Oxf. note.* (A, B, C, N give short text, E long text. D, F mixed).

[3] The Oxford translators have the following note: "Chrysostom seems to have read on to the end of the chapter. The rest of the citation being omitted in the MSS., the remodeller of the text makes alterations and adds matter of his own, to make the exposition run

It is better as it is. For, in the first place, they were engaged in other things ; secondly, of Christ's presence among them the greatest proof that could be given was this : as He had chosen when He was among them, so did He now being absent. Now this was no small matter for their consolation. But observe how Peter does everything *with the common consent, nothing imperiously* (οὐδὲν αὐθεντικῶς οὐδὲ ἀρχικῶς *long text*). And he does not speak thus without a meaning. [*Long text adds* : 'And he did not simply say, " Instead of Judas, we choose such a one." '] " But observe how he consoles them concerning what had passed. In fact, what had happened had caused them no small consternation."[4]

That St. Peter might have been expected to appoint a new apostle without betaking himself to lot, or consulting the brethren, is what strikes St. Chrysostom.

" Wherefore at the beginning he said : ' Men and brethren, it behoves us to choose from among you.' *He defers the decision to the whole body*, thereby making the elected objects of reverence, and himself keeping clear of all invidiousness with regard to the rest. . . . ' Must one be ordained to be a witness,' that their college (ὁ χορός) might not be left mutilated. *Then why did it not rest with Peter to make the election himself?*[5] What was the motive ? This : that he might not seem to bestow it of favour. And, besides, he was not yet endowed with the Spirit. 'And they appointed two, Joseph, called Barsabas, who was surnamed Justus, and Matthias.' Not he appointed them, but it was he that introduced the proposition to that effect, at the same time pointing out that even this was not his own, but from old time by prophecy, so that he acted as expositor not preceptor.[6]

" Again consider the moderation of James. He it was who received the bishopric of Jerusalem, and here he says nothing.

smoother. Why did he not ask of Christ, *alone*, to give him someone in the place of Judas ? And why of their own selves do they not make the election ? " Then instead of βέλτιον γέγονε λοιπόν, πρῶτον μὲν γὰρ, κ. τ. λ. he has βελτίων λοιπὸν ἦν γεγονὼς ὁ Πέτρος αὐτὸς ἑαυτοῦ. κ. τ. λ. " Peter has now become better than he was. So much for this point. But as to their request to have their body filled up, not simply, but by revelation, we will mention two reasons, first, etc."
[4] *Library of the Fathers. The homilies of St. J. Chrysostom on the Acts*, Oxford, 1852, hom. 3, p. 37 ; *Migne*, vol. ix, p. 33 (23).
[5] The Oxford translators give no note, but they apparently read τί οὖν ἑλέσθαι τὸν Πέτρον αὐτὸν οὐκ ἐνῆν; while the long text in Migne has τί οὖν; ἑλέσθαι τὸν Πέτρον αὐτὸν οὐκ ἐνῆν; καὶ πάνυ γε. *What then? Could not Peter himself elect? Of course he could.*" The sense is much the same, but the corrector has made the passage stronger.
[6] *Oxf. tr.*, p. 40. Migne, pp. 35-6 (25).

Mark, also, the great moderation of the other apostles, how they concede the throne to him [James] and no longer dispute with each other."[1]

3. " Here is forethought for providing a teacher ; here was the first who was ordained a teacher. He did not say : ' We are sufficient.' So far was he beyond all vain glory, and he looked to one thing alone. *And yet he had the same power to ordain as they all collectively.* [Oxford translator's note : "καίτοιγε ἰσότυπον ἅπασιν εἶχε τὴν κατάστασιν, which Erasmus justly renders, *Quanquam habebat jus consti-tuendi par omnibus ;* i.e the ordination by Peter singly, would have been as valid as the ordination by the whole body. DF have καίτοι οὐδὲ, i.e., and yet he possessed a power of ordaining, in which they were not all on a par with him ; which reading is accepted by Morel. Sav. and Ben., and is rendered by the last : *quanquam non pariforma apud omnes ejus uigebat auctoritas.* This reading originated in a mistake as to the meaning of the other, as if that asserted only that St. Peter had the same power of ordaining as *any* of the rest."] "But well might these things be done in this fashion, through the noble spirit of the man, and in regard that *prelacy* (ἐπιστασία)[2] *then was not an affair of dignity, but of provi-dent care for the governed.* This neither made the elected to become elated, for it was to dangers that they were called, nor those not elected to make a grievance of it, as if they were disgraced. But things are not done in that fashion now ; nay, quite the contrary. For observe they were a hundred and twenty, and he asks for one out of the whole body ; with good right, *as having been put in charge of them ;*[3] *for to him Christ had said : 'And when thou art converted, strengthen thy brethren '* " (*ibid.* p. 42. Migne p. 37 [26]).

Thus, if we prefer the Benedictine text, we have a rhetorical question with its answer : " Could Peter not have appointed Matthias himself ? Of course he could." If we prefer the short text, we have a plain statement, " And yet he had the same power [to appoint] as they all collectively."

---

[1] *Ox. tr.*, p. 42. Migne, p. 36 (26).

[2] Compare : "But let me say why it is that the episcopate has be-come a subject of competition ; it is because we come to the episcopate not as unto a work of governing and superintending the brethren, but as to a post of dignity and repose," Oxf. tr., p. 46. ὅτι οὐχ ὡς ἐπὶ ἀρχὴν καὶ προστασίαν τῶν ἀδελφῶν, ἀλλ' ὡς ἐπὶ τιμὴν καὶ ἀνάπαυσιν vol. ix, p. 39 [28]. So far is Chrysostom from imagining that Peter held a primacy of honour like that of the Duke of Norfolk among English peers !

[3] The Benedictine text has " ἅτε αὐτὸς πάντας ἐγχειρισθείς."

I know no more emphatic testimony to the supreme jurisdiction of St. Peter in any writer, ancient or modern, than the
view taken in this homily of the election of St. Matthias, for
I know of no act of jurisdiction in the Church more tremendous
than the appointment of an apostle.

Further, I will venture to say that perhaps St. John
Chrysostom goes too far. Would it not be more natural to
think that Christ only can make an apostle, and that it was
because the eleven knew this, that they did not venture to
elect one, but chose two, asking for a direct intervention of
the Divine Head of the Church in so great a matter ?

And, I ask, will anyone venture, after considering the last
sentence of the passage quoted, to maintain that the apostles
were excluded from the " brethren " over whom Peter was
told to rule, προΐστασο τῶν ἀδελφῶν.

Next in importance is St. Chrysostom's account of the
Council of Jerusalem. This was the matter of a very fruitless
discussion between Dr. Rivington and Mr. (now Bishop) Gore.
The latter scored heavily in a wholly unimportant point. He
showed that in the true text, St. James, not St. Peter, is said
to have the ἀρχή that is, the bishopric of Jerusalem. But he
certainly gained nothing for his general argument, for neither
he nor anyone else pretends that St. James had rule over St.
Peter, nor does he attempt to show that St. Chrysostom
thought so. If he had carefully considered the third homily
on the Acts, from which I have just been quoting, it is to be
hoped that he would have modified his opinions.

St. Chrysostom has perceived what some overlook, that in
the " council " St. Peter speaks at the end of the discussion.
And he notices also the vehemence of his speech. St. Peter
takes one side, and reproves the opponents with violence.
" See how terrible his conclusion." [1] And indeed his words
are not those of a debater, but of an inspired teacher : " Why
tempt ye God to place a yoke on the neck of the disciples,
which neither we nor our fathers have been able to bear ? "
(Acts xv 10). " Observe," says Chrysostom, " he first
permits the question to be moved in the Church, and then
speaks." [2] He was not obliged, then, to have a council.
The ruler who might have appointed an apostle might also
have decided himself the question of the obligation of the
ceremonial law.

[1] *Hom.* 32 *in Acta*, vol. ix, p. 236 (250)
[2] Oxf. trans. pp. 446-7.

" 'And after they (Barnabas and Paul) were silent.' He (James) was bishop of the Church of Jerusalem, and therefore he speaks last (p. 239 [253]). [What follows is Mr. Gore's translation from the ' shorter ' Greek text.]¹ ' There was no arrogance in the Church. After Peter, Paul speaks, and no one silences him. James refrains and does not leap up. Great is the orderliness. Nothing (speaks) John here, nothing the other apostles, but hold their peace ; for he (ἐκεῖνος) was invested with the chief rule (τὴν ἀρχὴν) and they think it no hardship.' Then after a sentence follows : Peter, indeed, spoke more strongly, but James more mildly ; for thus it behoves the one in great power to leave what is unpleasant for others to say, while he himself appears in the milder part."

Obviously, it is James who has the " rule " and the " great power " as bishop of those believing Pharisees who had initiated the discussion. But the idea that he had ἀρχή over Peter is, of course, ludicrous, and the notion that he could possibly be the president of the council certainly never occurred to Chrysostom's mind. He only draws out a moral lesson from the fact that James was mild for fear of offending his subjects and alienating their confidence.² But it was Peter who " allowed the discussion to arise " and who gave the decision.³

VI

The order of the twelve apostles, according to this doctor of the Church, is therefore that our Lord preferred three to the rest, and among them put Peter in the first place, giving to him, after the Resurrection, the government of the whole Church. We have yet to examine the relation of Peter to the

¹ *Roman Catholic Claims*, preface to third edition, p. ix.
² In reality, St. James modified St. Peter's decision by proposing a compromise, which was admitted. It does not appear that it was long observed, and we all eat chickens now without scruple.
³ Other passages from the commentary on the Acts cannot be wholly passed over. *Hom.* 26, 1, p. 198 (208) when prayer is offered up by the Church for Peter in prison, " The contest was now for life and death " (so Oxford trans., p. 370), περὶ τὰ καίρια (Dr. Rivington translated " a vital part," which is equally correct). There is a fine passage on Acts ix. 32. " Peter, as he passed through, visiting all," where he is described as a general visiting the ranks of bishops (!) always the first—first when an apostle was to be elected, first to speak to the Jews, to heal the lame man, etc. ; when there is no peril nor management of affairs, he is first ; yet he asked for no higher honour when there was peace, etc. *Hom.* 21, 2, vol. ix, p. 165 (170).

new apostle, who was the last in time, but the greatest in labours, and of whom St. John Chrysostom is especially the interpreter.

In a well-known homily on the words " I withstood him to the face " (Galat. ii, 11) St. Chrysostom explains the dissimulation of Peter at Antioch and the rebuke boldly administered by Paul as a sort of play got up for the edification of the Christians, since he holds it impossible that the two great coryphaei should have disagreed, that Peter should have been afraid, and that Paul should have been wanting in respect. The discussion of the same question by St. Jerome and St. Augustine in a series of letters, which passed (not always by the quickest route) between Bethlehem and Hippo, is sufficiently famous. St. Jerome in his study of Greek writers, had assimilated the same traditional Eastern exegesis which Chrysostom inherited, while the mystical Augustine is actually found on the side of plain literal interpretation against the greatest commentator of the school of Antioch !

" 'And when Peter was come to Antioch I withstood him to the face, because he was to be blamed.' Does not this trouble every man who hears it ? That Paul should have resisted Peter, that the pillars of the Church should collide and dash against each other ! For, indeed, these are pillars which uphold and support the roof of the Faith, and columns and bulwarks and eyes of the Body of the Church, and fountains of good, and treasures and harbours ; and whatever we may say, we shall not attain their worth."[1]

In the first place, who can believe that Peter really " feared them that were of the circumcision," Peter who confessed Christ before all the others, and was the first to break the onset of the Jews ?

" So that even though John, though James, *though Paul*, though any other whatsoever, appears to perform any great deed after this, yet Peter excels them all, he that was the first to make way for their boldness, and open the entrance, and to enable them to enter with great confidence, like a river carried in mighty flood. . . . Was he such after the Cross ? Before the Cross, also, was he not more fervent than all ? Was he not the mouth of the apostles ? Did he not speak when all were silent, etc. . . . And much more might he

[1] *In illud, " in faciem ei restiti "* vol. iii, p. 373 (363, *seqq.*).

have said about Peter, to show his fervour, his courage, and his love for Christ." [1]

Similarly St. Paul's habitual deference to St. Peter makes it impossible that he should have rebuked him :.

" Paul was the servant not only of the coryphæus of those saints, but absolutely of all the apostles, and this though he excelled all by his labours, in spite of which he thought himself to be the last. For he says : ' I am the least of the apostles, who am not worthy to be called an apostle,' and, the least, not only of the apostles, but simply of all the saints : ' To me,' he says, ' the least of all the saints, was this grace given '."

" You see his humble soul ? you see how he sets himself below all saints, not merely below all the apostles ? And feeling this towards all, he was aware how great a superiority (προεδρία) Peter must enjoy, and he reverenced him more than all men, and he esteemed him according to his dignity. The whole world was looking to Paul, the care of the Churches throughout the world was hung upon his soul, every day he transacted a thousand matters, all surrounded was he with business, presidency, corrections, counsels, warnings, instructions, the management ,of a thousand things ; and setting all this aside, he went to Jerusalem, and there was no other pretext for his journey but to see Peter, as he himself says : ' I went up to Jerusalem to visit Peter,' so greatly did he honour him and set him before all. And then ? When he had seen him, did he return at once ? By no means ; but he abode with him fifteen days. Tell me, then, if you should see some general, noble and famous, who when war was begun, when the armies were in array, when the fight was at its hottest, when a thousand matters called him, should leave the ranks to go off and find some friend—would you seek for a greater proof, tell me, of his goodwill to that man ? I think not. Think the same, then, with regard to Paul and Peter. For in this case, also, there was a cruel war, and battle array, and fighting not against men, but against principalities, against powers, against the world-rulers of the darkness of this world, and fighting for the salvation of men. Yet so much did he reverence Peter, that, with such necessity weighing upon him and pressing him, he ran for Peter's sake to Jerusalem, and remained with him fifteen days before returning " (p. 378 [368] seqq.).

[1] ibid, pp. 376-7 (365-7).

In his commentary on Galatians, St. Chrysostom deals with this passage in just the same way, but adds that in reality St. Paul had no need of Peter nor of his voice, being equal in honour, ἰσότιμος.[1] Here, also, he explains (ibid., p. 379 [367]) that our Lord committed the Jews to Peter, and over the Gentiles He set Paul :

" Christ [like a wise king who has one general for the cavalry and another for the infantry] divided His army, the Jews to Peter, the Gentiles to Paul."[2]

And elsewhere :

" ' For He who operated in Peter for the apostleship of the circumcision, worked also in me among the Gentiles.' As by the name of uncircumcision he means the Gentiles, so by the circumcision he means the Jews. And *he shows himself to be equal in honour* (ἰσότιμος) *and compares himself, not with the others, but with the coryphæus, showing that each enjoyed the same dignity* (τῆς αὐτῆς ἀξίας)." [3]

---

[1] " Commentary on Galatians," i, 11, vol. x, p. 631 [677] : " ' Then after three years I went up to Jerusalem to see Peter.' What could be more humble than this soul ? After such great deeds, *having no need of Peter, nor of his voice, and being equal in honour to him* (ἰσότιμος) —for I will say no more at present—yet he goes up as to the greater and elder, and the only cause of his journey is to visit Peter. Do you see how he gives him the proper honour (τὴν προσήκουσαν τιμήν) and not only thinks himself not their (sic) superior, but not even their equal. Thus, as many of our brethren journey to holy men, so Paul went then to Peter ; or, rather, with far greater humility. For they do it for the sake of advantage to themselves, but this saint went not to learn anything from him, nor to receive any correction, but for this alone, that he might see him, and honour him by his presence. ' To visit, ἱστορῆσαι (enquire, examine), Peter,' he says; he did not say to see Peter, but to ἱστορῆσαι Peter, which is the word employed by those who visit great and famous cities— so great was the trouble he thought fit to take merely to see him. And this is further evident from his actions. When he came to Jerusalem, after converting many of the Jews, and after doing greater works than any of the others, having brought Pamphylia, Lycaonia, Cilicia, and all that part of the world into the right path, and having converted them to Christ, he first goes up to *James, as to a greater and more honourable*, with much humility. Then he bears with him when he gives counsel, and counsel contrary to the doctrine of this epistle." Of course St. Paul had no need of Peter, nor could Peter teach him anything ; as to the promise to say more about ἰσότιμος (" I will say no more for the present "), it is apparently fulfilled in the passage given in the text from p. 638 of the same commentary, where it is explained as meaning that St. Paul had been made by our Lord apostle of the Gentiles, as St. Peter of the Jews.

[2] *ibid*, p. 379 (369).

[3] *In Galat*. ii, 3, vol. x, p. 638 (684-5).

Thus St. Paul looks up to all the apostles out of humility, to James, and especially to Peter, while at the same time he is well aware that he is the superior of all but Peter, and equal to him. This placing of Paul above the rest is not astonishing ; in East and West they are always " the princes of the apostles." We may, however, ask why he is twice called " equal in honour to Peter." The answer is plainly that St. Paul shares in that oecumenicity of apostleship which St. Chrysostom so frequently attributes to Peter, " to whom were committed the sheep," " who was entrusted with the whole world." St. Paul receives the Gentiles, as St. Peter the Jews. It did not, of course, enter into St. Chrysostom's head to doubt that Peter remained the " coryphaeus " of the apostles, or to suppose that Paul received any such jurisdiction over the others as he ascribes (as we have seen) to Peter. Still less is he likely to have asked himself whether Peter had theoretically any jurisdiction over Paul. We have learnt how inconceivable it is to him that they should disagree even about a matter of prudence and policy. He regards them here as two equally inspired captains of the Church : Peter, the original generalissimo, Paul, a colleague, sent afterwards to relieve him of half the command.

St. Chrysostom is careful to point out how St. Paul recognized the primacy of St. Peter over the others : " See Paul's wisdom," he says (after quoting 1 Cor. ix 5 : " Have we not power to carry about a sister,[1] as well as the rest of the apostles, and the brethren of the Lord, and Cephas "), he puts the coryphaeus last, for in that position he places his most powerful point. For it was not so wonderful to represent the others taking about a sister as the primate ($\pi\rho\omega\tauο\sigmaτάτης$), he who was entrusted with the keys of heaven.[2]

---

[1] Of course, $\dot{a}\delta\epsilon\lambda\phi\dot{\eta}\nu$ $\gamma\nu\nu\alpha\hat{\iota}\kappa\alpha$ means simply, " sister," as $\dot{a}\nu\delta\rho\epsilon\varsigma$ $\dot{a}\delta\epsilon\lambda\phiοί$ means " brethren."

[2] *Hom.* 21 *in* 1 *Cor.*, vol. x, p. 172 (181). Compare also *Hom.* 3, *in* 1 *Cor.*, p. 24 (16) (on " I am of Paul, I am of Apollo, I am of Cephas ") : " If they must not be partisans of the teacher and first of the apostles who had instructed so great a multitude, much more must they not attach themselves to nobodies. . . . It was not as preferring himself to Peter that he put him last, *but because he put Peter far above himself. For he arranged his sentence in an ascending scale*, that he might not be suspected of doing this out of envy, and to be taking away the honour of the others because he was jealous. This is why he places himself first. For he who discredits himself before the others, does so not for love of honour, but because he greatly despises all such glory. He therefore receives the whole shock himself, and next places Apollo, and then Cephas."

VII

The reader will ask what St. Chrysostom says of the successors of St. Peter. Fr. Puller remarks of the treatise *De sacerdotio* that, " when St. Chrysostom wrote this treatise, he neither was nor ever had been in communion with the Church of Rome, and, in fact, he remained outside of that communion for at least seventeen more years, perhaps for as many as twenty-six." As he proceeds to prove this in 146 large octavo pages, together with about fifty pages of extra notes, I cannot reply to it here. It is only necessary at present to state that there is no evidence that St. Chrysostom himself was ever out of communion with Rome. The bishops of the patriarchate of Antioch for the most part recognized St. Meletius and his successor St. Flavian as rightful patriarchs, while Rome and Alexandria (that is, St. Athanasius and his successors) thought that their rival Paulinus had the better title. But the rest of the East sided with Meletius, though remaining in full communion with Alexandria, Rome and the West. It is certain that neither St. Meletius nor St. Flavian was ever formally excommunicated by the Apostolic See. It is still more certain that their adherents—whether the bishops within the patriarchate, or the priests (including St. Chrysostom) and people within the city—were never excommunicated. When St. Chrysostom became Bishop of Constantinople, he was consecrated as a matter of course by Theophilus, patriarch of Alexandria. Paulinus was now dead, and Theophilus and Pope St. Siricius were induced by Chrysostom to recognize St. Flavian as patriarch of Antioch. The idea that there was any schism of the whole Church is absurd.[1] Still, we might expect St. Chrysostom to say little about Rome and Alexandria. As a fact, he is enthusiastic about Rome.

Antioch, where he was born, where he lived, and where he preached his most famous homilies, was the third see in Christendom, and claimed its high rank, as Rome and Alexandria did theirs, on the ground of its Petrine foundation :

" God has had great account of this city of Antioch, as He has shown in deed, especially in that he ordered Peter, *the ruler* (ἐπιστάτης) *of the whole world*, to whom He entrusted

---

[1] I am perfectly aware that so short an account of the difficulty is inadequate.

the keys of heaven, to whom he committed the office of bringing all in (ᾧ πάντα ἄγειν καὶ φέρειν ἐπέτεψε[1]) to pass a long time here, so that our city stood to him in the place of the whole world. And in mentioning Peter, I have perceived that a fifth crown is woven from this, for Ignatius received the episcopate after him."[2]

But as Peter could not make Jerusalem his see, because Christ " made him the teacher not of that throne, but of the world," so Antioch could not permanently " stand to him in place of the whole world."

" In speaking of Peter, the recollection of another Peter has come to me " (viz. St. Flavian, his bishop) " our common father and teacher, who has succeeded to the virtue of Peter, and also to his chair. For this is the one great prerogative of our city, that it received the coryphæus of the apostles as its teacher in the beginning. For it was right that she who first was adorned with the name of Christians[3] before the whole world, should receive the first of the apostles as her pastor. *But though we received him as teacher, we did not retain him to the end, but gave him up to Royal Rome.* Nay, but we did retain him till the end ; for we do not retain the body of Peter but we retain the faith of Peter as though it were Peter himself ; and while we retain the faith of Peter, we have Peter himself."[4]

And since Paul shared the world with Peter, so he also must go to Rome. " He prophesies, saying : ' I must also see Rome ' " ;[5] and in accordance with this prophecy, thither he goes, and there Peter and Paul, " greater than Kings and Princes,"[6] are buried :

" They who were dragged hither and thither, who were despised and bound with fetters, and who suffered all those thousand torments, in their death are more honoured than kings ; and consider how this has come to pass : in the most regal city of Rome to the tomb of the fisherman and the

---

[1] Better : " to sweep the whole world of its plunder."
[2] *Hom. in S. Ignat. M.* 4, vol. II, p. 591 (597).
[3] This reference to Acts xi. 26, in honour of Antioch is frequent, e.g., *Ad pop. Ant.* Hom. 3, vol II, p. 49 (37) ; Hom. 14, *fin.* p. 153 (150-1) ; Hom. 17, p. 176 (176) ; *In Matt.* Hom 7, 7, p. 81 (116).
[4] *Hom in inscr. Act* ii, 6, vol III, p. 86 (70).
[5] On Acts xix. 21, *Hom.* 42, 1, vol. IX, p. 295 (317).
[6] c. *Jud. et Gent.*, 6, vol. I, p. 821 (565).

tentmaker run emperors and consuls and generals " (c. *Jud. et Gent.* 9. vol. I, p. 825 [570]).

I need not apologize for quoting a longer piece of the magnificent peroration of the last homily on Romans :

" There (in heaven) we shall behold Paul, if we have heard him here, even though we be not near him ; yet shall we see him in glory by the Royal Throne, where the Cherubim praise, and the Seraphim fly. There we shall see Paul with Peter, (Paul) the coryphæus and leader (πρωτοστάτης) of the choir of the blessed, and we shall enjoy his true-hearted love. For if on this earth he so loved men, that when he might choose to be dissolved and to be with Christ, he preferred to be here, much more will he in heaven show his love yet more fervent. And for this it is I love Rome : though I might praise her on other grounds, for her greatness, her antiquity, her beauty, her numbers, her power, her wealth, her victories in war ; but passing over all these, I bless her because Paul, when living, wrote to the Romans, and loved them so much, and was among them, and spoke to them, and there ended his life. Whence also the city is more renowned for this than for all else ; and like a great and mighty body, she has two eyes, the bodies of those two saints. The heaven is not so bright when the sun shoots forth his rays as the city of the Romans, shedding forth the light of these two lamps throughout the world. Thence shall Paul be caught up, thence Peter shall rise. Consider and be amazed ! What a sight shall Rome then behold, when Paul sudden shall arise with Peter from the tomb, and be caught up to meet the Lord. What a rose shall Rome send forth to Christ ! What diadems are those two, with which the city is crowned, with what chains of gold it is girded ; what fountains it hath !¹ It is for this that I admire the city, not for its much gold, for its columns, or any other phantasy, but because of these two pillars of the Church. Who will grant me to embrace the body of Paul, to cling to his sepulchre, and to see the dust of that body which ' filled up what was wanting ' to Christ, which bore His stigmata, and sowed His teaching everywhere ! " (*Hom.* 32 *in Rom.* 2, Vol. IX, p. 678 [757]).²

¹ The chain of St. Paul is kept at S. Paolo fuori le mura, that of St. Peter (to which Eudoxia is said to have added the chain with which he was bound at Jerusalem, by gift to St. Leo the Great) is at St. Peter in Vincoli. The fountains are, of course, the *tre fontane* on the Ostian way on the spot where St. Paul was beheaded.

² Further on in the same splendid passage : " Would I could see his tomb, where are laid the arms of justice, the armour of light. . . . This body fortifies that city more surely than any tower or than ten

In the course of the terrible troubles which overwhelmed
St. Chrysostom's last years, he appealed for sympathy and
for assistance to the bishops of the West, and principally to
Pope St. Innocent, to whom he wrote a grateful letter in
return for the efforts made on his behalf. Of course he was
aware of the tremendous " papal claims " made by that great
Pope and by his predecessors. It would be mere special
pleading, without any ground whatever, to pretend that he
disallowed them. But it is to be remembered that the Popes
interfered very little in the East, except when the wrong-
doings of a patriarch were in question. It was on this ground
that Innocent rebuked the Patriarch of Alexandria for per-
secuting the bishop of the Imperial city, and after the saint's
death refused his communion to Theophilus, in token of his
displeasure.[3]

thousand circumvallations, and with it the body of Peter ; for while
living he honoured him : ' I went up to visit Peter.' Therefore when
Paul left this world, grace vouchsafed that he should share Peter's
resting place (ὁμόσκηνον αὐτῷ ποιῆσαι)."   *Ibid.* c. 4, p. 680 (759).
   [*] Note that the Pope did not *depose* Theophilus or deprive him of
jurisdiction, nor could the rest of the Egyptian bishops be said to be in
schism because they were necessarily in communion with him.   This
will help us to understand the case of St. Meletius and St. Flavian.   A
penal refusal of actual Papal communion, without deposition, was
common enough.   The punished bishop was in mediate communion
with Rome through his comprovincials.

V

ST. JEROME AND ROME

I

ERRORS die hard, especially Protestant fictions. One of the
strangest of these, and one of the hardiest, is the disguisal of
St. Jerome, *hominis Romani*, as a Protestant. I do not mean
that he is travestied as an opponent of monasticism and
virginity, or a preacher of the marriage of priests, or a de-
nouncer of the veneration of relics. But he is claimed, in
spite of his " advanced " views on these and similar points,
as a Protestant at bottom ; for he is represented as upholding
the fundamental dogma of Protestantism—the denial that the
Roman Church is infallible in her faith and the necessary centre
of Catholicity.

Now we should not *a priori* have expected to find such
explicit statements on this point in the works of the great
doctor as on those questions in which modern Protestantism
was anticipated by those glorious pioneers of free thought—
Helvidius, Jovinian, and Vigilantius. Nevertheless, a happy
chance led him to set down the most " ultramontane " views
in two famous letters to the reigning Pope. An ordinary
critic would consider the question of St. Jerome's belief to be
decided. Not so the Protestant controversialist. The witness
of this famous pillar of orthodoxy, and storehouse of Eastern
and Western learning, cannot be so easily renounced. St.
Jerome was young when he wrote thus ; he died an old man :
he must have changed his mind.

This brilliant idea occurred to Dr. Littledale—or, more probably, he found it in the works of preceding controversialists ;
but it is not worth while to trace the pedigree of his contention
to books which may now be presumed to be out of date. The
only proofs offered of St. Jerome's conversion to Protestantism

are two passages—one from his work against Jovinian, and the
other from a letter to Evangelus (or Evagrius) printed by
Vallarsi among the last of his letters as of uncertain date.
Dr. Littledale jumped to the conclusion that it was his last
word on the subject, and dated the letter in the year of the
saint's death, 420. This he altered in later editions, in
deference to Dr. Ryder's reply in the *Tablet*, afterwards republished in book form. But, notwithstanding the complete
refutation Dr. Littledale had received, he did not retract the
statement that St. Jerome changed his mind, but repeated it in
another publication called *Words for Truth*, a curious title for
such a singularly unveracious compilation.[1]

It would be of little importance what a writer of this
stamp might have admitted or not admitted, but that his book
was apparently the poisoned fountain whence more respectable
writers have drawn. Bishop Gore quoted the letter to
Evangelus in his " Roman Catholic Claims," and was very
completely answered by Dr. Rivington. Bishop Gore returned
to the subject in *The Church and the Ministry*, and referred to
this new discussion in a later edition of *Roman Catholic
Claims*.[2] This second attack on St. Jerome was more serious
than the former, as it occurred in a distinctly scholarly work,
with the greater part of which Catholics will be in complete
sympathy, and in the course of a discussion of St. Jerome's
views on the ministry which is as fair as it is careful. Yet it
has not provoked any reply, from the very fact of its position
in an uncontroversial work.[3]

From Bishop Gore the idea was borrowed by a writer whose

---

[1] *Tablet*, Feb. 28th, 1880. *Catholic Controversy*, by H. I. D. Ryder,
1884, pp. 21-25. Littledale, *Plain Reasons against joining the Church of
Rome*, S.P.C.K., 3rd ed. pp. 242-244. *Words for Truth*, 1886, p. 31.

[2] *Bishop Gore actually says :* " The passage (*i.e.*, from the letter to
Evangelus) is not quoted by Roman controversialists, for a very plain
reason : because it indicates that the authority of the Roman See rested
for Jerome on what is variable in a theologian—on sentiment, on
expedience, on feeling—not on what is invariable, the basis of doctrinal
authority." I do not know what Roman controversialists are referred
to. I only know that the answer to this wonderful discovery is given
by pretty well every one of those I have come across. Bishop Gore
might have known Dr. Ryder's admirable little book (l. c.). *Cf.* also
Stone, *The Invitation Heeded*, N.Y. 1870, p. 287 ; Archbishop Kenrick,
Vindication of the Catholic Church, Balt. 1855, p. 203, and plenty of
others ; not to speak of Father Rivington's reply, which Bishop Gore
ignores.

[3] *Roman Catholic Claims*, 3rd ed. 1890, p. 116. *The Church and the
Ministry*, 2nd ed. p. 172, note. *Authority*, by L. Rivington, 5th ed.
pp. 113-117.

piety does not make up for his want of learning,[1] and the
story was also repeated in Puller's *The Primitive Saints and
the See of Rome*. Then it gained the authority of Bishop
Moorhouse, whose assertions were effectively answered by
Fr. Bernard Vaughan in his very brilliant lectures.[2] Last
of all,[3] the episcopal chair of Manchester has been confirmed
by the professorial *cathedra* of Christ Church.[4]

And, after all, the whole thing is the most commonplace of
mare's nests, the most unkind of libels, the most grotesque of
perversions of a couple of quite harmless expressions. The
refutation has been so often repeated, and is so easy, that one
feels almost the need to blush in reiterating it. I wish to give
the answer here with all painstaking exactness, so that there
may be no room for any other reply than misrepresentation
or abuse ; but one feels as though one were using a steam-
hammer to kill a flea, or proving the multiplication-table by
counting it on one's fingers. And yet, of course, no one will
be convinced who does not wish it.

To begin with, I give the two passages in question :

A[5].—St. Jerome has been praising virginity, and exalting
St. John above the other Apostles. He anticipates the objection : ' But you say, the Church is founded upon Peter,'
and replies: "Although the same is done in another place
upon all the Apostles, and they all receive the keys of the
kingdom of heaven, and the strength of the Church is made
solid upon them all equally, *yet one of them is elected among
the twelve, that by the setting up of a head the occasion of schism
may be removed.* But why was not John, the virgin, elected ?
Deference was had to age, because Peter was older, in order
that a young man—almost a mere lad—should not be preferred
above men of advanced age, and that the good Master (whose
duty it was to take away all cause of dispute from His disciples,
and who had said to them : ' My peace I give you, My peace I
leave unto you,' and ' Whoso among you wishes to be greater,
let him be the least of all ') might not seem to afford a ground

---

[1] *The Roman Question*, T. T. Carter. Dr. Rivington (l. c.) quotes
p. 23, but in the 2nd ed. 1890 I can find nothing of the kind, so perhaps
the author omitted the passage. But he still quotes Gore on p. 87.

[2] *Ten Lectures delivered in Free Trade Hall, Manchester*, 1896, pp.
24-27, and 258-264.

[3] *Roman See in the Early Church*, by W. Bright, p. 106, note.

[4] St. Jerome. *Ep.* 97.

[5] " C. Jovin." *P.L.* 23, vol. ii, p. 279 (258), written A.D. 393. The
dates are those of Vallarsi, whose pages are given, with those of Migne
in brackets.

for jealousy in appointing the young man whom He had loved."

B.[1]—" We read in Isaias, 'The fool will talk folly.' I hear that someone has burst out into such madness as to prefer deacons before priests—that is, before bishops. When the Apostle clearly teaches that presbyters and bishops are the same, how can a server of tables and widows dare to exalt himself above those at whose prayer is made the Body and Blood of Christ ? You ask my authority ? Hear the proof." He then quotes Phil. i. 1, 1 Tim. iv. 14, 1 Pet. v., 2 John 1., 3 John 1., with comments, and continues : *"As for the fact that one was afterwards elected to be set over the rest, this was done as a remedy for schism ;* lest each one should draw to himself the (net of the) Church of Christ, and so break it. Besides, at Alexandria, from Mark the evangelist until the episcopates of Heraclas and Dionysius, the priests always took one of their own number, whom they elected, and placing him in a higher rank, called him bishop, as though an army should make a general, or deacons should elect one of themselves, whom they know to be a practical man, and call him arch-deacon. For what does a bishop do that a priest does not, except ordain? Nor is the Church of the city of Rome one thing, and the Church of all the rest of the world another. Gaul and Britain, and Africa, and Persia, and India, and all barbarian nations, adore one Christ and observe one rule of charity. If authority is looked for, the world is greater than the city. Wheresoever a bishop is—whether at Rome or at Eugubium, at Constantinople or at Rhegium, or at Alexandria, or at Tanis, he is of the same worth, and also of the same priesthood (*ejusdem est meriti, ejusdem est et sacerdotii*). The power of riches and the lowliness of poverty do not make a bishop more exalted or more low. Besides, they are all the successors of the Apostles (*ceterum omnes Apostolorum successores sunt*). But, you will say, how is it that at Rome a priest is ordained on the testimony of a deacon ? Why do you produce the custom of one city [or of the city alone] ? Why do you put forward that small number from which pride has arisen against the laws of the Church ? All rarities are more appreciated. Fleabane in India is more precious than pepper. The deacons are honoured from their fewness, the priests are looked down upon because of their numbers. Besides, even in the Church of Rome the priests sit, and the deacons stand, although by gradual growth of abuses I have seen a deacon sit among the priests when the bishop was absent, and give

[1] *Ep.* 146 *ad Evangelum*, vol. i. p. 1081 (1193). I will not discuss the date.

his blessing to priests at private banquets.   Let those who act thus learn that they do not rightly, and let them hear the Apostle," etc.

In both of these passages we find the same theory of St. Jerome, that a head is necessary for the prevention of divisions.

A. That was the reason, says he, that our Lord placed St. Peter above the other Apostles.   It was a necessity, and the age of Peter fitted him for the post.   The Apostles *qua* Apostles, he carefully explains (following St. Cyprian),[1] were all equal.   They had the same rank ; all were equally foundations of the Church (Eph. ii. 20, Apoc. xxi. 14), all received the keys (Mat. xviii. 18, John xx. 23).   St. Peter receives over and above the Apostleship a headship or primacy, to prevent a schism.

To suppose that by this is meant a primacy of honour and not of jurisdiction is to pay but a poor compliment to St. Jerome's sense.   Any one can see, if he chooses to see, that a primacy " such as that enjoyed by the Duke of Norfolk among English Peers " might conceivably be a fruitful source of jealousy, but could not conceivably be of any use to guard against divisions.

Beyond this, the conception of an empty primacy of honour being established by our Lord among His Apostles is so revoltingly anti-Christian as to be nothing less than blasphemous.   Only the exigencies of controversy could have driven sensible men to attribute such a view to St. Jerome or St. Cyprian.   Only the blindness of anti-Catholic rage could induce earnest and pious men to think they hold it themselves.

B. In the second passage the same necessity of avoiding divisions is said by St. Jerome to have induced the Apostles to set one of the bishops or presbyters above the rest in each city, and to this one was limited the title of *episcopus*, as that of *presbyter* remained peculiar to the rest, while the name *sacerdos* was in St. Jerome's time common to both.   This is a theory which St. Jerome is very fond of.[2]

---

[1] The passage : *De cath. eccl. unitate*, 4, was doubtless in St. Jerome's mind.   It is noticeable that St. Jerome does not understand St. Cyprian's words, as Anglicans do, to deny the primacy of St. Peter !

[2] The Western view, that the essence of Priesthood is the offering of Sacrifice, and that the High Priesthood or Episcopate is only a higher rank of Priesthood, and not a different order, was evidently current and dominant in St. Jerome's time, else he could not have appealed to it.   The more logical Eastern view counts three major orders : Bishops,

In the dialogue against the Luciferians, written about the year 379, he uses it as an argument for the necessity of Bishops :

" The safety of the Church depends on the dignity of the High Priest. If to him is not given a certain independence and eminence of power (*exsors et eminens potestas*), there will be made in the Church as many schisms as there are priests. This is the reason that without chrism and the command of a bishop neither a priest nor a deacon has the right to baptize. "[3]

In his commentary on the Ep. of Titus, written in 387, he uses the same view to give good advice to priests to be submissive, and to bishops to be humble and not arrogant :

"A priest is then the same as a bishop, and before party-spirit in religious matters arose by the devil's suggestion, and it was said among the peoples : ' I am of Paul, I of Apollos, and I of Cephas,' the Churches were governed by a common council of presbyters.   But after each of them came to think that those whom he had baptized were his own and not Christ's, it was decreed in the whole world that one of the priests should be elected *to be placed above the others, and that to him the whole care of the Church should belong,* and thus the seeds of division should be destroyed."

He then proves his point from Scripture, and proceeds :

" This was to prove that among the ancients, priests were the same as bishops ; but by degrees, in order that the young shoots of dissensions might be uprooted, *the whole solicitude was given to one man.* As therefore the priests are aware that by the custom of the Church they are subject to him who is set over them, so let bishops remember that it is rather by custom than by the truth of the Lord's disposition that

Priests, Deacons ; whereas the ancient Latin computation is still in force in the Latin Church, Priests (including Bishops), Deacons, Subdeacons.   Thus St. Jerome's argument " a Priest is the same as a Bishop," is still the teaching of Western theologians, and represents the official usage of the Latin Church.   There is, of course, no difference of doctrine on the subject, between Easterns and Westerns ; nor is St. Jerome's further statement that the distinction between Priests and Bishops is merely one of custom consistent with the teaching of the Church or with his own admission that only a Bishop can ordain or consecrate the Chrism.

[3] C. 9, vol. ii, p. 182 (173).

they are greater than priests, and that they ought to rule the Church in common with them, as Moses did, etc.[1]"

In accordance with this theory, St. Jerome always paid great respect to bishops at every period of his life,[2] but at the same time is very sensitive as to any depreciation of the priesthood. He holds this office to be distinguished from that of bishop by ecclesiastical custom only, which gives to the bishop, besides the exclusive right of ordaining (*Ep. ad Evang.* above) and of consecrating the chrism (*Dial. c. Lucif.* above),[3] the care and responsibility of the rule of the whole of his Church. It was this authority and jurisdiction which was rendered necessary, according to his view (with the truth of which we have nothing to do here) by the divisions of Apostolic times.

Now, like causes have like effects.

If, to avoid schism among the Apostles, St. Peter was given by our Lord a primacy of honour only, then among the priests the bishop need have received no more.

But if the avoidance of schism among the priests necessitated their subjection to a bishop, then the avoidance of schism among the Apostles involved their subjection to St. Peter.

We thus have obtained from passage B a confirmation of our interpretation of passage A; we must now consider passage B alone.

We learn from an anonymous contemporary writer[4] that a

---

[1] Vol. vii. pp. 694-695 (597).

[2] *e.g.*, in letter to Theophilus against his own bishop, John of Jerusalem : " We are not so puffed up as to ignore what is due to the bishops (*sacerdotes*) of Christ. For whoso receives them, receives not so much them as Him whose bishops they are. But let them be content with their due honour, and recognize that they are fathers and not lords." (*Ep.* 82, al. 62, p. 521 (743), A.D. 399). Or, in a rather sharp letter to St. Augustine : " Farewell, my dearest friend, in age my son, in dignity my father " (*Ep.* 105, al. 92, p. 641 (837) A.D. 403). If St. Jerome frequently lectures bishops in general (e.g., *Comm. in Ezek.*, c. xxxiv., A.D. 414), he still more often lectures priests, and sometimes both together—e.g., *Istum locum episcopi et presbyteri non intelligentes, aliquid sibi de Pharisaeorum assumunt superbia. In Matt.* c. xvi. v. 18, Bk. iii. p. 124 (122), A.D. 398.

[3] See Vallarsi's note there, and *cf. Comm. in Sophon.*, c. iii. vol. vi. p. 721 (1,443), A.D. 392. *Sacerdotes quoque, qui dant baptismum et ad Eucharistiam Domini imprecantur aduentum ; faciunt oleum chrismatis ; manus imponunt ; catechumenos erudiunt ; leuitas et alios constituunt sacerdotes,* etc.

[4] Ambrosiaster, *Quaestiones ex utroque mixtim,* 101, *inter opp. St. Augustini,* vol. iii. app. Souter's ed. (C.S.E.L., vol 50, p. 194). The passage should be read entire.

certain deacon,[1] " out of stupidity and the boastfulness of the city of Rome," taught the equality of deacons with priests, and almost their superiority. The original number of seven deacons was still retained at Rome, and they were set over the seven regions of the city, while the priests, many in number, were distributed in the various parishes. The deacons, called *diaconi regionarii*, or later, *cardinales*, were the chief officials of the Pope, and it was often from amongst their number that the Pope was elected. Owing to the many flatterers by whom they were surrounded, our anonymous informant tells us, they came to forget sometimes in practice their inferiority of order. What wonder if St. Jerome had seen a deacon sit in the presence of priests, when the Pope was absent, and the liturgical ceremonial was therefore less elaborate ; or if their host at dinner should have asked the great man, though a deacon, to say grace, instead of a humbler priest ? The thing was natural, and St. Jerome treats it as an abuse, though not with great violence. As a fact, the Church has not so treated it, and up to the present day has continued to look upon ecclesiastical rank as not altogether dependent on the degrees of holy orders ; so that a Cardinal Antonelli would rank not merely before priests, but before bishops, no more regard being had to his inferior order than to his personal merit. A lesser objection, met both by St. Jerome and by the author of the *Quæstiones*, is the fact that at Rome a priest was ordained on the testimony of a deacon. In this neither Anglicans nor Catholics can find any gross abuse, as the practice remains to this day in the directions of the Roman Pontifical and of the English Book of Common Prayer. In both, the candidates for ordination are presented to the Bishop by the Archdeacon. The author of the *Quæstiones* explains that this is a service which the deacon renders the priests, and not a position of superiority.

St. Jerome condemns these instances of pride in the Roman deacons as contrary to the laws of the Church. But his method of proving the inferiority of deacons to priests is at first sight somewhat surprising. Why does he not simply say, as in fact the anonymous writer does, that a priest is a deacon,

---

[1] The printed texts of Ambrosiaster, when I wrote this article in 1897, had *nomen Falcidii*, but the right reading is *nomen falsi dei*, and Prof. C. H. Turner has shown that the reference is to a Roman deacon under Damasus, whose name was Mercurius. He seems to have written his book under the pseudonym of Urbicus.

and something more, since he was ordained first deacon and then priest ?   Because then he might be answered, " For the same reason, then, a priest is below a bishop." And St. Jerome is most anxious to impress on every one his theory (doubtless not generally accepted or known) that while the distinction between priests and deacons is one of order, and of Divine institution, the distinction between priests and bishops is one of jurisdiction only, and of ecclesiastical, or at the utmost, of Apostolic institution.

He, therefore, at once enunciates against the deacon the dictum that bishops and priests are one, adding the minor premiss that of course deacons cannot compare themselves with bishops. The conclusion that they cannot compare themselves with priests is obvious. So St. Jerome proceeds to prove his major premiss from Holy Scripture, adding the explanation that bishops had been introduced as a remedy for divisions, though a college of priest-bishops had survived at Alexandria for two centuries and a half, with the right of electing the patriarch from among themselves.[1] " For what does a bishop do that a priest does not, except ordain ? " As to the deacon's argument from what took place at Rome, he says we cannot consider Rome apart and the rest of the world apart. There is one law for every nation under the sun ; and if we are looking for *auctoritas*, that is for *precedent*, the world is greater than the city. The local customs of Rome are not a law for the whole world. Twice St. Jerome says the same thing with regard to frequency of communion.[2] St. Augustine took the same view in his famous letter to Januarius ;[3] and against a Roman who wrote under the

[1] Bishop Gore's account (*Church and Ministry*, 2nd ed. pp. 137-139) is excellent. He gives good reasons also for thinking that St. Jerome was mistaken as to the fact.   But in reality Jerome only says the priests " nominated " one of their number to be bishop.   Elsewhere, though often the people and the clergy *chose*, the *appointment* rested with the metropolitan, or (in the case of metropolitans) with the Patriarch, and so forth.   In the case of the Patriarch of Alexandria, the actual appointment was not by any bishop or bishops, but by the Alexandrian priests—so St. Jerome believed.   His point is not that the Patriarch was not consecrated (as he assuredly was) but that he was *appointed* by inferiors, who were therefore not inferiors.   St. Jerome had been at Alexandria, and his statement had doubtless some foundation.   It is probably as near to the fact as an intelligent traveller would get.

[2] *Ep.* 48 (al. 50) *ad Pammach*, c. 15, p. 227 (506), A.D. 393 ; and *Ep.* 71 (al. 28) *ad Lucin.* p. 434 (672), A.D. 398.

[3] *Ep.* 54.

pseudonym Urbicus[1] to prove that all the world ought to
fast on Saturday, because St. Peter taught the Romans to do
so, he thinks ridicule the most suitable reply.[2]   So that even
the good customs of Rome are not binding on the rest of the
Church ; nor are we Catholics bound in England to observe
the feast of St. Philip Neri as a bank-holiday,[3] or to cease
putting real flowers on our altars.

"Wheresoever," continues St. Jerome, "a bishop may be,
whether he be the successor of Peter at Rome or a suffragan at
Gubbio, bishop of the imperial city Constantinople or of
Rhegium, Patriarch of Alexandria, the second see of Christendom, to which jurisdiction over Libya and Pentapolis had been
confirmed by the Council of Nicæa, or simple bishop of a small
Egyptian town—he has just the same worth, the same
sacerdotium.   Similarly, riches and poverty make no more
difference than does jurisdiction, and they are all successors
of the Apostles."[4]

All this glorification of the episcopal office is meant to
emphasize the difference between bishops—" that is, priests "
—and deacons.   A priest is the same so far as order is concerned as a bishop, notwithstanding the difference of jurisdiction ; and one bishop has the same orders as another, even
though the see of Rome or Alexandria may have more authority, and the see of Constantinople more riches.   It follows that
every priest and St. Jerome himself has the same spiritual
dignity by his ordination as a patriarch or a pope.   Surely
this is majesty enough to make even a Roman deacon feel
shy !

For the rest, he explains that, though these Roman deacons
had gained importance and pride from their limited number,
yet even in Rome the theory of their spiritual inferiority was
observed, so that a few obvious abuses ought not to have been
quoted as customs.

The above paraphrase gives the sense of the passages as St.
Jerome intended it.   About this there can be no question.
The Anglican interpretation was that St. Jerome denied the

---

[1] Urbicus is evidently the same as Mercurius ; thus his book is
refuted by Augustine as well as by Jerome and Ambrosiaster.

[2] *Ep.* 36.

[3] When I wrote in 1897, this holiday of obligation was still kept in
Rome.   But the new Canon Law has abolished it.

[4] *Cf. Ep.* 41, 3, p. 189 (476) : *Apud nos Apostolorum locum episcopi
tenent.*   (Written at Rome, A.D. 384.)

Bishop of Rome to have any more authority than the Bishop of .Gubbio. There are four objections to this view.

First, he does not say so; for he says *ejusdem sacerdotii*, not *ejusdem auctoritatis*.

Secondly, he would have had no object in saying so ; for he does not even suggest that the Bishop of Rome was answerable for the conduct of his deacons, still less that he approved the theory of Mercurius, which, of course, no pope ever did or could.

Thirdly, he could not have said so, or he would be also denying that the Bishop of Alexandria had any more authority than the Bishop of Tanis, and thus contradicting the Council of Nicæa. Besides Gubbio was under the Pope as metropolitan.

Fourthly, St. Jerome's point is that bishops have exactly the same powers by their ordinations, whatever the immense difference in their jurisdiction. This point is lost unless we realize that the difference between the bishop of Rome, the successor of the Prince of the Apostles, or the Pope of Alexandria, who ruled the bishops of Egypt with despotic power, and an ordinary bishop of Tanis or Rhegium or Eugubium was enormous, and similarly with the bishop of Constantinople, the Emperor's adviser and a would-be Patriarch.

If St. Jerome had invented a new heresy to the effect that all bishops had equal authority, he would have expressed it with his usual plainness of speech, and (I suppose) would have been condemned by the Church. If two canons of Westminster and Christ Church and the Bishop of Manchester wish to uphold the same view on St. Jerome's authority, I suppose they will hardly expect the Archbishop of Canterbury to be pleased.

Out of all this discussion, what can we gather as to St. Jerome's opinion of the Church of Rome ? Presumably that he had felt some personal irritation at its deacons, and certainly that its local customs are not laws for the whole Church, especially if they are abuses—a very obvious remark. I do not see what more against Rome can be got out of the passages.

In favour of Rome, on the contrary, we have extracted the statement that while all the Apostles, as apostles, are exactly equal, yet St. Peter had from our Lord Himself a primacy of jurisdiction over the others, in addition to his apostleship. Further, while all bishops, as bishops, are exactly equal, some of them have also a similar primacy of jurisdiction by ecclesiastical law. So far then we have the distinct assertion of the primacy of St. Peter, and the distinct implication of at least patriarchal authority for the Bishop of Rome.

But a very little logic will carry us a great deal further.

No one doubts that St. Jerome believed St. Peter to have been the first Bishop of Rome, even though they think him mistaken. He said so in 376 (" chair of Peter," " successor of the fisherman "),[1] in 380[2], in 387 (*Romam translatum*)[3] in 389,[4] in 392, in his short Life of St. Peter,[5] in 402 (*cathedra Petri*),[6] in 411,[7] and he implies it in using the common title " Apostolic See," and in many important passages which will be quoted later on.

Since, therefore, St. Jerome believes one bishop to be the successor of St. Peter, will he not believe him to succeed to his primacy as well as to his episcopate ? Since he declares that a primate was necessary even among the Apostles, and that without a monarchy over the priests of one city there " will be as many schisms as there are priests," it follows that he must *a fortiori* believe in the necessity of a primacy over the universal Church.

Our Protestant friends believe that external unity is not necessary to the Church, and that in the midst of mutually exclusive schisms an inexplicable and transcendental unity is preserved. A head therefore is unnecessary, as schisms, though regrettable, are not destructive of unity.[8] But no one will pretend that St. Jerome ever dreamt of such a theory ; and his belief (unquestioned by any one, so far as I know) of the necessity of external unity imperatively demanded a central and supreme authority.

St. Peter was, according to St. Jerome, apostle, primate, and bishop. In his apostleship, strictly speaking, he had no successor, any more than the other Apostles ; but he had successors in his episcopate. That these successors succeeded to his primacy also is proved to have been the belief of St. Jerome, not merely by a logical deduction from the two passages which Protestants have brought forward to prove

---

[1] *Ep.* xv.
[2] *Chron. Euseb.*, transl.
[3] *In Galat.*, vol. vii. p. 410 (366).
[4] Transl. *Orig. in Luc. hom. vi.* vol. vii. p. 261 (245).
[5] *De uiris ill.*," c. i. p. 828 (638).
[6] *Ep.* 97.
[7] *Comm. in Isai.*," c. 52, 15, p. 612 (523).
[8] As to this Anglican theory, I never have understood what can destroy unity if schism does not.

the contrary, but by the direct evidence of many other passages scattered throughout his works. It remains to examine these.

II

The two famous letters to St. Damasus were written about the years 376-377. St. Jerome was then twenty-nine years old, if we follow Cavallera. Born in Pannonia, he had passed his youth at Rome, and was converted to a life of holiness while journeying in Gaul. His baptism at Rome is considered to have been subsequent to this by Tillemont; but Vallarsi shows that it probably took place earlier. In 372-373 he journeyed to the East, and retired to the Syrian desert to lead a life of asceticism. It is from thence that he wrote his two famous letters to St. Damasus, before referred to.

In these he begs for the Pope's decision as to which of the three claimants of the patriarchal see of Antioch is to be communicated with. Vitalis was an Apollinarian; St. Meletius he suspected of Arian heresy, on account of the circumstances of his election; but he was afraid of embracing the party of Paulinus, because the East in general sided with Meletius. The ambiguity of the word *hypostasis* increased his distress, for the followers of St. Meletius, by whom he was surrounded, refused to accept the explanation he gave of his belief on the subject, and he complains bitterly of the persecution he underwent from them, declaring that Arian tendencies were latent beneath their rejection of the expression " one hypostasis " in the Holy Trinity.

The letters are written in the elaborate style of St. Jerome's early years, and are of startling vigour and cleverness, in spite of their affectations and exaggerations :

" Since the East, dashed against itself by the accustomed fury of its peoples, is tearing piecemeal the undivided tunic of Christ, woven from the top throughout, and foxes are destroying the vine of Christ, so that among the broken cisterns which have no water it is hard to know where is the sealed fountain and the garden enclosed, I have considered *that I ought to consult the Chair of Peter and the faith praised by the mouth of the Apostle* (Rom. i. 8), asking now the food of my soul where of old I received the garment of Christ. Neither the vast expanse of ocean nor all the breadth of land which separate us could preclude me from seeking the precious pearl. Wheresoever the body is, thither will the eagles be gathered together. Now that an evil progeny have dissipated their patrimony, with you alone is the inheritance of the Fathers preserved uncorrupt.   There the fertile earth reproduces a hundredfold the purity of the seed of the Lord.   Here the corn cast into the furrows degenerates into lolium and wild oats.   It is now in the West that the sun of justice rises ; whilst in the East, Lucifer, who fell, has set his seat above the stars.   You are the light of the world, the salt of the earth. Here the vessels of clay or wood will be destroyed by the rod of iron and the fire everlasting.

Therefore, though your greatness makes me fear, yet your kindness invites me.   From the priest I ask the salvation of the victim ; from the shepherd the safety of his sheep.   Away with envy, away with all canvassing of the Roman power ; it is but with the successor of the fisherman and the disciple of the Cross that I speak. *Following none in the first place but Christ, I am in communion with your beatitude, that is, with the Chair of Peter.   On that rock I know the Church is built.   Whosoever shall eat the Lamb outside that house is profane.   If any be not with Noe in the ark, he shall perish beneath the sway of the deluge.*   And because for my sins I have migrated to this solitude, where Syria borders on the barbarians, and I cannot always at this great distance ask for the Holy One of the Lord from your holiness, therefore I follow here your colleagues the Egyptian confessors ; and under these great ships my little vessel is unnoticed. Vitalis I know not, Meletius I reject ; I know not Paulinus. *Whoso gathereth not with thee scattereth ; that is to say, whoso is not with Christ is of Antichrist.*

Now, alas ! after the creed of Nicæa, after the decree of Alexandria joined to the West, the new expression of three hypostases is required of me, a Roman, by that progeny of Arius, the *Campenses* [i.e. the followers of Meletius]. What new Paul, doctor of the nations, has taught this ? . . .

Decide so, I beseech you, if you will, and I will not fear to acknowledge three hypostases. If you order it, let a new creed be composed, after that of Nicæa, and we orthodox will confess our faith in the words of the Arians.   But the whole literary faculty uses *hypostasis* in the sense of οὐσία etc.

Are we to be separated from Arius by walls [i.e. in different Churches], but united in heresy ?   As well might Ursicinus be joined to your beatitude, Auxentius to Ambrose !   Far be this from the faith of Rome ; may the religious hearts of the people drink no such impiety !   Let three hypostases be

no more mentioned, if you please, and let one be held. . . .
Or if you think fit that we should say three hypostases with the
necessary explanations, we do not refuse. But, believe me,
there is a poison hidden beneath the honey. . . .

. . . Wherefore I beseech your holiness by the crucified
Salvation of the World, by the Trinity of one Substance,
that you will write and give me authority to say or to refuse
to say three hypostases. And lest perchance the obscurity
of the place in which I dwell may escape the letter-carriers,
please send your letters to the priest Evagrius, whom you well
know. At the same time let me know with whom to communicate at Antioch ; for the Campenses having joined the
heretical Tharsenses desire nothing but to preach three
hypostases in their old sense, supported by the authority
of communion with you.[1] "

A few months later he wrote again, having received no
answer :

"The importunate woman in the Gospel merited at length
to be heard, and, though at midnight, the door being closed,
the friend received bread from his friend. God Himself,
who can be overcome by no adverse power, is conquered by
the prayers of the publican. The city of Ninive, which was
to be destroyed by its fault, was saved by its prayer. Why
commence with this long list ? So that your greatness may
look upon my littleness, the rich shepherd not despise a sick
sheep. Christ brought the thief into Paradise from the cross ;
and thus, lest any should think repentance can come too late,
the reward of murder was changed into a martyrdom, etc., etc.

I, therefore, as I wrote before, who received the garment of
Christ in the city of Rome, now am dwelling at the barbarian
limit of Syria, and (that you may not think I received this
sentence from another) I myself decided my own punishment.
But, as the gentile poet says : *Coelum non animum mutant*
qui trans mare currunt. My incessant enemy has dogged my
steps, so that I have but fiercer battles in the desert. On the
one side storm the raging Arians, supported by the powers of
the world. On the other, a Church, torn in three parts, tries
to seize me. The authority of ancient monks who dwell
around rises against me. *Meantime I cry aloud : If any is*
joined to the Chair of Peter, he is mine !

Meletius, Vitalis and Paulinus say that they adhere to you.
If one of them asserted it, I could believe him. But now either

[1] *Ep.* XV (al. 57), vol. i, p. 38 (355), c. A.D. 376.

two of them or all three are lying. Therefore I beseech your beatitude by the Cross of the Lord, by the essential glory of our Faith, the Passion of Christ, that you who are the successor of the Apostles in dignity should be their successor in merit also. May you sit in judgment on a throne with the Twelve, may another gird you with Peter in old age, may you gain with Paul the citizenship of Heaven, if you will tell me by letter with whom I ought to communicate in Syria. Despise not a soul for which Christ died."

Passing over the difficulties of translation and of exact date, let us sum up the doctrine which the letter implies concerning the Pope.

That the Pope sat in the Chair of Peter, and was successor of the fisherman, was repeated frequently by St. Jerome in later years, as we have seen. But some more remarkable points may be gathered.

First, the Chair of Peter is the rock on which the Church is built. Everyone knows that the Rock is, in the first place, Christ ; and Peter, or Peter's faith, from his likeness and union with Christ ; *Petrus a Petra*, says St. Augustine often, and St. Leo explains the same thing in a passage too well known to need quotation.[1] As a foundation must be permanent, St. Peter's successors, or their faith, remain the Church's foundation in the same sense. St. Augustine's words are well known :[2]

Numerate sacerdotes uel ab ipsa Petri sede,
Et in illo ordine patrum quis cui successit uidete ;
Ipsa est Petra quam non uincunt superbae inferorum portae.

Secondly, the Roman See is consequently the centre of communion for the whole Church ; and any one who is out of

---

[1] *St. Aug. Serm.*, 295, vol. v, p. 1349 (Migne) *et alibi* ; *St. Leo, Serm.* 3 *in Anniu. Assump."* ; *Ego inuiolabilis Petra*, etc.

[2] *Ps. c. partes Donati.* We know that St. Augustine did not change his view in later years as to the substance of this saying, for his actions prove it ; and no doubt, had he done so, his Retractations would have been most explicit on the subject. As a fact, though he came to prefer the view (untenable though it will appear to most), that the words *super hanc petram* refer to our Lord Himself, yet he not only did not reject his former interpretation, but he assumes that there was no fault to be found with the doctrine he had based upon it and upon the following words. I have to say this because of Fr. Puller's remark that St. Augustine was young when he wrote this, and changed his mind later. (See " Retract. I.," xxj. vol. i, p. 618.)

communion with it is outside the Church. " I am in communion with your beatitude, that is, with the Chair of Peter,
on that rock I know the Church is built. Whosoever shall
eat the Lamb—that is, receive communion—outside that
house is profane (Exod. xii. 45-6). If any be not with Noe in
the Ark he shall perish." " Whoso gathereth not with Thee
scattereth ; whoso is not with Christ is of Antichrist." And
it appears that the Easterns agreed with this view. St.
Jerome is unconscious of any dissension with them on this
vital point, and would have at once declared that they were
not in the Ark, had they denied this necessity of union with
Rome. The followers of St. Meletius " desire nothing else
than to preach three hypostases in the heretical sense, *auctoritate communionis uestrae fulti.*" And in the second letter, the
answer to St. Jerome's cry, " If any be joined to the Chair of
Peter he is mine," is an assertion from the three rival claimants
of the Petrine chair of Antioch that they have that communion
with St. Damasus which will authorise both their claim and
their teaching, *tibi haerere se dicunt.* Dr. Bright coolly
says[1] : " This obviously means to agree with Damasus as
to the faith ; which, indeed, Meletius did." This is really
unpardonable carelessness. " I could believe it," continues
St. Jerome, " if one of them asserted it ; now either two of
them are lying, or else all three." This " obviously means "
that only one of three rival bishops could be in communion
with Rome, and not that only one of three could possibly
be orthodox ! Nor did St. Jerome's exclamation mean :
" I will communicate with whosoever is the lawful bishop,"
proved to be so by communion with Rome," for no one had
ever suspected the orthodoxy of Paulinus,[2] and he has not
ventured finally to condemn his two rivals, or there would have
been no need to write to the Pope. He meant, of course,
" I will communicate with whosoever is the lawful bishop."
There was no metropolitan or patriarch above Antioch, and
the question was one for Rome to decide.[3]

[1] *Roman See in the Early Church,* p. 107.
[2] The accusations of Sabellianism were not quite serious, but a sort
of *tu quoque.*
[3] As a fact, none of the three was lying, since Rome had as yet
excommunicated none. Later on, as every one knows, Damasus, like
Athanasius, gave full communion to Paulinus, without venturing to
excommunicate St. Meletius, whose adherents were tolerated, and who
was upheld by the entire East. It was an uncomfortable state of things,
but perhaps, after the long and unfortunate delays which made St.

Thirdly, as the See of Rome is the necessary centre of orthodoxy, Roman faith must be perfect and unalterable. The bishop and his Church are one ; for he is the representative of her faith, and its teacher.   In early centuries, therefore, " Roman faith " was a proverb for its purity and indefectibility.   When the Bishop of Rome decided a point of faith, he was declaring the unalterable faith of his Church ; the faith of Peter praised by Christ, the faith praised by Paul in his epistle.   It was the pride of every Roman to share this faith, and it is a pride that St. Jerome felt throughout his life. This is the first place in which he speaks of the Chair of Peter and the faith praised by Paul, but we shall see that it is the first in a long series.   " The evil progeny have dissipated their patrimony," in the midst of heresy the East has lost the inheritance of faith ; at Rome only is the true seed sown and nurtured to full growth ; " you (the whole West might be meant) are the light of the world, the salt of the earth.   A new creed is taught me, *hominem Romanum*—a Roman by spiritual birth—in the words of the Arians.   Far be this from Roman faith !   May the religious hearts of the people drink no such impiety ! "   For to the Roman people St. Jerome attributes a special gift of devotion and simplicity of faith which guards them from error.   Individuals, and even large numbers, might, of course, go wrong; and we shall see later the distress of St. Jerome when he thinks that the Roman faith is being deceived and misled by Rufinus or the Pelagians.

Lastly, St. Jerome implies two powers in the Pope ; the one, as we have seen, of deciding which is the true Bishop of Antioch, the other of deciding a point of doctrine.   Was it right or not to say there are three hypostases in the Blessed Trinity ?   He will obey even if the Pope's decision is an addition to the creed of Nicæa, and contrary to literary usage, though he argues strongly against an affirmative decision. In the second letter he begs the Pope, who follows Apostles in office, to follow them also in goodness (*ut qui apostolos honore sequeris sequaris et merito*).   We cannot take *apostolos* for all the Apostles ; since the Pope has not succeeded to their

Basil so angry, there may have been no better way.   If any one chooses to find fault with the policy and conduct of Rome and Egypt, I have no objection to make, for St. Basil was on the spot.   But a Catholic is more inclined to think Rome's proverbial slowness was more prudent than the impetuosity of so great a saint ; and St. Basil was less careful than St. Athanasius about orthodoxy.

office, and is not strictly an Apostle. St. Peter and St. Paul
are probably rather meant. But the expression is only an
oratorical amplification of the habitual *apostolica sedes*,
apostolatus uester (as a form of address). Yet it certainly
implies more than that the Pope is bishop of a see founded by
an Apostle.

I do not wish to press all this as being a distinct statement
of the Pope's infallibility *ex cathedra*, or of his superiority to
the only General Council. These are modern expressions ; I
only suggest that the idea of them was not very far off from
St. Jerome's mind.

What are we to think of Janus's remarks : " He then urges
the Pope with courtly and high-sounding professions of un-
conditional submission to his authority, but at the same time
in a strictly menacing tone, to pronounce upon this term in the
sense needed for justifying him." Fancy a young layman
threatening the Pope !¹

With these letters may be compared *Ep.* 17, *ad Marcum*,
while the elaborate enumeration of Scripture texts in request-
ing an answer can be paralleled by *Ep.* 11, *ad Virgines
Aemonenses*, written also in the saint's youth. But we have
now his later life to consider.

In September 382, after the Council of Constantinople, St.
Jerome, who had in the meantime sat at the feet of " the
theologian," Gregory of Nazianzum, accompanied St. Epiphanius and Paulinus to Rome. He had been ordained priest by
the latter some time before at Antioch. He was appointed
his secretary by St. Damasus, as he tells us when relating the
story of the woman who was buried in a sort of public triumph
by her twenty-third husband, she being his twenty-second
wife ; " when I assisted Damasus, Bishop of Rome, in his
ecclesiastical papers (*in chartis ecclesiasticis iuuarem*),

---

¹ *The Pope and the Council*, Engl. transl., Rivingtons, 1873, pref.
p. xxv, note. He continues : " In fact he gave St. Cyril of Jerusalem
to whom he had sent his profession of faith, as high a place as the Pope.
But Cyril, with good ground, thought the case a suspicious one, and
gave him no answer." The reference is to *Ep.* 17, 4, where an unknown
Cyril is mentioned, probably (as Cavallera says, p. 55) a bishop or
priest of the neighbourhood. The whole sentence is of course a tissue
of absurdities and has no foundation but the ingenious imagination of
the apostate who penned it.

May I be pardoned here for mentioning myself, and rendering to
Dr. Littledale and to Janus the thanks which are their due for the help
they gave me when a Protestant towards my conversion ? The attempt
to verify some of their statements was most enlightening.

and answered the synodical consultations of East and West."[1]

The letters of St. Damasus have nearly all perished, but many of those of his immediate successors have survived. All are in the same style : assuming and often stating the pre-rogatives of the Apostolic See, and exercising a jurisdiction over the whole Church, deposing bishops, enforcing laws under excommunication, confirming or annulling the decisions of synods, reproving, praising, and exhorting in all parts of the world. It is this kind of decretal letter which St. Jerome had to write. Did he come to look upon them afterwards as Fr. Puller and Dr. Bright would do, as mere examples of arrogance contrary to the laws of the Church ? He does not, at least, show any sign of repentance in this bare mention, written in old age, A.D. 409.

At Rome St. Jerome continued his ascetic habits, and was much courted as a favourite with the Pope. But when he undertook to be the spiritual guide of the noble lady Paula, he declares that he suddenly found the adulation of the city turned to abuse. The death of the Pope had doubtless something to do with the change, and the holy man's violent tongue still more. He found Rome unbearable, and returned to the East. In a letter written at Rome,[2] he refers to the *Aristippi and Epicuri* of the Roman clergy, but in his farewell letter to Asella[3] he speaks of Roman society in general as his detractors. He says that till lately *omnium pene judicio dignus summo sacerdotio decernebar.* Hence Bishop Gore's note :[4]

" In Jerome's earlier years his tone is papal, e.g. in his letters to Damasus from the East, A.D. 375-380 (*Epp.* xv-xvi). Afterwards, disgusted with Roman manners and disappointed of the Roman episcopate, he broke with the Church there A.D. 385, and his abusive tone about the Roman clergy is subsequent to this date, e.g. *Ep.* 52, *ad Nepotian.* is after A.D. 393. His commentaries on the N.T., which contain the passages minimising the episcopal office by comparison with the presbyterate, date A.D. 386-392. His letter to Evangelus (*Ep.* 146) is marked by its hostile tone towards Rome to belong to the period subsequent at any rate to A.D. 385, and *Ep.* 69 *ad Oceanum* is about A.D. 400."

[1] *Ep.* 123, al. 11, c. 10, p. 907 (1052).
[2] *Ep.* 33, p. 154 (447).
[3] *Ep.* 45, al. 99, August 385.
[4] *The Church and the Ministry*, 2nd ed., chap. iii, p. 172, note.

There is a ring of scholarship about this elaborate note which is calculated to deceive the unwary. But (a) St. Jerome could hardly mention disappointment at not being elected Pope in so open a manner. He is merely relating what was said of him, and said insincerely. (b) St. Jerome's abuse of the Roman clergy was written before he left Rome, and was the cause of his being persecuted and of his leaving, and not its effect. The famous letter to Eustochium on virginity contains a passage[1] which was a great cause of offence.[2] The preface to the translation of Didymus *De spiritu sancto* was written not long after his departure, and need not refer principally to the clergy. (c) The letter to Nepotian, written nine years later at Bethlehem, and sent to Altinum, contains nothing whatever about the Roman clergy, though it does include certain warnings against the arrogance of bishops, which would be more probably suggested by his quarrel just commencing with John of Jerusalem than by any disappointment at not being made Pope. One gathers that Bishop Gore regards his depreciation of the episcopal office as a question of the fox and the grapes. But we have seen above that this depreciation is grounded on a theory which appears in the dialogue against the Luciferians, which was written before he even went to Rome ; though he uses the theory there to show the necessity of episcopacy, a necessity which he never doubted at any time of his life. (d) As to the commentaries on the N.T., it is evident that the passage from that on the Epistle to Titus, already quoted, is intended. What on earth has this " depreciation of the episcopal office " to do with the Pope ? (e) The letter to Evangelus we have seen to be marked by no hostile tone towards Rome ; while its date is quite unimportant in view of other evidence, even if it were really anti-papal. (f) The letter to Oceanus does indeed mention St. Jerome's view of the identity of bishops and priests, but, I repeat, he had held that view before he went to Rome.[3]

Soon after St. Jerome's arrival in the East, he wrote a letter in the names of Paula and Eustochium, who had rejoined him,

---

[1] *Ep.* 22, c. 28, p. 112 (413). A.D. 384.

[2] *Cf. Ep.* 27, al. 120, and *Ep.* 40, al. 100, both written shortly before leaving Rome. See also Vallarsi's life of the Saint, c. xvi.

[3] This letter (*Ep.* 69, written after 395 and before 401) upholds a view as to second marriage which is contrary to the decision of Siricius in his decretal to Himerius, written Feb. 385. St. Jerome was perhaps just in the first troubles which succeeded the death of St. Damasus, and apparently he knew nothing of the letter.

to Marcella, to invite that noble and saintly lady to join their incipient community at Bethlehem. He contrasts the noisiness of the great capital with the quiet and the holy memories of the Saviour's birthplace. But there is no depreciation of Rome from an ecclesiastical point of view :

"There, indeed, is a holy Church, and the trophies of the Apostles and martyrs, and the true confession of Christ ; there is that faith which was praised by the Apostle, and that name of Christian which daily rears itself upon the ruins of paganism ; but,"[1] etc.

Somewhat later St. Jerome addresses Paula and her daughter in a similar strain :

"Do you wish to know, O Paula and Eustochium, how the Apostle has noted each province with its own particular characteristic ?   Even till our own day the vestiges of the same virtues or faults may be traced.   It is the faith of the Roman people which he praises.   And where else can we see so fervid a concourse to the churches and the tombs of the martyrs ? Where does the ' amen ' thus resound like the thunder of heaven, and shake the temples of the idols ?   Not that the Romans hold another faith than that of all the Churches of Christ, but that they have a greater devotion and simplicity[2] in believing.   The Apostle accuses them also of being easygoing, and also proud," etc. (Rom. xvi. 17-19, xii. 15-16.)[3]
Here there is no question of irritation with Rome, nor of change in his estimation of the Roman gift of faith.
In the same commentary we find much about St. Peter. In the first chapter St. Jerome enunciates (with Origen, Apollinarius, Chrysostom and others) the view to which St. Augustine later objected, viz., that the reprehension of St. Peter by St. Paul at Antioch was only a make-believe. Here is a characteristic passage :

" Then, after three years, I came to Jerusalem to see Peter." Not that he might see his eyes and cheeks and countenance, whether thin or fat, whether his nose was curved or straight, whether his forehead was covered with hair, or (as Clement says in the *Periodi*) if his head was bald.   Nor do I think it

---

[1] *Ep.* 46, al. 17, c. 11, p. 208 (490).   Written about 386.
[2] The word *simplicitas* is the constant expression of St. Jerome for unhesitating faith.
[3] *Comm. in Gal. II*, vol. vii, p. 427 (381).

consistent with the gravity of an Apostle that he should have
desired to see anything human in Peter, after this long three
years' preparation.   But he wished to see him with those eyes
with which he himself is seen in his epistles.   Paul looked on
Cephas with those eyes by which he himself is seen by the
wise.   If any one disagrees, let him join this passage with the
preceding words, that the Apostles taught him nothing.
For that he thought fit to go to Jerusalem, that he went for
the purpose of seeing the Apostle, was not for the desire of
learning (for he also had the authority of Christ for his teaching), but of giving honour to the earlier (or *more eminent,
priori*) Apostle." [1]

So much for the superiority of St. Peter to St. Paul.
Further on he quotes Origen as to the translation of St. Peter
from Antioch to Rome, as was mentioned above.

In 393 St. Jerome wrote the book against Jovinian, who
had published at Rome heresies till then unheard of, but now,
alas, too well known.   One passage of it has already been
discussed at length.   I quote further from it :

"Was there no other province in the world to receive this
panegyric of voluptuousness into which this adder could have
crept, but that one which was founded on Christ the Rock
by the doctrine of Peter ? " [2]

No wavering to be traced here in his trust in Roman faith.
He ends the book by the following appeal :

"Thee I address, who hast blotted out by the confession of
Christ that blasphemy which was written upon thy head ; city
of power and dominion, city praised by the Apostle's voice.
Interpret thy name, Rome, name of strength in the Greek,
of loftiness in the Hebrew.   Preserve that which thy name
signifies, and let strength exalt thee, and not pleasure abase
thee." [3]

In the year 392 was published the book, *De uiris illustribus,*

---

[1] l.c. Bk. I, c. i, v. 18, vol. vii. p. 394 (354).   On ancient views of
this passage of St. Paul and the testimony they give to the supremacy
of St. Peter, see by all means Passaglia's great work, *De praerogatiuis B.
Petri,* Ratisb. 1850, Bk. I, c. xxiv, pp. 217-245.   With *priori Apostolo
cf. praecessori Apostolo, p.* 402 (360) ; and *posteriores*—inferiors, *Ep.* 116
(Aug.), p. 774 (947).
[2] Bk. II, vol ii, p. 381 (350).
[3] p. 383 (352).

the first biography being that of " Simon Peter, prince of the Apostles," who held the sacerdotal chair at Rome for twenty-five years.

At the end of 397 he writes to St. Pammachius, who after his wife's death was living an ascetic life at Rome, praising Rome, which now possessed what once the world knew not, viz., monastic life ;[1] and in a letter to Theophilus, patriarch of Alexandria, during his dispute with his bishop, John of Jerusalem, he says :

"For your admonition concerning the canons of the Church we thank you, for whom the Lord loveth He chasteneth . . . but know that we have nothing more at heart than to observe the laws of the Church, and not to move the landmarks of the Fathers, and ever to be mindful of that Roman faith which the Church of Alexandria boasts of participating."[2]

So the faith of Rome, kept pure by a special gift of devotion, founded on the Rock, Christ, by St. Peter, and praised by St. Paul, which it was folly in Jovinian to try and disturb, is the norm for the world, and the second see of Christendom glories in sharing it.   What more is said in the letters to Damasus than is implied in these later passages ?

In the book against John of Jerusalem he thus reproves his time-serving bishop :

"He (Bishop John) writes an apology to Bishop Theophilus which commences thus : ' You as a man of God and endowed with Apostolic grace sustain the care of all the Churches, especially of that which is in Jerusalem, though yourself disturbed by many solicitudes in that Church of God which is subject to you.'   He flatters him and treats him as a prince ! You who seek for ecclesiastical rules, and who quote the canons of the Council of Nicæa, and who try to appropriate the clerics of other bishops who are dwelling with them, answer me, how does Palestine appertain to the Bishop of Alexandria ? If I mistake not, it was decided in that Council that Cæsarea should be the metropolis of Palestine, and Antioch that of the entire East.   Therefore, either you ought to have referred the case to the bishop of Cæsarea, with whom you know that we are in communion, though we have rejected yours ; or else, if the judgment was to be sought afar off, you should rather

---

[1] *Ep.* 66, al. 26, p. 395 (641).
[2] *Ep.* 63, al. 68, p. 353 (607), A.D. 397.

have sent your letter to Antioch. But I know why it was you would not send to Cæsarea or Antioch ; well did you know what you were escaping. You preferred tiring the ears of one who was already occupied, to rendering the due honour to your own metropolitan."

John had accused St. Epiphanius of violating a Nicene canon by ordaining Paulinian, brother of St. Jerome, in Palestine. As a fact, Paulinian was not a subject of John, and the ordination did not take place within his diocese. St. Epiphanius for his part accused John of holding the errors of Origen. The Bishop of Jerusalem tried to get a testimony to his orthodoxy from Theophilus of Alexandria ; hence his polite language to that prelate. It is noticeable that John, Epiphanius, and Theophilus all wrote to Pope St. Siricius, trying to get his influence on their side in this purely Eastern quarrel.[1]

Of course St. Jerome knew quite well that John was far from intending to treat Theophilus as his metropolitan. The " care of all the Churches " refers to the paschal letters which Theophilus had published according to custom. The reminder that Jerusalem was subject to Cæsarea, Cæsarea itself to Antioch, would be particularly galling to the bishop of a see which within fifty years after was acknowledged as a patriarchate.

The importance of this passage is merely that it shows how far St. Jerome was about the year 399 from saying that the bishop of Alexandria had no more authority than the Bishop of Tanis. The bishop of Jerusalem was as much a bishop as the bishop of Cæsarea or of Antioch, but was inferior in jurisdiction.

A more serious quarrel was to disturb the serenity of Bethlehem. Rufinus published towards the end of 398 a translation of the περὶ ἀρχῶν of Origen, in the preface of which he referred to St. Jerome, then at the height of his fame, as his example and model, thus seeming to accuse St. Jerome of approving the errors of Origen, because he had translated many of his homilies. Pammachius and Oceanus wrote from Rome to St. Jerome, sending him this preface, and asking him to clear himself.

---

[1] *C. Joannem Hieros*, c. xxxvii, vol. ii, p. 447 (406). I will not omit an anecdote from the same treatise (c. viii, p. 415 (377) : " A heathen and idol-worshipper used to say in joke to B. Pope Damasus : ' Make me Bishop of Rome, and I'll be a Christian on the spot.' "

In St. Jerome's reply to this letter, he says :

"Whosoever you be who assert new dogmas, I beg you to
spare Roman ears, spare that faith which was praised by the
mouth of the Apostle.   Why after four hundred years do
you try to teach us what we knew not till now ?   Why do you
produce doctrines which Peter and Paul did not think fit to
proclaim ?   Up to this day the world has been Christian
without your doctrine.   I will hold to that faith in my old
age in which I was regenerated as a boy."[1]

No question here about changing his mind.   The faith of
Rome which he received at the font is still his.   He had
learnt at Rome (Dr. Bright vouches for this) those strong
expressions about the necessity of communion with the Holy
See and the inviolability of her faith which he had used to
St. Damasus when he was thirty ; at fifty he is as proud as
ever of being a Roman.

Rufinus sent an apology to the Pope, and finding Rome too
hot for him, obtained a letter from St. Siricius (merely an
ecclesiastical passport, like a modern *celebret*) and went to
Aquileia, the place of his baptism.   But St. Siricius soon died,
and Anastasius, his successor, condemned his translation.   In
401 Rufinus published three books against St. Jerome, which
the latter answered without having seen them by two books
Contra Rufinum, and he soon afterwards added a third.

Rufinus said in his preface that Jerome, in translating
more than seventy homilies of Origen, had carefully purged
them from all error.   He cannot then, argues the saint, accuse
me of being a heretic :

"'Nothing,' says he, 'will be found in them by a Latin
reader which is in disaccord with our faith.'   What does he
call his faith ?   That which the Roman Church possesses ?
Or that which is contained in the volumes of Origen ?   If he
answers, the Roman, it follows that he and I are Catholics,
since we have translated none of Origen's errors."[2]

There is more about Roman faith and Roman ears than it
is worth while to quote ; but here are instances :

" When I read this and had compared it with the Greek, I

[1] *Ep.* 84, al. 65, c. viii, p. 531 (750), c. A.D. 400.
[2] *C. Ruf.*, I, iv. vol. ii, p. 461 (418).

perceived at once that Origen's impieties as to the Father, the Son, and the Holy Ghost, which Roman ears could not have borne, had been changed for the better by the translator."[1]

" Never was any question raised about my translations of Origen : Rome never rose against them." [2]

St. Jerome urges Rufinus with the letters of St. Epiphanius and Theophilus against him, and with those of Pope Anastasius which follow up the heretic in the whole world. [3] Rufinus had addressed an apology to the Pope, just as Pelagius, Celestius and Bachiarius did under similar accusations, and, like them, declares that he holds the Roman faith. He does not " wish to wipe any blot of suspicion from the Pope's holy mind, which, like some shrine of God, would receive nothing unjust, but to give him this confession of faith as a stick wherewith to beat off his enemies and rivals when they bark against him."[4] He concluded :

" And I, besides this faith which I have exposed, that is, which the Roman Church, and the Alexandrian and my own Aquileian hold, and which is preached at Jerusalem, have never held any other, nor do I, in the name of Christ, nor ever will."

Of all this St. Jerome makes fun,[5] and continually refers to the letters of St. Anastasius, which condemned his translation, though as a fact they did not condemn Rufinus himself. The principal of these letters, that to John of Jerusalem, and another to Simplicianus of Milan, are extant. I do not quote them as no one can doubt the decided way in which the popes of that day gave their decisions, and the view they held as to their prerogatives. If St. Jerome, who had once composed similar letters for St. Damasus, had come to disbelieve in the Papal supremacy, he was not a man to hold his tongue ; and though the letters were in his favour, he would have protested against the insolent assumption of authority which they implied with that frankness which loves to call a spade by a more forcible name.

Rufinus had also translated an apology for Origen under

---

[1] *Ibid.* I, vi, p. 462 (420).
[2] *Ibid.* I. viii, p. 464 (421) ; *cf.* further on, p. 464 (422).
[3] *Ibid.* I, x, p. 465 (423), and I, xii, p. 468 (425).
[4] Ruf. : *Apol. ad Anast.* I, Migne, vol. xxi, p. 623.
[5] *cf. C. Ruf.* II, i, p. 491 (444-5) ; x, p. 498 (451) ; xiv, p. 505 (527).

the name of St. Pamphilus, the friend of Eusebius. St.
Jerome denies its authenticity :

" Know that the Roman faith, praised by the voice of the
Apostle, does not accept these stratagems [viz. a heretical
treatise under the name of a martyr].   Even though an angel
[not merely a martyr] should announce another gospel than
that once preached, know that, relying on the text of St. Paul
(Gal. i. 8), it could not be altered.   Wherefore, brother,
whether the book was forged by yourself (as many believe)
or by another, and you were so rash as to believe the composition of a heretic to be by a martyr, at all events change
the title of the book, and deliver Roman simplicity from so
great a peril."[1]

" I wonder how Italy can have approved what Rome has
despised, and how bishops can have accepted what the
Apostolic See condemned."[2]

Rufinus accused St. Jerome of having forged the letter of
St. Anastasius which condemned him.   " Why," says the
holy doctor, " don't you go and ask for it in the Roman
chartarium ? "

" You should go to Rome, and cross-examine Anastasius
face to face, why it is he has insulted you, being innocent and
absent ; first, in that he would not receive the exposition of
your faith, which all Italy, according to you, had approved,
and that he would not use your letter ' as a stick to beat your
dogs ' ; next that he sent letters against you to the East,
and branded you with the stigma of heresy without your knowledge, and declared that the Περὶ ἀρχῶν of Origen had
been translated by you and given to the ' simple ' Roman
Church, in order that by your means they might lose that truth
of the faith which they had learned from the Apostles. . . .
It is no light matter which the Pontiff of so great a city lays
on your shoulders. . . ."[3]

"You bring up the letter of Siricius, already asleep in the Lord,
and you despise the words of the living Anastasius.   For you
say, What can that harm you which he wrote or did not write
in your absence ?   And again, if he wrote it, ' the testimony

[1] *Ibid.* III, xii, p. 542 (487).
[2] *Ibid.* III, xv, p. 545 (489).
[3] *cf. C. Ruf.* III, xx, p. 549 (493).

of the whole world suffices you, in that it appears credible
to no one that the bishop of so great a see could do injury either
to an innocent or to an absent man.' You call yourself
innocent, when Rome trembled at your translation ? Absent,
because you dared not answer the charges against you ?
And so anxious are you to fly from the judgment of the city
of Rome that you can easier endure a siege by barbarians in
Aquileia than the sentence of a peaceful city. Suppose it
true that I forged the letter of last year. Who sent the recent
writings against you to the East ? In these Pope Anastasius
pays you such compliments that when you have read them
you will begin rather to defend yourself than to attack me."[1]

" If you can produce even a short note against me by the
Bishop of Rome or any other Church, I will confess that all
the crimes you are charged with were my own ! "[2]

" Because you had a letter from Siricius, was not Anastasius
allowed to write against you ?[3] O what a wealthy ship,
which came to enrich the poverty of Rome with Oriental and
Egyptian merchandise ! ' You are that Maximus who restores
the commonwealth by—writing ! ' Alexandria [i.e. Origen]
has taught you what Rome was ignorant of ; Egypt has
enriched you with what Rome had not ! "[4]

Enough of quotations from this witty and unkind book,
which was hardly calculated to restore that faith and friendship which Rufinus had betrayed.

St. Jerome wrote a most fulsome letter to Theophilus of
Alexandria to congratulate him on his paschal letter against
the Origenists, using such language as this :

" The voice of your beatitude has resounded throughout the
world, and whilst all the Churches of Christ rejoice, the devils
cease to utter their poison. . . . The priest Vincent who has
just returned from Rome . . . continually repeats that
Rome and almost all Italy has been freed by your letters on
Christ's behalf."

He begs him to write to the Western bishops and to send
him any synodal letters he may have composed, that he may
be the bolder *tanti Pontificis auctoritate firmatus.* He himself
has just written to the West, and he considers that it is a

[1] *Ibid.* III, xxi, p. 550 (494).
[2] *Ibid.* III, xxii, p. 552 (495).
[3] *Ibid.* III, xxiv, p. 553 (496).
[4] *Ibid.* III, xxix, p. 558 (501).

special Providence that Theophilus should have written to the Pope just at the same time.[1]   St. Epiphanius also writes to St. Jerome in delight at what Theophilus had written to the whole world.[2]

St. Jerome turned these paschal letters into Latin, and speaks of them with effusion when sending one of them to SS. Pammachius and Marcella :

" Again I enrich you with Oriental merchandise, and in early spring I send the wealth of Alexandria to Rome. . . . Origen, who was banished from Alexandria by Demetrius, is driven from the whole world by Theophilus, the same, doubtless, to whom Luke addressed the Acts of the Apostles, whose name speaks of the love of God ! Where is the heresy ? . . . It is smothered by his authority and eloquence."

" Pray, therefore, that what is approved of in Greek may not displease in Latin, and that what the whole East admires may be joyfully received in the bosom of Rome. *May the Chair of Peter the Apostle confirm by its preaching that of the Chair of Mark the Evangelist.*   Though it is also noised abroad everywhere that Pope Anastasius, too, has with the same fervour, for he is of the same spirit, followed the skulking heretics to their lairs ; and his letters tell us that what has been condemned in the East [viz. by Theophilus in a synod, and by the bishops assembled at the Encænia at Jerusalem] has been condemned in the West as well."[3]

A pleasanter quarrel to look back upon is the unfortunate misunderstanding between St. Jerome and St. Augustine, which the gentlemanly and Christian courtesy of the latter brought to a friendly termination, followed by sincere admiration on the part of the generous if excitable Jerome for the younger doctor.   The respect shown by Jerome for the episcopal dignity of Augustine *communionis meae episcopum,* and the view of the former as to St. Peter's reprehension of St. Paul, has already been touched upon.   It only remains to remark that upon one point they were quite agreed, that is, upon the pre-eminent dignity of St. Peter.

St. Jerome on the one hand argues that St. Peter could not have been really corrected by St. Paul, for St. Peter was the true author of the decree of the Council of Jerusalem on which

---

[1] *Ep.* 88, al. 71, p. 537 (755), A.D. 400.
[2] *Ep.* 91, al. 73, *inter* Hieron.
[3] *Ep.* 97, al. 78, p. 581 (790), and 583 (792), A.D. 402.

St. Paul's reproof reposed. After a long demonstration, he concludes: " It is, therefore, doubtful to no one that the Apostle Peter was the first author of this decision, which he is now accused of transgressing."[1]

St. Augustine, on the other hand, does not deny this statement, but argues that " Peter gave a rarer and holier example to posterity that men should not disdain to be corrected by their inferiors (*a posterioribus*) than did Paul, that the lesser should resist the greater for the defence of evangelical truth, saving fraternal charity."[2]

Here are a few scattered quotations :—In 403 he again praises the devotion of the Roman people :

" The gilded Capitol is unswept; all the temples of Rome are covered with soot and cobwebs. The city is moved on her foundations, and a deluge of people pour past the decaying temples to the tombs of the martyrs."[3]

In the commentary on Isaias, A.D. 411 :

" This house (Is. ii. 1) is built upon the foundation of the Apostles and Prophets, who are themselves mountains, as imitators of Christ. . . . Wherefore upon one of these mountains Christ founds the Church, and says to Peter, ' Thou art Peter,' "[4] etc.

He speaks of St. Peter and St. Paul as *duo apostolorum principes*,[5] elsewhere as *ecclesiarum principes*.[6] But more often St. Peter alone is *princeps apostolorum*,[7] e.g., in the dialogue against the Pelagians, one of St. Jerome's very last writings, A.D. 415 : " As Plato was prince of philosophers, so is Peter of the Apostles upon whom the Church is founded in massive solidity, which is shaken by no surge of floods nor any storm."[8]

[1] *Ep.* 112, p. 742 (920), A.D. 404.
[2] *Ep.* 116, *inter* Hieron, p. 774 (947), A.D. 405.
[3] *Ep.* 107, al. 7, p. 678 (868).
Also writing in 406 against Vigilantius, St. Jerome mentions how Jovinian had been condemned " by the authority of the Roman Church," *C. Vigil.* I, vol. ii, p. 387 (355).
[4] Vol. iv, p. 31 (44).
[5] *Ibid.* c. liv., p. 627 (535).
[6] *cf.* also *Ad Gal.* vol. vii, p. 372 (336).
[7] *Ibid.* p. 373 (335), *De uiris illustr.*, c. i, in Isai, *ut supra*, p. 609 (521), etc.
[8] I, 14, vol. ii, p. 707 (529). In the preface, p. 695 (519), St. Jerome again speaks of *Romana fides*,

In the year 412 St. Jerome wrote a panegyric of St. Marcella, addressed to her daughter Principia :

" From priests of Alexandria and from Pope Athanasius, and afterwards from Peter, who to avoid the persecution of the Arians had fled to Rome, as to the safest port of their communion, St. Marcella had learned the life of St. Antony, then still living, and the discipline of the monasteries in the Thebaid of Pachomius, and of virgins and widows."[1]

She made of Rome a very Jerusalem, says St. Jerome. He then recounts her services in fighting the Origenists, and in frightening Rufinus out of Rome :

" In this tranquillity and service of the Lord the storm of heresies which arose in these provinces turned all upside down, and grew to such violence that it spared neither itself nor any good person.   And, as if it were a light thing to disturb all here, it carried a ship full of blasphemies into the port of Rome.   And the dish soon found a cover to fit it, and muddy footsteps defiled the pure fountain of Roman faith.   What wonder if in the streets or market a mountebank plays his shameless and silly tricks, if this poisonous and filthy doctrine could find at Rome people to follow it.   Then was the ill-famed translation of Περὶ ἀρχῶν ; then the disciple who would have deserved his name of Macarius had he never fallen in with such a master.   The opposition to our friends was broken up, and the school of the Pharisees was upset. [Apparently Roman clerics, as in pref. to Didymus De Sp. S., who had till then been detractors of St. Jerome.]   The holy Marcella, who had long restrained herself lest she should seem to act out of rivalry, when she saw that the faith praised by the Apostle was violated in very many, so that even priests [no mention of bishops or deacons here !] and some of the monks, and especially men of the world, were being drawn to agree, and that the simplicity of the bishop (Siricius) was being played upon, who valued others at the rate of his own goodness, Marcella, I say, publicly resisted it, preferring to please God rather than men."[2]

" Not long afterwards the illustrious Anastasius succeeded to the Pontificate.   Rome did not merit to possess him long, lest the world's head should be severed under such a bishop [when Alaric took Rome, A.D. 410].   Nay, he was taken away, lest

---

[1] *Ep.* 127, al. 16, p. 954 (1089).
[2] *Ibid.* c. ix, p. 957 (1092).

he should essay by his prayers to bend the sentence once decided, as the Lord said to Jeremias : ' Pray not for this people.' . . . You say, what has this to do with the illustrious Marcella ? She was the cause of the heretic's condemnation, by producing witnesses ' "[1] . . . etc.

In 414, being then nearly seventy years of age, St. Jerome wrote to Demetrias the often-quoted passage, which I cannot omit :

" I had nearly left out what is most important. When you were a child, and Bishop Anastasius of holy memory ruled the Roman Church, a fierce storm of (Origenist) heretics from the East tried to sully and destroy the simplicity of faith which was praised by the mouth of the Apostle. But that man of richest poverty and Apostolic solicitude straightway smote the noxious head and stopped the mouth of the hissing hydra. And because I am afraid, nay, I have heard the rumour, that these poisonous shoots are still alive and vigorous in some, I feel that I ought with the deepest affection to give you this advice, to hold the faith of holy Innocent, who is the successor and son of that man, and of the Apostolic See, and not to receive any foreign doctrine, however prudent and clever you may think yourself to be."[2]

In the forty years since he wrote to St. Damasus, St. Jerome's views do not seem to have changed. He was the *protégé* of Damasus ; we have just heard him praise the next Pope Siricius, and extol still higher his successor Anastasius ; now St. Innocent is the representative of the faith taught by Peter and praised by Paul.

It is doubtless the Pelagians who are referred to in the above quotation. Three years later they stormed the monasteries of St. Jerome and St. Eustochium, and the old man only escaped their hands by shutting himself up in a tower. The Pope wrote a very strong letter[3] to John of Jerusalem, whom he suspected of worse than negligence in not preventing this outrage, remonstrating as his superior and threatening him with ecclesiastical law. He wrote also to console St. Jerome,[4] saying that he would have " seized the authority of the Apostolic See to restrain all wickedness," had he known the

[1] *Ep.*, 127, c. x, p. 958 (1093).
[2] *Ep.* 130, al. 8, p. 992 (1120),
[3] *Ep.* 137, *inter* Hieron.
[4] *Ep.* 136.

names of the offenders. " But if you will depose an open and plain accusation against certain persons, I will either appoint competent judges, or, if anything else more urgent or more careful can be done by us, I shall not be behindhand, beloved son."   Such is the affection of St. Innocent for the aged saint, who is supposed to have been openly crying " no Popery." Nor did St. Jerome, any more than St. Augustine or St. Aurelius, the aged primate of Carthage (to whom these two letters were sent by St. Innocent as an enclosure, to be sent on to St. Jerome) protest against this assumption of lecturing and threatening an Eastern bishop and of instituting a court of inquiry into his action in his diocese.   Yet such procedure goes far beyond the warrant of the Sardican canons.   Such was the protection asked for by St. Jerome's pupils, Eustochium and Paula the younger, and apparently by St. Jerome himself, for " *tuus gemitus* " in the Pope's letter implies that he had written.

The aged saint's life was drawing to a close ; in 420 he died, worn out by troubles and old age.   We have seen his relations with four successive popes, and a love of Rome and a tenacity of Roman faith which was as fresh at the end of his life as when he received the garment of Christ in the Lateran baptistery.

VI

THE CONDEMNATION OF PELAGIANISM

I

THE anti-papalism of the African Church has been a fruitful theme for Protestant controversialists. St. Cyprian has been, since the days of Dodwell, their pet instance of resistance to Roman claims. Apiarius they are never tired of. St. Augustine is quoted as a Protestant in the Thirty-nine Articles. "The advocates of Papal Infallibility are obliged to give up St. Augustine," said the reckless Janus.[1] " England," wrote Dr. Pusey,[2] " is not at this moment more independent of any authority of the bishop of Rome than Africa was in the days of St. Augustine." Fr. Puller has followed of late years by warning " honourable men " to " refrain from pretending that the Church of North Africa, in the time of St. Augustine, believed in the principles laid down by the Vatican Council " : it would be " an impertinence and an act of folly." Fr. Rivington ventured to commit this impertinence in spite of so solemn a warning ; and Dr. Bright retaliated in the *Church Quarterly Review,* and later republished his apparently hasty articles in *The Roman See in the Early Church.*

The best answer to such wild statements is a mere relation of facts. I propose to give the history of the condemnation of Pelagianism, so far as possible in the words of the original authorities, giving references for every fact. These may easily be verified by anyone who has access to the second and tenth volumes of St. Augustine's works, the former containing his letters, the latter comprising his treatises against the

---

[1] p. 67, Engl. tr. note.
[2] *Eirenicon,* p. 66.

Pelagians, together with an appendix of documents concerning the history of that heresy.[1]

It is not to be gainsaid that the African Church looked upon the Roman Church as ever free from heresy, or as possessing an especial gift of faith. Tertullian signalled it among Apostolic Churches as that into which the Apostles poured forth their faith with their blood.[2] To the Romans, whose faith was praised by the Apostle," says St. Cyprian, " heresy can have no access." [3]   And this because it was the See of Peter—*locus Petri*,[4] *cathedra Petri, ecclesia principalis unde unitas sacerdotalis exorta est.*[5] There the very chair of Peter was preserved,[6] *in qua una cathedra unitas ab omnibus seruaretur ;* [7] *ipsa est petra quam non uincunt superbae inferorum portae.*[8] In the Roman Church *semper apostolicae cathedrae uiguit principatus,*[9] and the succession of its bishops is one of the marks of the true Church as opposed to heresy.[10]

The Roman Church and the See of Peter are therefore the divinely appointed centre of unity, and at the same time, and consequently, incapable of error. Dr. Bright and Fr. Puller, following the example of a long series of Anglican writers, explain away St. Cyprian's words as if they were dealing with the Thirty-nine Articles ; but the above thesis will be confirmed by the evidence brought forward in the following pages, in which the bishop of Rome will appear as the final and inerrant judge of questions of faith.

---

[1] The pages given are those of Migne. Once for all I acknowledge my debt to the invaluable Benedictine preface to vol x which I have continually used. The disquisitions of the Ballerini have, of course, been a necessary accompaniment, with Pagi, Tillemont, Hefele, Jungmann, etc.

[2] *De Praesc.* 36 ; *cf. Adu. Marc.* iv, 5.

[3] Referring to Rom. i, 8, a text constantly quoted by the Fathers, Eastern and Western, in this way ; *cf. Revue Bénédictine* of Maredsous, Dec. 1895, pp. 547-557.

[4] *Ep.* 59. Ed. Hartel, p. 683, *cf. Ep.* 60, p. 692.

[5] *Ep.* 55, p. 630.

[6] St. Optatus ii, 2. Ed. Vindob. (Dr. Bright's attempt to explain away this well-known passage need not detain us here) and *Tert. de Praesc. loc cit.* ; *cf. Cypr. Ep.* 59, *loc. cit. cf. Roma Sotteranea,* vol. i, appendix ii, note A.2, p. 488.

[7] Opt. *loc. cit.*

[8] *Augustine Ps. c. partes Donati*, str. 18, vol. ix, p. 30. Migne, *cf. Opt.* ii, ix. *Per cathedram Petri, quae nostra est, et ceteras dotes apud nos esse.*

[9] *Aug. Ep.* 43, 3, 7, vol ii, p. 163.

[10] *Aug c. Ep. Fund. Man.* iv, 5, vol. viii, p. 175 ; *cf. Ep.* 53, i, vol. ii p. 196 and *De util. cred.* xvii, 35, vol. viii, p. 91.

The honour of producing Pelagius appears to belong to our own island. A monk and a layman, he resided long at Rome, and achieved some reputation for sanctity. A big, fat man, Orosius says he was ; weighed down, adds St. Jerome, with the porridge of the Scots. He came from Rome to Carthage in 410, at the time that the Eternal City was sacked, and he met St. Augustine there once or twice during the following year. He was already reputed to have heretical opinions, but the Saint was too much occupied in discussions with the Donatists to take much notice of him.[1] From Africa Pelagius seems to have gone to Egypt and Palestine.

Celestius, his disciple, seems to have left Rome with his master, or about the same time, and was at Carthage by the year 411.[2] He had been born an eunuch, but was of considerable talents and of noble birth. He hoped to attain the priesthood, but was brought to the notice of Aurelius, bishop of Carthage, as a preacher of heresy. At a Council in the same year[3] he was accused by Paulinus, a deacon of Milan, who had been ordained by the great St. Ambrose, and had written his life at St. Augustine's request. Celestius was condemned and excommunicated, being obstinate in his errors. " From this sentence," says Marius Mercator, the disciple of St. Augustine and contemporary, " he thought fit to appeal to the examination of the bishop of Rome." Yet shortly afterwards, neglecting this appeal, he went to Ephesus, and there tried to obtain the priesthood by fraud.[4] " I could do nothing at that time," Paulinus himself wrote later on, " for he, who had appealed to the Apostolic See, was not forthcoming when he ought obviously to have defended the rights of his appeal ; and especially since, even according to civil laws, when the appellant takes no steps, it is always the gainer of the original trial who is winner."[5]

No one made the slightest objection to this appeal ; and we

---

[1] *Aug. De gestis Pel.* xxii, 46.

[2] The Benedictines and Quesnel gave 412, as the date of the Council which condemned Celestius, since the Council of Carthage in 417 calls it about five years ago. The Ballerini have shown (*Opp. S. Leon.* iii, p. 845. *P.L.* 56, p. 1008) that 411 is more likely.

[3] St. Augustine was not present. *De gestis Pel.* xi, 23.

[4] *Comm. secundum,* 2 in append, vol. x. *S. Aug.* p. 1687, and *P.L.* xlviii. Zosimus (*ibid.* p. 1726) calls it *appellatio pristina* and later, Facundus (*lib.* 7, c. 5, *ibid.* p. 1723) *in ecclesia Carthaginensi conuictum atque appellantem apostolicam sedem.*

[5] *Ibid.* p. 1725, in the *libellus,* sent by Paulinus to Pope Zosimus in Nov. 417.

see that Mercator and Paulinus blame Celestius for not daring to follow it up at the time. Had the case been one of discipline, like that of Apiarius, it is possible that the Africans might have requested the Pope to refuse to hear him, though it is hardly probable, as Celestius was not an African. But the question, whether or no the Africans in their letter of 424 or 425 to St. Celestine denied the right of the Pope to hear appeals, does not touch the present matter, as from the facts before us and from the whole history we are about to relate, it is evident that a case of faith was naturally referred to Rome ; while the appeal of the priest Apiarius was an unusual measure, being an appeal after condemnation on a criminal charge. Further, the objections against the deciding of a matter of discipline out of the country do not apply to a matter of faith ; for the chief witness both for and against the accused on a charge of heresy is the heretic himself. The question discussed in this article is not whether the Africans recognised in the Pope an ordinary jurisdiction with regard to discipline in every diocese, but what position they attributed to the Holy See with regard to questions of faith and morals.

After the Council, St. Augustine, like the other Bishops of Africa, opposed the doctrine of Celestius in his sermons [1] ; and later in the same year, 412, he wrote the book *De peccatorum meritis et remissione* in which, however, he mentions by name neither Celestius nor Pelagius, and, in fact, appears to praise the latter for his piety and learning. He added to this the book *De spiritu et littera*, and on the feast of St. John Baptist and again, three days later, he preached at Carthage against the same heresy.[2] Pelagius also wrote him a most complimentary letter, which he answered by a short note, saying that he had received the letter, and asking Pelagius to pray for him that he might be worthy of such compliments.[3]

It is about this time that St. Jerome addressed his well-known letter to the virgin Demetrias, whose renunciation of great wealth and position by her veiling had lately caused the admiration of all Christendom. In it he cautions her against certain heretics, who were doubtless the Pelagians. He says :

" I had nearly left out what is most important. When you were a child, and Bishop Anastasius, of holy memory,

---

[1] *Serm.* 170, 174, 5, 6.
[2] *Serm.* 293, 4.
[3] *Ep.* 146, *cf. De gestis Pel.* 26, 51, p. 349.

ruled the Roman Church, a fierce storm of (Origenist) heretics from the East tried to sully and destroy the simplicity of faith which was praised by the voice of the Apostle (Rom. i. 8). But that man of richest poverty and Apostolic solicitude (2 Cor. xi. 28) straightway smote the noxious head and stopped the mouths of the hissing hydra. And because I am afraid, nay, I have heard the rumour, that these poisonous shoots are still alive and vigorous in some, I feel that I ought with the deepest affection to give you this advice, *to hold the faith of holy Innocent,* who is the successor and son of that man and of the Apostolic See, and not to receive any foreign doctrine however prudent and clever you may think yourself to be."

It may seem probable that Pelagius had already addressed to Demetrias the letter quoted by St. Augustine and Orosius. St. Augustine and St. Alypius, by the advice of whom she had taken the veil, wrote to her later on (417 or 418) an antidote to the heretic's epistle.[1] Later still, after the condemnation of Pelagianism by Zosimus, another letter was addressed to her by an author (thought by Quesnel to have been St. Leo the Great, then a young man, by the Ballerini and others St. Prosper, but probably neither) who refers thus to this heresy :

" This impiety was resisted by the hearts of innumerable saints, and not only by every learned bishop ; but even the rank and file of the Church, following the example of the Apostolic See, abhorred the madness of the new doctrine."[2]

We return to Pelagius, who on leaving Africa in 411, proceeded to Palestine, where he seems first to have been friends with St. Jerome.[3] About 414 St. Jerome wrote a letter to Ctesiphon against Pelagius, promising a fuller treatise, which he commenced in July, 415. About 414 St. Augustine wrote a letter against the Sicilian Pelagians,[4] and in 415 the treatise *De natura et gratia,* addressed to Timasius and Jacobus, two young men of good family, who were much troubled by a book

[1] *Ep.* 188.
[2] *P.L.* vol. lv, p. 269 (170), *cap.* 10.
[3] *Veterem necessitudinem,* Aug. vol. x, app. 52, from Jerome, *in Jerem.* Bk. iv, vol. iv, p. 967. *P.L.* xxv, p. 825. But Vallarsi remarks that the Bishop of Jerusalem may be meant.
[4] *Ep.* 156, 7.

ascribed to Pelagius. At the end of the year he wrote *De perfectione justitiae.*

About the middle of this year, Paulus Orosius, a Spanish priest, and later a famous historian, who had come as a disciple to St. Augustine, was sent by him to Bethlehem, that he might sit at the feet of Jerome, then the most eloquent and learned divine in the whole Church. About the 29th or 30th of July a discussion was held at Jerusalem, under the presidency of John the bishop. The apology addressed later on by Orosius to the same assembly gives an account of its first sitting : [1]

"I was in retirement at Bethlehem, having been sent by my Father Augustine that I might learn the fear of God sitting at the feet of Jerome ; from thence I came at your bidding to Jerusalem. I sat down with you in the assembly at the command of the Bishop John. Thereupon with one accord you demanded of my littleness to relate faithfully and simply whatever had been done to my knowledge in Africa as to this heresy sown by Pelagius and Celestius. I exposed shortly, as best I could, how Celestius, who was then intending to creep into the order of priesthood, was at Carthage, before many bishops in judgement, exposed, heard, convicted, that he confessed, was excommunicated, fled from Africa ; and how the blessed Augustine had most fully answered the book of Pelagius, at the request of the heretic's own disciples (viz. Timasius and Jacobus) ; and that I had in my hands a letter of the said bishop, which he had lately sent into Sicily, in which he mentions many of the heretic's views. You ordered me to read the letter, and I read it. Upon this John the bishop asked for Pelagius to be introduced. You gave him your consent, both for the reverence due to the bishop, and because the thing was itself good, for you thought he would be more rightly refuted in the bishop's presence. When Pelagius was admitted, you inquired of him unanimously whether he acknowledged that he had taught the doctrines which Bishop Augustine had confuted. He replied at once : 'And what is Augustine to me ?' And when all cried out that a man who blasphemed against a bishop by whose mouth God had vouchsafed to heal the unity of Africa (viz. by the conversion of the Donatists) ought to be expelled not only from that assembly but from the whole Church, Bp. John thereupon told him to sit down, he a layman in the midst of

[1] *In Aug.* vol. x, app. ii.

priests, he accused of manifest heresy in the midst of Catholics, and then said : ' I am Augustine,' forsooth, that assuming his person he might the more easily pardon the wrongs which he took to himself, and so soothe the minds of his sorrowing audience. After making Pelagius acknowledge his doctrine, I continued : ' This is what the African Synod condemned in Celestius ; this is what Bishop Augustine rejected in his writings as you heard ; this is condemned by Pelagius in his own writings by his present answer ; this is condemned by blessed Jerome, whose words are waited for by the whole West as the dew upon the fleece. . . ."

The Bishop then tried to get Orosius and the rest of the assembly to pose as accusers, while he should judge. They declined, on the ground that the question was already decided. And to his objections in favour of Pelagius, Orosius replied : " We are sons of the Catholic Church ; do not you, our Father, ask us to set ourselves up as doctors above doctors or as judges above judges. The Fathers who are approved by the universal Church (viz. whom he had before referred to, Cyprian, Hilary, Ambrose, Aurelius, Augustine and Jerome), to whose communion we rejoice to belong, have declared these doctrines damnable : we must obey their decision." The interpreter (for Orosius spoke in Latin) continually gave a wrong idea of the views of Orosius. At length Orosius cried : " The heretic is a Latin, we are Latins ; the heresy, which is better known in Latin regions, should be set aside to be judged by Latin judges." Eventually, " after many other things had passed, Bishop John brought forth the final sentence, confirming at last our demand and intention *that brethren and letters should be sent to B. Innocent, Pope of Rome, for all to follow what he should decide ;* but that the heretic Pelagius should until then be silent," and to this all assented. John of Jerusalem, however, himself broke this silence by violent objurgations addressed to Orosius, when the latter came to pay him a complimentary visit at the dedication festival (September 13th) and by accusations of heresy ; to this Orosius replied by writing his apology. St. Jerome about the same time composed his dialogues against the Pelagians.

About December 20th in the same year, 415, a synod was convened at Diospolis (Lydda) to consider the charges brought against Pelagius by Heros and Lazarus, bishops of Arles and Aix, who were dispossessed and travelling in Palestine. Owing to the illness of one of them neither was present at the

Council, nor was Orosius. Before fourteen bishops Pelagius explained away or anathematized the errors attributed to him, and was absolved by the Council. He tried to prevent its acts being made public, but published a short account himself, of which he sent a copy to St. Augustine. He also wrote a book, *De libero arbitrio*, against St. Jerome, who was also attacked on the same subject by Theodore of Mopsuestia.

At the beginning of 416 Orosius returned to Hippo, bringing with him those relics of St. Stephen (whose body had just been discovered at the time of the Council of Lydda) which worked so many miracles during the next few years.[1] He also brought letters from Heros and Lazarus, who complained of the harm Pelagius was doing in Palestine. These he exhibited to a provincial synod of Africa Proconsularis, which met about June at Carthage, and consisted of sixty-eight bishops.

The letter written by the council to Pope Innocent I. explains their action :

"We had come according to custom to the Church of Carthage, and a synod was held for various affairs, when our fellow-priest Orosius presented us with letters from our holy brothers and fellow-bishops Heros and Lazarus, which we enclose. These having been read, we perceived that Pelagius and Celestius were accused of being authors of a wicked error, which must be anathematized by all of us. Wherefore we asked that all which had been done with regard to Celestius here in Carthage about five years ago should be gone through. This having been read, as your holiness can perceive from the acts which we append, although the decision was clear, by which so great a wound was shown to have been cut away from the Church by an episcopal judgement, yet we thought good by a common deliberation, that the authors of this persuasion (although it was said that this Celestius had arrived since then at the priesthood), unless they openly anathematized these things, should themselves be anathematized in order that, if their salvation cannot, at least that of those who may have been or may be deceived by them may be procured, when they know the sentence against them. This act, lord brother, we thought right to intimate to your holy charity, in order that to the statutes of our littleness might be added the authority of the Apostolic See (*ut statutis nostrae mediocritatis etiam apostolicae sedis adhibeatur auctoritas*) for the preservation of the safety of many, and the correction of the perversity of some. "

[1] *De Civ. Dei*, xxii, 8. *Serm* 319-324 ff.

The Fathers next expose the errors of Pelagius, and after refuting them by a string of Scripture texts, they continue :

" And we fear lest by repeating to you these very things which you preach with more grace from the Apostolic seat (*quae majore gratia de sede apostolica praedicas*), we should seem to act inconveniently. But we do so because, just on account of our greater weakness, the more zeal we show in preaching the Word of God, the more constant and bold are the attacks of the heretics. If, therefore, Pelagius seems to your Holiness to have been justly absolved by the Episcopal acts which are said to have been transacted in the East, at all events, the error itself and impiety which has now many assertors in divers places, ought to be anathematized by the authority of the Apostolic See also. Let your Holiness consider and feel with us in your pastoral heart how baneful and destructive for the sheep of Christ is that which follows of necessity from their sacrilegious disputations.

After more theological argument, they conclude thus :

" Wherefore, even if Pelagius and Celestius have amended their ways or say that they never held such opinions, and deny to be theirs whatever writings are brought as evidence against them, and if there is no way of convicting them of falsehood— yet in general whoever asserts dogmatically, etc. . . . let him be anathema. Whatever other things are objected against them, we doubt not that your reverence, after perusing the Episcopal acts which are said to have been drawn up in the East in the same cause, will make such a judgement that we shall all rejoice in the mercy of God (*id judicaturum unde omnes in Dei misericordia gaudeamus*)."[1]

At the same time was held a provincial council of the province of Numidia at Milevis,[2] attended by sixty-one bishops, including St. Augustine. Imitating that of Proconsular Africa, they also wrote to Pope Innocent :

" Since God has by a special gift of His grace set you in the Apostolic See, and has given such a one as yourself to our

[1] *Ep.* 175, *inter Aug.* (vol. ii, p. 758, *seq.*). A better text is given by the Ballerini of this and the five following letters. They may also be found in Mansi and Coustant. (*P.L.* vol. xx).
[2] I write *Milevis* because it seems to be the commonest spelling. I do not pretend to know which is most correct of the five or six forms of the name.

times, so that it could rather be imputed to us as a fault of
negligence if we failed to unfold to your Reverence whatever
is to be suggested for the Church, than that you should be
able to receive the same with contempt or negligence,[1] we
beseech you to apply your pastoral diligence to the great peril
of the weak members of Christ."

After exposing the heresy, they continue :

" In insinuating these things to your Apostolic breast we
have no need to say much, and heap up words about this
impiety, since doubtless they will move you in such wise
that you will be altogether unable to refrain from correcting
them, that they may creep no further. . . . The authors of
this most pernicious heresy are said to be Pelagius and Celestius, whom, indeed, we should prefer to be cured with the
Church, rather than that they should be cut off from the
Church, if no necessity compels this.   One of them, Celestius,
is even said to have arrived at the priesthood in Asia.   Your
Holiness is better informed by the Council of Carthage as
to what was done against him a few years back.   Pelagius,
as the letters of some of our brethren say, is in Jerusalem,
and is said to have deceived many there.   Many more, however, who have been able to examine his views more closely,
are fighting him on behalf of the Catholic Faith, but especially
your holy son, our brother and fellow-priest, Jerome.   But
we consider that with the help of the mercy of our God, whom
we pray to direct your counsels and to hear your prayers,
those who hold such perverse and baneful opinions will more
easily yield to the authority of your Holiness, which has been
taken from the authority of the Holy Scriptures (*auctoritati
sanctitatis tuae, de sanctarum scripturarum auctoritate depromptae facilius . . . esse cessuros*), so that we may be rather
rejoiced by their correction than saddened by their destruction.
But whatever they themselves may choose, your Reverence
perceives that at least those many must be cared for whom
they may entangle in their nets if they should not submit
straightforwardly.   We write this to your Holiness from
the Council of Numidia, imitating our fellow bishops of the
Church and province of Carthage, whom we understand to
have written of this affair to the Apostolic See which your
Blessedness adorns."

These two letters were carried to Italy by Julius, an African
bishop.

[1] The sentence is not quite logical as it stands ; I translate literally.

The least that we can gather from them as to the Pope is that he has " more grace " [1] than the two provincial councils, and that, while the judgment of these is braved by the heretics, the authority of the Apostolic See, founded on Scripture,[2] will strike terror into them, and perhaps convert them. The Africans ask for an authoritative condemnation by the Pope of those doctrines which they had themselves condemned, in order that the evil may be entirely cut away. They imply the view that we shall find more clearly exemplified later on, that their decision was strictly binding only in Africa, while that of Innocent would have an oecumenical force.

But we may learn more from a third letter, longer and less formal, which was taken by Bishop Julius to Rome, signed jointly by five Bishops—viz., Aurelius the Primate, Augustine, Alypius, Evodius and Possidius, five great names. They say :

" We send to your Holiness letters from the two Councils of the provinces of Carthage and Numidia, signed by no small number of bishops, against the enemies of the grace of Christ.... Many of these rise up against us and say to our soul, ' There is

[1] For the sense of *majore gratia* compare St. Augustine's well-known comparison of St. Peter with St. Cyprian : " Si distat *gratia cathedrarum una est tamen martyrii gloria.*" *De. bapt. c. Don.* ii, 1,vol. ix, p. 127.

[2] It would need more prejudice in Dr. Bright's readers than he has any right to presume, for them to believe that *de s. scripturarum auctoritate depromptae* means merely that Innocent would rest his decision upon scriptural quotations. Doubtless the word *auctoritas* may mean a quotation (we should expect *auctoritatibus*), but also doubtless the Numidians mean the same by the *auctoritas* of the Pope as did their Carthaginian brethren (*ut statutis nostrae mediocritatis etiam apostolicae sedis adhibeatur auctoritas*, and *impietas etiam auctoritate ap. sedis anathematizanda est*) ; while if we translate, " the authority of your Holiness, which you have drawn from the fountain of the sacred Scriptures," it is absurdly implied that the Pope has no authority beyond the value of his quotations. In either case, if the Pelagians were so Protestant that they would yield to nothing but " texts " one does not see why they should " yield more easily " to the open bible of Innocent than to that of the Africans. So far it is clear that Dr. Bright makes nonsense of the passage. But yet more. Why should Dr. Bright be afraid to accept the ordinary and obvious translation ? He knows that the Africans really did regard the authority of Rome as founded in Holy Scripture. Compare together the following passages of St. Augustine : *Quis nesciat primum apostolorum esse beatissimum Petrum? Quis nescit illum apostolatus principatum cuilibet episcopatui esse praeferendum ? In qua (Romana ecclesia) semper apostolicae cathedrae uiguit principatus.* It follows that the primacy of Peter, which (however much Dr. Bright may object) St. Augustine finds in Scripture—*quis nescit ?*—is continued to the Bishops of Rome (*tract* 56 in *Joann.* vol. iii, p. 788 ; *de bapt. c. Don. ubi supra* ii, 1, vol. ix, p. 127, and *Ep.* 43, 3, 7, vol. ii, p. 163),

no help for him in his God.' Therefore the family of Christ, which says, ' When I am weak then am I strong,' and to whom the Lord says, ' I am thy salvation,' with suspense of heart, with fear and trembling, *waits for the help of the Lord also by the charity of your Reverence.* For we have heard that there are many in the city of Rome, where Pelagius long lived, who favour him for various causes, some because he is said to have persuaded them of his doctrine, but a larger number because they do not believe him to hold it, especially since it is boasted that ecclesiasical acts were drawn up in the East, where he is living, by which he is declared innocent. If indeed the bishops there pronounced him Catholic, we must believe that it was for no other reason than because he said he acknowledged the grace of Christ . . . it is not a question of Pelagius only, but of so many others of whose loquacity and contentiousness . . . the world is full. Therefore either he should be sent for to Rome by your Reverence and carefully examined as to what grace he admits when he admits (if he does admit) that men are by grace aided to avoid sin and live justly, or else this must be transacted with him by letter. And when it has been proved that he means that grace which is taught by ecclesiastical and apostolic truth, then without any doubt on the Church's part, without any lurking ambiguity, he must be absolved, and then we must really rejoice in his acquittal. [Much further on, *c.* 15 :] If his supporters knew that the book which they think or know to be his has been anathematized and condemned by himself on the authority of Catholic bishops, and especially that of your Holiness, *which we do not doubt will be of greater weight with him,* we think they will not dare further to disturb faithful and simple Christian breasts. . . . Wherefore we have thought it best to send to your beatitude a letter written by one of our number [St. Augustine] to Pelagius, who had sent him by a certain deacon (ordained in the East, but a citizen of Hippo) some writing to justify himself, since we think it better that you should send it to him yourself ; and we pray you to do so, for so he will the rather not disdain to read it, regarding more in it him who sent it than him who wrote it."

Thus the five bishops say just the same as the two Councils in which they had borne a part, that the Pope's greater authority will doubtless be respected where their own might be despised.[1]

[1] The intentions and opinion of one of the five bishops—Possidius—are testified in his life of St. Augustine, *cap.* xviii, The passage will be quoted later on.

They do not so far state explicitly that his judgment is final or infallible. But the last sentence of their letter suggests something of the sort :

" Of the rest of the accusations against him doubtless your beatitude will judge in the same way as the acts of the two Councils. Doubtless your kindness of heart will pardon us for having sent to your Holiness a longer letter than you might perhaps have wished. For we do not pour back our little stream for the purpose of replenishing your great fountain (*non enim riuulum nostrum tuo largo fonti augendo refundimus*) ; but in the great temptation of these times (from which may He deliver us to whom we say, " and lead us not into temptation ") we wish it to be approved by you whether our stream, though small, flows from the same head of water as your abundant river, and to be consoled by your answer in the common participation of the same grace.[1]

We cannot but compare the words in which St. Augustine later sends his writings to the Holy See, *non tam discenda quam examinanda, et ubi forsitan aliquid displicueret emendanda*,[2] which are similar words to Pelagius' insincere protestation : *emendari cupimus a te qui Petri et fidem et sedem tenes.*" [3]

At the same time Augustine was writing to a certain Bishop Hilary, perhaps of Narbonne, warning him against the Pelagians :

" Already, as I am writing this, we have heard that in the Church of Carthage a decree of the council of bishops has been made against them[4] to be sent by letter to the holy and vener-able Pope Innocent ; and we have similarly written from the Council of Numidia to the same Apostolic See."[5]

He also wrote to John of Jerusalem, explaining the heresies contained in the books attributed to Pelagius in Africa, and asking for a correct copy of the acts of Diospolis, which he as yet knew only from Pelagius' own fraudulent account.[6]

[1] *Ep.* 177, vol. ii, pp. 764-772.
[2] C. 2, *Epp. Pell.* i, l. vol. x, p. 551.
[3] *Libellus in App.* vol. x, p. 1718.
[4] These words sufficiently dispose of the supposition of Garnier, Tillemont and others, that St. Augustine composed the decree and letter of the Council of Carthage.
[5] *Ep.* 178, p. 773.
[6] *Ep.* 179.

The answers of Innocent to the three letters addressed to him from Africa are all dated January 27th, 417. To Carthage he writes (and the letter probably emanates from a Roman Council, according to custom in grave matters) :

" In making inquiry with respect to those things that should be treated with all solicitude by bishops, and especially by a true and just and Catholic Council, by preserving, as you have done, the example of ancient tradition, and by being mindful of ecclesiastical discipline, you have truly strengthened the vigour of our religion, no less now in consulting us than before in passing sentence. For you decided that it was proper to refer to our judgement, knowing what is due to the Apostolic See, since all we who are set in this place, desire to follow the Apostle from whom the very episcopate and whole authority of this name is derived. Following in his steps, we know how to condemn the evil and to approve the good. So also, you have by your sacerdotal office preserved the customs of the Fathers, and have not spurned that which they decreed by a divine and not human sentence, that whatsoever is done, even though it be in distant provinces, should not be ended without being brought to the knowledge of this See,[1]

---

[1] Dr. Bright (*loc. cit.* p. 129) says : " Swelling words these, which it would have been impossible for Innocent to verify : the Fathers had never made any such decree, and if ' this one rescript contains the teaching of the Vatican Council entire ' that teaching rests, as indeed we have already seen, on apocryphal history. The plain English of the matter is that Innocent, in true Roman fashion, was interpreting an application as broadly as suited him, and adding a broad assertion to match " ; and in a note, " the language goes far beyond the provisions called Sardican. So does that of Innocent, *Ep.* 2, 3." I quite agree with the last note. Innocent is referring to inveterate custom up to his own time. As to " apocryphal history," St. Innocent knew more than Dr. Bright about the frequency of appeals to Rome, and the principle involved in them. It was not only at Rome such statements were made. A dozen years afterwards Socrates (*H.E.* ii, 8 and 17), a Greek, and twenty years after him Sozomen (iii, 10, *cf.* Theodoret. *H.E.* ii, 4), another Greek, made just the same statement. Dr. Bright (p. 84), says that these two Greeks have " gravely misapprehended " the letter of St. Julius, to which alone he supposes them to refer. What if he (following Coustant) is right ? It remains to explain why they so " gravely misapprehended " a (to Dr. Bright) perfectly plain passage, unless they themselves were accustomed to the doctrine which they state, that ecclesiastical law forbids any canons to be made without the consent of the Bishop of Rome (see p. 59 above). What Innocent, Zosimus, Boniface, Celestine, and their successors throughout this century all repeated and acted upon in East and West was at least not looked upon as apocryphal history in their time, for they were disobeyed frequently, but they were never contradicted. Dr. Bright is at liberty to disbelieve them. He is not at liberty to imply that the Church of the fifth century disbelieved them.

that by its authority the whole just pronouncement should be strengthened, and that from it all other Churches (like waters flowing from their natal source and flowing through the different regions of the world, the pure streams of one incorrupt head), should receive what they ought to enjoin, whom they ought to wash, and whom that water, worthy of pure bodies, should avoid as defiled with uncleansable filth. I congratulate you, therefore, dearest brethren, that you have directed letters to us by our brother and fellow-bishop Julius, and that, while caring for the Churches which you rule, you also show your solicitude for the well-being of all, and that you ask for a decree that shall profit all the Churches of the world at once ;[1] so that the Church being established in her rules and confirmed by this decree of just pronouncement against such errors, may be unable to fear those men, etc."[2]

The Pope goes on to declare that men who deny the necessity of grace must be cut off from the Church, lest the festering wound should corrupt the rest of the body. Should they, however, repent, he concludes, it will be in the power of the Pontiffs to assist them to a certain extent, and to give some care to these great wounds, such as that kindness which the Church is not wont to deny to the lapsed when they repent.

To Milevis he writes :

" Among the cares of the Roman Church and the occupations of the Apostolic See in which we treat with faithful and medicinal[3] discussion the consultations of divers, our brother and fellow-bishop Julius has brought me unexpectedly the letters of your charity which you sent from the Council of Milevis in your earnest care for the faith, adding the writing of a similar complaint from the Council of Carthage. [He praises their zeal and continues :] It is therefore with due care and propriety that you consult the secrets of the Apostolic office (*apostolici consulitis honoris* [al. *oneris*] *arcana*) that office, I mean, to which belongs, besides the things which are without, the care of all the Churches, as to what opinion you should hold in this anxious question, following thus the ancient rule which you know has been observed with me by the whole

---

[1] This is exactly the expression of what the Africans wanted. Their decision was for Africa only, and might be appealed against. That of the Pope was for the whole Church, and final.

[2] *Ep.* 181.

[3] *Medica*, Ball ; *modica*, Bened. ; *non modica*, conj. Garnier.

world.[1] But this subject I dismiss, for I do not think it is
unknown to your prudence ; for else, why did you confirm it
with your action, if you were not aware that responses ever
flow from the Apostolic fountain to all provinces for those
who ask them ? Especially *as often as a question of faith is
discussed*, I think that all our brothers and fellow-bishops
should refer to none other than to *Peter, the author of their
name and office*, even as now your charity has referred to us
a thing which may be useful throughout the world to all the
Churches in common. For all must of necessity become more
cautious when they see that the inventors of evil, at the relation
of two synods, have been cut off by our sentence from ecclesiastical communion. Your charity will therefore do a
double good. For you will obtain the grace of having preserved the canons, and the whole world will share your benefit."

Further on he gives his decision. "We judge by the
authority of Apostolic power (*apostolici uigoris auctoritate*)
that Pelagius and Celestius be deprived of ecclesiastical
communion, until they return to the faith out of the snares
of the devil. . . ." [2]

To the five bishops he writes that " some laymen or other "
had given him acts, purporting to be those of a Council wherein
Pelagius was acquitted. The judgment he can neither praise
nor blame, since he knows not whether the acts are genuine ;
or if they are, whether Pelagius did not merely escape condemnation by subterfuge.[3] A fourth letter was addressed to
the Primate Aurelius alone.

We have seen what the Africans asked. We see now that
Rome gave exactly the answer they wished. The Pope
compliments them on their adherence to ancient custom in
referring the matter to himself, approves their action with
regard to the heretics and their heresy, and accedes to their
request that he should excommunicate them.

The doctrine of St. Innocent as to the rights of the Apostolic
See is more explicit but hardly wider than that of the letters
to which he replies. It would need no special comment had

---

[1] Among such of St. Innocent's letters which remain to us we find
answers or directions sent to Africa, Jerusalem, Constantinople, Moesia,
Thessaly, Rouen, Toulouse, Toledo, etc. Traces of others may be
found in Jaffé. The real amount of the correspondence of the Popes
at this time must have been very great. *Cf.* Jerome, *Ep.* 123, 10, vol. i,
p. 907. *P.L.* xxii, 1052 (p. 117 above).
[2] *Ep.* 182.
[3] *Ep.* 183.

it not raised the indignation of most modern heretics. Dr. Bright assumes that the Africans felt as he does, only that they dissimulated their disgust, because it was so important for them to secure the influence of " the Apostolic and Petrine See " against Pelagianism.   " They would not in such circumstances, feel bound to criticize its language about itself, but would dwell on its Catholic view of the question at issue " (p. 129). There is absolutely no evidence for this view of Dr. Bright's, while the letters of the Councils and of the five bishops alone are decisive against it.   It is useless to protest against this *a priori* method of writing history.   Nevertheless I will be at pains to complete the proof as carefully as though a refutation were needed.

In the first place it must not be overlooked that the African bishops knew perfectly well the *stylus curiae* of their time. The epistles sent to East and West from Rome on the business of some particular province or diocese were usually published to the world at large. Sometimes the bishop who received them was expected to publish them ; sometimes the letter was sent elsewhere from Rome, with a mere change in the greeting, while the contents betray their original destination.

The Africans must have been familiar with many other letters of Siricius, Innocent and their predecessors, most of which are lost to us ; but we can judge of their claims by the existing letters,[1] and by those of the succeeding Pontiffs, Zosimus, Boniface, Celestine, Leo, Hilarus, and so on. As for the predecessors of Siricius, their letters are few and far between, but those we possess of Damasus make no lesser claims. And who can forget the two famous letters sent to Africa, which roused the wrath of Tertullian and St. Cyprian ? These epistles, so far as we can gather, were just in the style of the letters before us; the former was as from a *Pontifex maximus* and *episcopus episcoporum ;*[2] the latter enjoined obedience to ancient custom under pain of excommunication, by the authority of that rock on whom Christ built His Church.[3] The African Bishops therefore knew perfectly well what style of answer they would get, and we should be surprised if they did not receive the answers with joy. We shall, in fact,

---

[1] We possess six letters of Siricius, three of his successor Anastasius, two in Coustant, another published by Pitra (*Analecta Nouissima*) as of Anastasius II, and thirty-four of Innocent.
[2] *De puducitia*, c. 1.
[3] St. Cyprian. (Firmilian) *Ep.* 75 (Hartel, p. 821).

presently come upon many proofs that they did, and even upon many direct approvals of the Pope's claims. I simply defy Dr. Bright or anyone else to find any ancient authority for his theory that in the view of the Africans the decision of their two Councils were a co-ordinate element with the letters of Innocent in the condemnation of the heresy. Such a theory would force us to ignore the meaning of the words *relatio*, *referre*, constantly and consistently used of the action of these Councils, which imply the reference of a matter to a higher authority, and correspond with the words *rescripta*, *rescribere*, applied to the letters of the Pope. One would be obliged also to forget the words of the five Bishops given above, implying the possibility (however improbable) of their decision being *corrected* by the Pope's reply. Here are some of the passages in which the decision is ascribed by contemporaries to St. Innocent alone.

St. Prosper, the devoted admirer of St. Augustine, writing twelve years later, has the following reference :[1]

> *Pestem subeuntem prima recidit*
> *Sedes Roma Petri, quae pastoralis honoris*
> *Facta caput mundo, quicquid non possidet armis*
> *Relligione tenet.*[2]   *Non segnior inde Orientis*
> *Rectorum cura emicuit, etc.*

The same writer has the expressions : " At that time the Pelagians, who had already been condemned by Pope Innocent were being resisted by the vigour of the Africans and above all by the learning of Bishop Augustine " ;[3]   and

---

[1] *De ingratis*, i. 39.

[2] The same epigram that Rome rules by her faith what once she ruled by arms, occurs in the contemporary book *De uocatione gentium*, ii.16. *P.L.* 51, p. 905 (704), *quae tamen (Roma) per apostolici sacerdotii principatum amplior facta est arce religionis quam solio potestatis*, and a few years later by St. Leo in one of his finest sermons (*in Nat App. Petri et Pauli*, lxxii.   *P.L.* 54, p. 422 [321]), *Isti sunt (P. et P.) qui te ad hanc gloriam prouexerunt, ut gens sancta, populus electus, ciuitas sacerdotalis et regia, per sacram beati Petri sedem caput orbis effecta, latius praesideres religione diuina quam dominatione terrena.   Quamuis enim multis aucta uictoriis jus imperii tui terra marique protuleris, minus tamen est quod tibi bellicus labor subdidit quam quod pax Christiana subjecit.*   With the word *recidit, cf. Apostolicus gladius* or *mucro*, used by St. Prosper elsewhere three times (*Chron. ad. ann.* 439, and two more passages quoted in text).   In an epigram (*P.L.* 51, p. 190 [150]), *Stratosque rebelles, oris apostolici fulmine ubique uide*, may *possibly* refer to St. Augustine, " apostolic " being used in a different sense, as " Augustinus . . . apostolice asseruit."   (*Resp. ad cap. Gall. praef.*)

[3] *Chron. in ann.* 416 (i.e., 417).

"They fell when Innocent, of blessed memory, struck the heads of the deadly error with the apostolic sword, *apostolico mucrone percussit*, when the synod of Palestinian bishops drove Pelagius to condemn himself and his followers ; when Pope Zosimus, of blessed memory, joined the strength of his sentence to the decrees of the African Councils (i.e. those of next year), and armed the right hands of all bishops with the sword of Peter for the cutting off of the impious. When Pope Boniface, of holy memory, rejoiced in the devotion of the most pious emperors, and made use against the enemies the grace of God, not only of apostolic, but also of royal edicts ; and when, though himself most learned, he asked for answers to the books of the Pelagians from blessed Bishop Augustine.[1]

Here is Marius Mercator's account (the explanations in brackets are mine) :

"Celestius and Pelagius were not then for the first time condemned by Zosimus of blessed memory, but by his predecessor Innocent, of holy memory, by whom Julian had been ordained. And Julian, after their condemnation, until the death of Innocent, remained in his communion and persevered in the true faith ; and since he communicated with him who had condemned Pelagius and Celestius, doubtless he condemned them himself ; and what he wants now, or of what he complains, I do not know. Now the reason for this condemnation by Innocent, of blessed memory, was the following : After the devastation of Rome (by Alaric in 410) Pelagius was living in Palestine. His books were discovered by certain careful bishops (viz. Heros and Lazarus) in which he has evidently written many things against the Catholic faith. These books were sent, together with letters, to the Fathers and bishops in Africa, where the books were read at the three Councils which were assembled (i.e. those of Carthage, Milevis, and of the five Bishops). From thence relations were sent to Rome, together with the books ; the apostolic sentence in reply to the Councils followed, which deprived Pelagius and Celestius of ecclesiastical communion, and we have in our hands copies of these writings" (i.e. the letters of Innocent).[2]

---

[1] *C. Collat*, c. xxi (al. xli). *P.L.* 51, p. 362 (271) and *in App. S. Aug.* vol. x, p. 1831.

[2] *Exinde relationibus Romam missis, ipsis quoque libris pariter. destinatis, apostolica sententia rescribentis ad praedicta concilia emanauit,* etc. (*Commonitorium C. Pel.* 10, 11, *in App. S. Aug.* vol. x, p. 1689 and *P.L.* xlviii, p. 70).

Here, again, the whole sentence is ascribed to Innocent, and the African Councils are merely represented as referring the matter to him.

In the book called *Praedestinatus,* written some twenty or thirty years after, and attributed to Arnobius the younger, we find the following :

"Pope Innocent, when the matter was referred to him by nearly all the African Bishops, wrote the condemnation of both Pelagius and Celestius.   These latter, however, whether before they were condemned by the universal Church, or after they were condemned, did not cease to write," etc.[1]

Here again the judgment of Innocent is simply treated as final ; while apparently it is considered to be a condemnation by the universal Church.   The subsequent sentence of Pope Zosimus may, however, be meant, which was signed by all bishops.   But Gennadius, at the end of the century, the later author of the *Liber Pontificalis,* and the contemporary Possidius have similar expressions.[2]

Again the Council of 214 Bishops which met early in the next year at Carthage has : " We decide that the sentence against Pelagius and Celestius promulgated by the venerable Bishop Innocent from the See of the blessed Apostle Peter remain firm, until they shall confess," etc.[3]   Again Paulinus,[4] in his account (which will be quoted further on) of the trial of Celestius before Pope Zosimus, has no mention of the African Councils, but openly professes belief in the inerrancy of the Roman See.

To make the proof complete let us look at St. Augustine's statements on the subject.   We have already seen him at the Council of Milevis and in the private letter of five bishops referring the matter to the Pope in terms which alone totally

[1] *Tunc ad relationen pene omnium Africorum episcoporum Papa Innocentius damnationem et Pelagio et Coelestio conscripsit.* (*Praedest. haer.* 88.   P.L. 53, and *App.* vol x, Aug., p. 1682.)
[2] " Innocentius . . . scripsit decretum, occidentalium et orientalium ecclesiis aduersus Pelagianos datum.   Post quem successor ejus papa Zosimus latius promulgauit " (Gennad. *De. uiris illustr.* c. 43).   " Hic constitutum fecit de omni ecclesia " (*Lib. Pontif*), and *Possid,* c. 18.   On all of which see Pagi, in Baron, ann, 417, 14, 15.
[3] *Prosper. c. Collat.* c. v. 15.   P.L. 51, p. 319 (227), or in *App. St. Aug.* vol x, p. 1808.
[4] *Ibid. Append.* p. 1724.   " Pel. Celestiusque quia . . . papa Innocentio . . . damnati sunt," and the words of Zosimus which follow.

exclude Dr. Bright's view.   He was also the prime leader of
the 214 Bishops just cited, and St. Prosper, Marius Mercator
and the Milanese Paulinus were proud to be his disciples.
Yet I add his express words :

" Do you think these Fathers—viz. Irenaeus, Cyprian,
Reticius, Hilary, Ambrose [whom he had been quoting] are
to be despised because they all belong to the Western Church,
and I have mentioned no Eastern Bishop among them ?
What are we to do, since they are Greeks and we are Latins ?
I think that you ought to be satisfied with that part of the
world in which our Lord willed to crown the chief (*primus*)
of His apostles with a glorious martyrdom.   If you had been
willing to hear blessed Innocent, the president of that Church,
you would have long ago disengaged your perilous youth
from the nets of the Pelagians.   For what could that holy
man answer to the African Councils, except what from of old
the Apostolic See and the Roman Church with all others
perseveringly holds ?   And yet you accuse his successor
Zosimus of prevarication, because he would not allow the
apostolic doctrine and the decision of his successor to be
rescinded.   But I say no more of this, that I may not, by the
praise of him who condemned you, irritate your mind, which
I desire rather to heal than to wound.   See what you can
reply to St. Innocent, who has no other view than have those
into whose council I have introduced you (viz. the Fathers
whom he had quoted) ; with these he sits also, though after
them in time, before them in rank (*etsi posterior tempore,
prior loco*) . . . answer him, or rather our Lord Himself,
whose words he alleges. . . . What will you say ? what can
you answer ? for if you should call blessed Innocent a
Manichean, surely you will not dare to say it of Christ ?[1]

---

[1] *C. Julian.* i, c. iv. 13, p. 648.   Julian had called St. Augustine's
doctrine Manichean.   The saint shows that in that case the above-
mentioned doctors and Pope Innocent, nay, Christ Himself, were
Manicheans.   He adds some Greek doctors to the list, and then the
Council of Diospolis, and goes back to St. Ambrose, of whom Pelagius
had said : *in libris ejus praecipue fidem lucere Romanam* (*ibid.* c. vii, 30,
and *de Nupt. et Conc. T.* 35, 40, and elsewhere).   In the second book
he continues the same argument, and adds the authority of St. Jerome,
*Clarissimi sacerdotes, Irenaeus, Cyprianus, Reticius, Olympius, Hilarius,
Ambrosius, Gregorius, Innocentius, Joannes, Basilius, quibus addo
presbyterum, uelis nolis, Hieronymum* (c. 10, 33), *ex quibus papam
Innocentium et presbyterum Hieronymum retrahere fortasse tentabis ;
istum quia Pelagium Celestiumque damnauit ; illum, quia in oriente
contra Pelagium catholicam fidem pia intentione defendit.   Sed lege quae
dicat in laudem beati papae Innocentii Pelagius, et uide utrum tales facile
possis judices inuenire* (c. 10, 36, p. 699).

Again St. Augustine relates that while Celestius refused at Rome to condemn the views which Paulinus accused him of holding, which was equivalent to denying the authority of the Council of Carthage in 411, from which he had appealed, yet " he did not dare to resist the letters of the blessed Pope Innocent,"[1] Innocent who condemned Pelagius and Celestius.[2]

"And the words of the venerable Bishop Innocent to the Council of Carthage. . . . What more plain and clear than this sentence of the Apostolic See ? To this Celestius professed to consent when . . . he answered : " I condemn them according to the sentence of your holy predecessor Innocent." . . .
"What of that which the same Pope wrote in answer to the Bishops of Numidia also (because he had received letters from both Councils—that is, both of Carthage and Milevis) does it not speak clearly of infants ? "[3]

Again : he speaks of Celestius seeming to be Catholic " when he answered that he consented to the letters of Pope Innocent, of blessed memory, *by which all doubt about this matter was removed.*"[4] This last sentence alone is sufficient proof.

The following passage is also to be noted, written at the end of the Saint's life. " Let blessed Innocent also reply, the prelate of the Roman Church, who in answering (*rescribens*) the African Episcopal Councils in your case said : (he then quotes a passage from the letter to the Council of Carthage). " Do you see what the Catholic Faith holds by her minister ? " " *Videsne quid sapiat per ministrum suum catholica fides ?* "[5] Other equally strong passages will be quoted shortly, while St. Augustine's treatment of the decisions of Innocent's successor will also throw light on the subject later on.

Let us continue the interrupted history. Before receiving the Pope's answers, St. Augustine had at length received authentic copies of the acts of the synod of Diospolis, which Innocent himself had not yet been able to procure, and which St. Augustine had besought John of Jerusalem to send him. He found in them, as he had already divined, that Pelagius

[1] *De pecc. orig.* c. vii, 8, p. 389.
[2] *C. Julian.* ii, c. x. 36, p. 699, etc.
[3] *Ibid.* c. iv, 6, 7.
[4] *Ibid.* c. iii, 5, p. 574.
[5] *Op. imperf.* bk. vi, c. xi, p. 1520.

had only been acquitted because he feigned to accept Catholic doctrine. He thereupon wrote the book *"De gestis Pelagii,"* in which he shows that in the absence of his accusers, Heros and Lazarus, and in the presence of judges who could not read the book in question because they did not know Latin, Pelagius had evaded condemnation without difficulty.

About the same time the followers of Pelagius in Palestine wreaked vengeance on their vigorous opponent St. Jerome, by storming his monastery and that of his disciples, Eustochium and Paula, a deacon being killed and St. Jerome himself taking refuge in a tower.[1] This grievous outrage, writes St. Augustine, does not concern himself, but must be punished by the local bishops. The Pope, to whom Eustochium and Paula appealed, wrote a severe letter to rebuke John of Jerusalem who had taken no measures to protect the servants and virgins of Christ, and another letter to St. Jerome, saying that he had hastened to seize the authority of the Apostolic See to repress all wickedness, only that the name of the author of the crime had not been divulged, nor had a formal accusation been lodged. John of Jerusalem was perhaps already dead when the letter of St. Innocent reached Palestine. This great Pope himself died on March 12th of this year, 417.

Not long after this date St. Augustine and St. Alypius wrote to St. Paulinus of Nola,'whom they knew to have been formerly a friend of Pelagius, to warn him against his doctrines, which were said to be spreading among the citizens of Nola, and of which St. Paulinus himself appears to have been claimed as protector. They gave him an account of the Synod of Diospolis, and enclosed copies of the letters of the African councils to St. Innocent, and of the Pope's replies. They say :

" After letters had come to us from the East, discussing the case in the clearest manner, we were bound not to fail in assisting the Church's need with such episcopal authority as we possess (*nullo modo jam qualicumque episcopali auctoritate deesse Ecclesiae debueramus*). In consequence, relations as to this matter were sent from two Councils—those of Carthage and of Milevis—to the Apostolic See, before the ecclesiastical acts by which Pelagius is said to have been acquitted had come into our hands or into Africa at all. We also wrote to Pope Innocent, of blessed memory a private letter, besides

---

[1] *De gestis Pel.* c. xxxv, p. 358. See above, p. 131.

the relations of the Councils, wherein we described the case at greater length. TO ALL OF THESE HE ANSWERED IN THE MANNER WHICH WAS THE RIGHT AND THE DUTY OF THE BISHOP OF THE APOSTOLIC SEE (*Ad omnia nobis ille rescripsit eo modo quo fas erat atque oportebat Apostolicae sedis Antistitem*). All of which you may now read, if perchance none of them or not all of them have yet reached you ; in them you will see that, while he has preserved the moderation which was right, so that the heretic should not be condemned if he condemns his errors, yet the new and pernicious error is so restrained by ecclesiastical authority that we much wonder that there should be any still remaining who, by any error whatsoever, try to fight against the grace of God. . . .[1]

Here two Saints writing to another Saint explain the African method of using episcopal authority for the good of the Church. It consists in sending an authoritative account of the heresy rampant in their province to the Apostolic See, that the Pope may ratify their action and publish an anathema to the whole Church. His " swelling words " and "apocryphal history " are described as what was fitting and proper from the successor of St. Peter.[2]

It was on Sunday, September 23rd, 417, that St. Augustine, being at Carthage, preached "̣ at the table of Cyprian " the famous sermon against Pelagianism which concludes with these words : " My brethren, be of one mind with me. Wheresoever you find such men do not hide them, have no perverse pity. Refute those who contradict, and bring to us those who resist. For already two Councils have sent to the Apostolic See concerning this matter, and rescripts have come from thence. The case is concluded ; would that the error would soon cease also. *Causa finita est, utinam aliquando finiatur error.*[3]

True, the question of dogma was decided for ever, but yet the case was not finished. While Augustine spoke, letters were on their way from the new Pope, declaring that Celestius

---

[1] *Ep.* 186, i. 2, 3, p. 817.

[2] Further on (viii. 29) in the same letter we find again mention of submission to the Apostolic See. *Si autem cedunt sedi Apostolicae (Nolani)uel potius ipsi Magistro et Domino Apostolorum qui dicit . . .*"

[3] *Serm.* 131, 10, vol. v, p. 734. As for Dr. Bright's amusing burst of indignation against those who think St. Augustine meant what he said in this passage, I have dealt with it in the *Dublin Review* for July, 1896, pp. 8, 10. St. Augustine's words are the origin of the common saying : *Roma locuta est, causa finita est.*

and Pelagius were innocent victims of malicious calumny, and had never taught the errors attributed to them ; while they most humbly submitted to past and future judgments of the Holy See.

II

Pelagius and Celestius had been condemned by St. Innocent, but they had no intention of submitting in silence. The former had already imposed successfully upon the council of Diospolis, and both were now ready to assure the Pope that they had never taught the heresies which had been proscribed.

The moment was a propitious one, though they did not know it. Only four days after his consecration,[1] the new Pope St. Zosimus sent a letter to the bishops of Gaul, confirming the " ancient right " of the bishop of Arles, as Primate of Gaul, to consecrate the metropolitans of Vienne and of the two Narbonnenses, and stating that he would receive henceforward no cleric coming from Gaul who was not furnished with *litterae formatae* from Patroclus, Bishop of Arles, " to whom we have conceded this privilege in special contemplation of his merits." [2] Now the new privilege was as undeserved as the ancient right was apocryphal.[3] Patroclus was an intruder, and the lawful bishop whom he had dispossessed was no other than Heros, the accuser of Pelagius. The cause of the Pope's favour for Patroclus is hard to discover. It has been said, but without proof, that Patroclus was present in Rome at the time of the papal election, and had worked for Zosimus. He was the intimate friend of the powerful Count Constantius, now the real ruler of the empire, and for this reason was a man to be favoured.[4] But anyhow we can see that the infamous bishop of Arles, who dared, says Tiro Prosper,[5] to sell the sacerdotal office, had somehow persuaded the good-natured Pope of merits and rights which had no existence, while he had represented Heros as a disgrace to the episcopate. Besides this, the other accuser of Pelagius,

---

[1] According to Coustant's reckoning. Innocent died March 12th, according to the Martyrologies. Zosimus's letter to Gaul is dated March 22nd. The only intervening Sunday fell on the 18th.
[2] Zosimus, *Ep.* i, Migne, vol. xx, p. 462.
[3] St. Leo (*Ep.* x, 4) declares that no Bishop of Arles before Patroclus exercised the right. The successor of Zosimus reversed his decision.
[4] So St. Prosper, Chron. *P.L.* li. p. 578.
[5] *P.L.* li. p. 86.

Lazarus, Bishop of Aix, was also an enemy of Patroclus, as was proved a few months later. Heros and Lazarus being thus in disgrace at Rome, the moment was a happy one for those whose condemnation they had compassed.

It was just then that Celestius arrived in Rome. He had been ordained priest while at Ephesus, and from thence had sought Constantinople. From that city Atticus the bishop had expelled him, writing letters concerning him to the bishops of Ephesus, Thessalonica, and Carthage.[1]

He now presented himself to the judgment of the new Pope, on the ground that he had formerly appealed to him when condemned at Carthage seven years before, a fact which until now he had found it convenient to ignore. We have an account of his trial, written by St. Zosimus himself to the African bishops immediately after. He begins :

" Great matters demand a great weight of examination, that the balance of judgment be not less weighty than the matters dealt with. In addition there is the authority of the Apostolic See, to which the decrees of the Fathers have in honour of St. Peter sanctioned a particular reverence. We must pray, therefore, and pray incessantly, that by the continued grace and unceasing assistance of God, from this fountain the peace of the faith and of Catholic brotherhood may be sent into the whole world, *etc.* Celestius, priest, presented himself to us for examination, asking that he might be acquitted of the things of which he had been wrongfully accused to the Apostolic See. And although many occupations distracted our care and solicitude with greater bonds of ecclesiastical business, yet that the expectation of your fraternity as to his arrival and trial might not be delayed, we put them all aside, and on the day of examination we sat in the basilica of St. Clement . . . in order that the authority of so great a bishop might be an example for salutary discipline to the present investigation.

Therefore we discussed all that had been done heretofore, as you will learn from the acts appended to this letter. [These acts are lost.] Celestius being admitted, we caused the *libellus* which he had given in to be read ; and not content with this, we repeatedly inquired of him whether he spoke from his heart or with his lips only the things which he had written."

---

[1] M. Mercator. *Commonitorium,* c. 3. The Bishop of Ephesus had ordained Celestius, the Bishop of Carthage had condemned him ; Rufus of Thessalonica was Papal legate for Illyria and Achaia. Atticus may well have been shy of writing to Rome, where St. Chrysostom was not forgotten.

The Pope goes on to inveigh against Heros and Lazarus for not appearing at the Synod of Diospolis. They had rightly been deposed from their sees, and Celestius had scarcely seen Heros, and never Lazarus ; the latter, however, he had satisfied of his orthodoxy. The Africans had attended too easily, continues St. Zosimus, in the fervour of their faith, to the letters of these two bishops, and he proves from Scripture that even the wise may err through want of caution. For this very reason the Pope had come to no hasty or immature decision, but merely wrote an account of the trial. The former *libellus*, which Celestius had presented at Carthage in 410, ought to have been a testimony in his favour, against accusers of doubtful reputation. (This looks as if Celestius had deceived the Pope as to his condemnation on that occasion.) Within two months let these accusers come forward, otherwise Celestius will be formally acquitted. Further, Celestius and his friends had been recommended to avoid these dangerous questions for the future.[1]

The *libelli* and confession here referred to have not come down to us. With regard to the former *libellus* of 411, since Celestius had appealed to Rome, it probably concluded with a humble act of submission to the Pope. So certainly did the new *libellus*, of which we have the following account and quotation in St. Augustine :[2]

" In the *libellus* which he gave at Rome when he had explained his faith from the Trinity to the Resurrection (about all of which no one had asked him, and as to which no question had been raised), when he arrived at the crucial question he said : " If any questions have arisen beyond that which is of faith, about which there should be contention among many, I have not decided these matters with definite authority as the originator of any dogma, *but what I have received from the fountain of the Prophets and Apostles, we offer to be approved by the judgment of your Apostleship ; in order that if by chance any error of ignorance has crept in upon us being but men, it may be corrected by your decision.*" Here you see that in this introduction he takes care that, if any error should be found, he may seem to have erred not in faith, but in questions which are beyond the faith."

No wonder that Zosimus absolved from formal heresy the

[1] Zosimus, *Ep.* 2 (*in App. Aug.*, vol. x, p. 1719).
[2] *De pecc. orig.* xxiii. 26.

author of so complete a submission to Apostolic authority,
and so seemingly generous a submission of private judgment.
Doubtless the insinuation that the question was not one of
faith was not noticed at the time, and St. Augustine assures
us that he was repeatedly called upon to make the same submission by word of mouth.   For in one place of his *libellus*,[1]
he denied original sin most clearly so far as words go, though
he explained this away in the presence of the Pope.   Here is
St. Augustine's account :

"This opinion Pelagius was afraid or ashamed to bring out
to you ; but his disciple without any dissimulation was neither
afraid nor ashamed to publish it openly before the Apostolic
See.   But the very merciful prelate of that See, when he saw
him carried headlong with such presumption like a madman,
until he might come to himself, if that were possible, preferred
binding him bit by bit by question and answer to striking
him with a severe sentence, which would thrust him down
that precipice over which he seemed to be already hanging.
I do not say ' had fallen,' but ' seemed to be hanging ' ;
for earlier in the same *libellus* he had promised before speaking
of such questions : ' If by chance, being but men, some error
should creep in, let it be corrected by your decision.'
*So the venerable Pope Zosimus holding to this preparatory
statement, urged the man inflated with false doctrine, to condemn
what he was accused of by the deacon Paulinus, and to give his
assent to the letters of the Apostolic See which had emanated
from his predecessor of holy memory.*   He refused to condemn
what the deacon objected, but *he dared not resist the letters of
Bl. Pope Innocent, nay, he promised to " condemn whatever
that See should condemn."*   Thus gently treated, as if a madman, that he might be pacified, he was still not thought fit to
be released from the bonds of excommunication.   But a delay
of two months was decided, that an answer might be received
from Africa, and so an opportunity of coming to his senses

----

[1] *Aug.   De Pecc. Orig.* vi. 6.   *Celestius dicit : In remissionem autem
peccatorum baptizandos infantes, non idcirco diximus, ut peccatum ex
traduce firmare uideamur ; quod longe a catholico sensu alienum est.
Quia peccatum non cum homine nascitur, sed postmodum exercetur ab
homine : quia non naturae delictum, sed uoluntatis esse monstratur.
Et illud ergo congruum, ne diuersa Baptismatis genera facere uideamur, et
hoc praemunire necessarium est, ne per mysterii occasionem, ad Creatoris
injuriam malum antequam fiat ab homine, tradi dicatur homini per
naturam.*   Yet it is obvious that Celestius is speaking of actual sin,
and therefore might seem to be denying a doctrine which is not the
Catholic one.

was given him by a medicinal gentleness in his sentence. For, indeed, he would be cured, if he would lay aside his obstinate vanity, and attend to what he promised, and would read those letters [of St. Innocent], to which he professed to consent.[1]

St. Augustine, with the acts before him, is making here an excuse for the Pope, who had been accused by the Pelagians of approving Celestius' doctrine of original sin. What these heretics might have said would have been neither here nor there, had not modern Protestant writers (such as Dr. Pusey, Dr. Bright, and *Dict. of Eccl. Biography*, art. " Zosimus ") taken up the same strain. One cannot but feel pain every time that one finds estimable and well-meaning historians taking the side of ancient heretics against the Church. In this case Dr. Bright admits that this approval of Celestius' heresy was not *ex cathedra*, so that his argument is useless against Catholics. But he accuses St. Augustine of making an excuse for the Pope which he knew to be false (commonly called lying), entirely on the evidence of St. Zosimus' letter, which speaks quite vaguely. If he is right, St. Zosimus also must have lied, when in his third letter he denies that he had ever approved every word of the *libellus*. Mercator and Paulinus must be lying, for they are in exact agreement with St. Augustine.[2] " *Quidquid interea lenius actum est cum*

---

[1] *De pecc. orig.* vi-vii, 6-8, pp. 388-9.

[2] Paulinus' *libellus* is given further on. Here is Mercator's account : " The same Celestius, having been ejected from Constantinople, made his way with all possible speed to Rome, in the time of Bp. Zosimus of blessed memory. He was there questioned (according to the acts of which we possess copies), and being considerably terrified by such an examiner, he gave rise to hope by a great number of answers, promising that he condemned those chapters about which he had been accused at Carthage. For he was earnestly ordered and *expected to do so*, and *for this very reason* was judged worthy of much gentleness of treatment by the Holy Pontiff, which kindness he abused, or, rather, abuses still, to the deception of many." *Commonit. P.L.* vol. xlviii, p. 75, and in *App. S. Aug.* vol x, p. 1687.

The passage quoted by Dr. Bright in his note (p. 134) from Tillemont rightly implies that St. Augustine avoids mentioning the personal mistake of the Pope ; but Tillemont is always edifying, and would never accuse St. Augustine of *suggestio falsi*. Still Tillemont exaggerates, on the page referred to (xiii, 726) the approbation of Zosimus. The *libellus* was called perfectly Catholic, because its submission enabled the doubtful part to be interpreted favourably. Another passage should also be quoted : *Quale est autem quod beatae memoriae Zosimi apostolicae sedis episcopum, ut in tua prauitate persistas, praeuaricationis accusas ? Qui non recessit a suo praecessore Innocentio, quem tu nominare timuisti ; sed maluisti Zosimum, quia egit primitus lenius cum Caelestio :*

Caelestio, seruata dumtaxat antiquissimae et robustissimae fidei firmitate, *correctionis fuit clementissima suasio, non approbatio exitiosissimae prauitatis,*[4] says St. Augustine, and he absolutely denies that any approbation of the denial of original sin can be found either in the acts of the trial of Celestius or in the letters of the Pope to Africa.[5]   On Dr. Bright's theory this is definitely a falsehood ; but what a silly falsehood, if it could be refuted out of the very documents to which it appeals.   St. Augustine must have been not merely a liar (like St. Leo and Father Rivington), but a fool.

Since the Pelagians and Dr. Bright are interested accusers, we may acquit the saint on both counts. *Voluntas emendationis, non falsitas dogmatis approbata est ;* that is to say, his profession of submission (like that of St. Bernard in his famous letter on the Immaculate Conception), made the whole document Catholic ; and with this was joined his acceptance of Pope Innocent's letters, which had, incidentally and by implication,[6] condemned his error as to original sin.   But he was further urged to condemn the doctrines condemned at Carthage in 411.   This he refused to do at once, but gave hopes of submission.   In these counts of accusation was certainly included the denial of original sin, since St. Augustine quotes the acts of the council.[7]   There is, therefore, no doubt whatever that Dr. Bright is wrong, and Tillemont also, in saying that Zosimus approved the error ; while Mercator, St. Augustine, Paulinus, and later, Facundus of Hermiane,[8]

---

quoniam se in his sensibus vestris si quid displiceret, paratum esse dixerat corrigi, et Innocentii litteris consensurum esse promiserat.   C. Julian., VI, xii. 37, p. 842.

   [5] *C. duas Epp. Pel.* II, iii. 5, p. 575.

   [4] *l. c.* p. 575, *Nusquam prorsus hoc dixit, nusquam omnino conscripsit.* But it may be replied, St. Zosimus, in his third letter, is angry with the Africans for having misunderstood his first letter, as though he had approved every word of the *libellus.*   But he evidently means that they only implied this, not that they said so.   St. Augustine says that they urged in their letter that *homines tardiores et solicitiores* would think Celestius' submission insufficient, unless he openly anathematized the doctrine contained in his *libellus ;* for *multi parum intelligentes* would think it was the poison that was approved, and not the final clause of submission.   The Pope replies that he gave no formal approval at all. Notice, however, the judgment of the Africans on the modern Protestants : *homines tardiores—parum intelligentes !*

   [6] In the letters to both councils.   *Pariter hunc errorem damnaverat,* says St. Augustine, *C. duas Epp. Pel. l.c.,* and gives an extract.

   [6] *De pecc. orig.* i-iv, p. 385-7.

   [7] See the passage quoted *ap. Aug.* vol. x, append. p. 1723, ending, *non debet crimini deputari simplicium non intellecta versutia malignorum.*

are right.   The mistake of Pope Zosimus, and it was serious enough, was to believe Celestius to be sincere in his submission.

The above letter of the Pope was written some time in September 417,[1] and was soon followed by another written on the 21st of that month.[2]

"After the priest Celestius had been heard by us and had professed plainly his sentiments as to the faith, and had confirmed the statements of his *libellus* with repeated protestations, we wrote fully of him to your charity.   And now, behold, we have received a letter from Praylius, bishop of Jerusalem (who has been appointed in the room of the late B. John), who intervenes most earnestly in the cause of Pelagius.   The latter has also sent a letter of his own, containing his complete apology, and he has appended a profession of faith—what he holds and what he condemns—without any deceit, in order that all difficulties of interpretation may cease. These were publicly read ;   all their contents corresponded with what Celestius had produced previously,   and were in the same sense and tenor.   Would that any one of you, beloved brethren, could have been present at the reading of these letters !   What joy was there on the part of the holy men present !   How they wondered !   Scarcely could any refrain even from tears ! "

The Pope then accuses Lazarus of having on a former occasion been condemned by the Council of Turin for bearing false witness against St. Britius of Tours, and declares that both he and Heros were unlawful bishops set up by the usurper Constantine.   Into the truth of these statements we need not enter here.[3]   He goes on :

" See, Pelagius and Celestius present themselves before the Apostolic See by their letters and confessions.   But where is Heros ?   Where is Lazarus ?   Shameful names.   Where are those young men, Timasius and Jacobus, who produced writings, as it was said, of Pelagius ?   When these accused make such Catholic confessions before the Apostolic See, you yourselves judge whether the things reported of them by men of evil character and of no weight, and by vague rumour, should be believed.   Love peace, love charity, study concord.

[1] So the Ballerini have shown, *Opp. St. Leon.* vol. iii, p. 853 (1012).
[2] Aug. vol. x, p. 1721.
[3] See my article *Pope Zosimus and the C. of Turin, Dublin Rev.* Oct. 1904, and Duchesne in *Rev. Hist.* 1905, p. 278.

For it is written : ' Thou shalt love thy neighbour as thyself. Who are more neighbours one to another than we, who ought all to be one in Christ ? Not every wind that enters your ears is a messenger of the truth."

With Scripture texts St. Zosimus urges the danger of receiving false witness and the duty of caution. He enclosed the letter of Pelagius, addressed by him to Pope Innocent, of whose death he was not yet aware,[1] and his *libellus*. The letter is lost, save for some quotations in St. Augustine.

The *libellus* has been preserved, and is quite free from heresy so far as it goes.[2] But the Pope had not before him the detailed accusations of the heretical opinions of Pelagius, and was the more easily imposed upon by the rejection of every heresy except Pelagianism, which Pelagius, like Celestius, had set down.[3] He concludes, again like Celestius, with unreserved submission to the infallible decision of the Holy See.

"This is the faith, most blessed Pope, which we have learned in the Catholic Church, which we have ever held and hold. If we have by chance set down aught in it unskilfully or without due caution, we desire to be corrected by you, who hold both the faith and the See of Peter, *emendari cupimus a te qui Petri et fidem et sedem tenes*. If, however, this confession of ours is approved by the judgment of your apostleship, then, whosoever desires to blacken me, will prove not me to be a heretic, but himself unskilful, or else ill-willed, or even not a Catholic."

The African bishops may well have been disturbed at the receipt of these two letters. They could see at once that the submission of Celestius was insincere, and that Pelagius had carefully omitted in his *libellus* the condemnation of the particular heresies with which he was charged. It was on September 24th that St. Augustine preached at Carthage, saying, *causa finita est*. The former letter had not then arrived, and Paulinus received his summons to Rome as accuser only on November 2nd, from Basiliscus, the bearer of it. This is about the date that the second letter, written

---

[1] *De gratia Christi*, xxx, 32. *De pecc. orig.* xvii. 19.
[2] *In app. Opp. St. Aug.* vol x, p. 1716
[3] " In quo ea de quibus non interrogabatur multa disseruit," says St. Augustine, *De gr. Christi*. xxxii. 35.

September 21st, would have arrived ; so it may be presumed that both came by the same messenger.[1]

An answer appears to have been sent at once by Aurelius. probably with the help of some neighbouring bishops. St, Augustine may have been still in Carthage. The letter begged the Pope to lengthen the insufficient delay of two months, which had already nearly lapsed, in order that a full report might be sent.[2]

The council which met in December or January consisted of no less than 214 bishops, and is called by St. Augustine *Africanum concilium*,[3] as being representative of all Africa. But it apparently did not comprise a sufficient number of the regularly elected deputies from each province to deserve the title of *plenarium* or *universale*. It sent, by the subdeacon Marcellinus, a letter to the Pope, which contained or was accompanied by certain constitutions or decrees, of the length of which the Pope appears to complain. One of the decrees is twice quoted by St. Prosper :

"We establish that the sentence against Pelagius and

---

[1] The sequence of events is hard to follow with certainty. We know that Paulinus, being unable to go to Rome at once, wrote a *libellus* (shortly to be quoted) and entrusted it on November 8th to the sub-deacon Marcellinus. We know from the next letter of St. Zosimus (written March 18th or 21st) that Marcellinus was also the bearer of the letter from a council, and seemingly had only lately arrived, while another letter from the African bishops had come somewhat earlier. The messenger carrying this earlier letter must have started before November 8th, else Paulinus would have given him his *libellus* also. Basiliscus may have taken this letter back with him to Rome, and have started before the *libellus* of Paulinus was ready. But though the latter gave it to Marcellinus on November 8th, having seen Basiliscus on the 2nd, he must have known that Marcellinus would not be able to start at once, and that is doubtless the reason he mentions both dates in the *libellus* itself, to show that the delay was due to the messenger and not to himself. For if Marcellinus only arrived in Rome in March, he is not likely to have started earlier than the end of January. The council can hardly have come together by November (as Coustant, Quesnel, and the Benedictines supposed), but must have been held in December, or even in January. See Ballerini, *Obs. in Diss.* xiii. Quesnel. (*Opp. St. Leon*, vol. iii.)

[2] The fact of this letter is gathered from Zosimus' reply of March 18th or 21st, " Satisque illis scriptis quae ad illas rescripseratis novimus esse responsum. Sed *post missae* per Marcellinum subdiaconum uestrum epistolae " ; that is, " We considered that your reply was sufficiently answered by the letter to which it was the answer, but your new letter," etc. Further on, in the same letter (*St. Aug.* vol. x, app. p. 1726) he says that he had acceded to their *obtestatio* that the *status quo* might not be altered.

[3] *De pecc. orig.* vii, 8, viii. 9, xx. 24 ; *Ep.* 215, 2, etc.

Celestius published by the venerable Bishop Innocent *from the See of B. Peter*, remain firm, until they confess that by the grace of God," etc.[1]

This was nothing more than St. Zosimus himself had decided, since he had insisted on Celestius declaring his assent to the letters of St. Innocent, and even then had not released him from excommunication, so that he might also deny the doctrines Paulinus had accused him of, and meet any further objections the Africans might bring.

They further explained to the Pope that it was not sufficient for slow-minded men that Celestius should say in general that he consented to the letters of Pope Innocent, but that he ought openly to anathematize such false teaching as was contained in his own *libellus*, lest, if he did not, it should be supposed by the unlearned that the poison was approved by the Apostolic See, because the *libellus* was itself declared Catholic, rather than that it was atoned for by his consent to St. Innocent's letters.[2] They reminded Zosimus how his predecessor had judged that Pelagius had rather escaped condemnation at Diospolis by subterfuge than had been acquitted,[3] and they tried to show him the deceitful and evasive nature of the profession of faith which Pelagius had sent to Rome.[4] They also sent the acts of the council which had condemned Celestius in 411, and suggested to the Pope that perhaps it was rather he who had been hasty in acquittal than they in judgment. The loss of this important document is much to be regretted.

At the same time Paulinus sent the following *libellus :*

" I beseech justice of your blessedness, Lord Zosimus, venerable Pope. *The true faith is never disturbed, and above all in the Apostolic Church, in which teachers of false faith are as truly punished as they are easily discovered*, that they may die in the evils they have committed, unless they correct them, so that in them may be *that true faith which the Apostles taught, and which the Roman Church holds together with all the doctors of the Catholic faith.* And if like the other heresiarchs (who, long since judged by the Apostolic See or by the Fathers,

---

[1] *C. Coll.* v. 15, *P.L.* vol. li, p. 319 (227), or in App. vol. x, St. Aug. p. 1724 and 1808.
[2] *C. duas Epp. Pel* II, iii. 5.
[3] *De pecc. orig.* viii. 9.
[4] *Ibid.* xxi. 24.

and expelled from the bosom of the Catholic Church, are given over to eternal death) these also, who are or shall be discovered, remain in their perfidy, let them be delivered to the spiritual sword to be destroyed ; even as now Pelagius and Celestius, who were condemned by the predecessor of your blessedness, Pope Innocent, of blessed memory, if they cast off the true faith, and remain in their perverse doctrine."

Here is a disciple of Ambrose and friend of Augustine, a deacon of Milan and dweller in Africa, declaring with the decision of a Cyprian that " the true faith is never disturbed in the Apostolic Church," by which he means that of Rome, otherwise " especially," *maxime*, has no sense. He attributes to that Church the right and duty of cutting off heretics with the " spiritual sword," of which St. Prosper spoke, viz., excommunication. He continues :

" Following his sentence, your blessedness gave Celestius the following command, among others, when he was heard by the Apostolic See : ' Do you then condemn all those things which are contained in the *libellus of* Paulinus ? ' And in another place : ' Are you acquainted with the letters which the Apostolic See sent to our brothers and fellow-bishops of the African province ? ' And then : ' Do you condemn all that we have condemned, and hold all that we hold ? ' And, again, ' Do you condemn all the doctrines to which your name is given ? ' And, again, ' Or those things which Paulinus exposed in his *libellus* ? ' And when he said that I might be proved a heretic by my accusations of himself, you, filled with the Holy Spirit, by your Apostolic authority, rejected his wild and calumnious words, and gave a judgment by which at once I was declared Catholic, and he might be cured if he would. ' I will not have you lead us in a circle ; do you condemn all that was objected against you by Paulinus, or spread about by rumour ? ' To whom is this decision not sufficient ? Who would reject so healthy, so fit to be embraced, so pious a decision, except one who is astray from the faith ? And he who had above confessed that he would condemn whatever was objected against him, if you judged it to be contrary to the faith, hears the word ' condemn,' and not only does not condemn, but to the insult of so great a See (reading *injuriam tantae*, for *tantam*, *sedis*), he contests your judgment. Whence the Roman Church is no longer ignorant of the character of the accused, who has dared in so audacious a spirit to contradict, and not to condemn what your holiness decreed he should condemn."

Thus Paulinus proves that the Pope did urge Celestius to condemn his denial of original sin explicitly, as it stood in the former *libellus* of the deacon. Still more to our purpose is his comment on Celestius's refusal. It was an insult to the Apostolic See to doubt its judgment ; to contradict it by mere hesitation was to show himself a heretic ; *unde non ignorat jam Ecclesia Romana reum suum.*[1]

Paulinus goes on to thank God that the doctrines he had accused Celestius of holding should have been thus condemned by the Apostolic See, " by which this heresy was to be condemned, by the mouth of two Pontiffs." Pelagius also holds these doctrines, and both of them are refuted by the Council of Diospolis, by many doctors of east and west, south and north, Cyprian, Ambrose, Gregory, Innocent, and also by many yet alive,

" or, rather, since he ought to follow you, if he prefers learning the truth to teaching falsehood, he has, which is first of all, *quod primum est*, your blessedness, whose sentence he ought to have obeyed, when he heard you say ' condemn.' . . . Wherefore I pray your Apostleship to receive this *libellus* of mine, that I may be able to give thanks to your great See (*tantae sedi*), and to its most just decisions given in my favour. I write it because the subdeacon Basiliscus summoned me, though only by word of mouth, at Carthage, on behalf of your holiness, with acts of the Apostolic See addressed to me, on November 2, to be present before the Apostolic See and your holiness's judgment, to which it was implied that I had appealed. I should promise (reading *promitterem*) not to be wanting, if the sentence had been given against me, and not in my favour. On the former occasion (in 411) I could do nothing, for after he had appealed to the Apostolic See he was not forthcoming. . . ."

Paulinus continues, that by Zosimus' order to condemn, and Celestius's refusal, Celestius's insincerity is clear :

"Let that which could no longer be hid, but has been publicly brought to light, *be now cut off by your holiness with the spiritual sword*, that the flock of the Lord, which you govern as a good Shepherd with anxious solicitude, may no longer be torn by this wild beast's teeth."[2]

---

[1] Compare the final sentence of Pelagius' *libellus*, quoted above.
[2] *Libellus Paulini diaconi, in App.* vol x, St. Aug. p. 1724.

The " flock of the Lord " is here clearly the whole Church. Doubtless this document was seen by some of the Fathers of the African Council, with whose letter it was sent to Rome, and its doctrine as to the Papal prerogative cannot reasonably be supposed different to their belief.   The *libellus* is a clever one, justifying its author by the orders given by Zosimus himself.   Apparently Celestius had not absolutely refused to obey, but had delayed, and was expected to condemn these points at the next trial.[1]

Let us now sum up the situation arrived at.   At Rome the Pope feels certain that Pelagius and Celestius are orthodox ; but he will not declare them relieved of their excommunication without hearing from Africa, and until after a solemn trial. The two heretics had seemed to prove their innocence by the unhesitating and complete submission they had made in the usual form of a *libellus*,[2] directly they had been excommunicated by St. Innocent.   Pelagius was further recommended by the Bishop of Jerusalem and a council of Palestine, and by the supposed bad character of Heros and Lazarus, his accusers, Celestius, by his acceptance of the letters which had condemned him, and his promise to condemn all the doctrines he had been accused of holding.   What more could the Pope ask for ?

In his fatherly joy he writes the two gushing letters above quoted to Africa, and waits for a reply tuned in a similar key. Instead of this he receives a damping answer, warning and incredulous, asking for longer delay.   He waits six months, and then come the letters and lengthy decrees of the council, and Paulinus' *libellus*.   St. Zosimus is disappointed.   He is angry with the Africans for suggesting that his language might seem to some to approve every word of Celestius' *libellus*, and he understands them to mean that they think he really did so. He thinks their letters do not show sufficient recognition of the great condescension he had shown in consulting them on this matter.   He resumes, therefore, in his reply the stately official style of the Roman court, and evidently feels ashamed of his former outburst of feeling, which had met with so little response in Africa.   Yet contemporary evidence assures us that it was the explanation sent by the council which changed his mind ; and, in fact, reading between the lines, it is clear

[1] So Mercator, *id uehementius expectabatur.   Commonit. cap.* 1.
[2] Other instances are those of Rufinus, earlier, and Bachiarius, later, both extant.

that the change has already come.   He seems half to excuse
himself for his kindness to Celestius, and is evidently on the
point of taking up the matter afresh, now that there is nothing
more to wait for.   The text of the letter is very corrupt :

"Although *the tradition of the Fathers has attributed to the
Apostolic See so great authority that none would dare to contest
its judgment, and has preserved this ever in its canons and rules,
and current ecclesiastical discipline in its laws still pays the
reverence which it ought to the name of Peter,* from which it has
itself its origin, for canonical antiquity (*canonica antiquitas*)
willed that this apostle should have such power by the decisions of all (*per,* or *super sententias omnium*) ;   and by the
promise of Christ our God, that he should loose the bound
and bind the loosed, and *an equal condition of power has been
given to those who with his consent have received the heritage
of his See.*   For he himself has care over all the Churches,
and above all of that in which he sat, nor does he suffer anything of its privileges or decisions to be shaken in any wind,
since he established it on the foundation, firm and immovable,
of his own name, which no one shall rashly attack but at his
peril.   Since, then, Peter is the head of so great authority,
and has confirmed the suffrages of our forefathers since his
time, so that the Roman Church is confirmed by all laws and
disciplines, divine or human ;   whose place we rule, and the
power of whose name we inherit, *as you are not ignorant, my
brethren, but you know it well, and as bishops you are bound to
know it ;* yet, though such was our authority that none could
reconsider our decision, yet we have done nothing which we
did not of our own accord refer to your cognizance by letter,
giving this much to our brotherhood, in order that by taking
counsel in common, not because we did not know what ought
to be done, or because we might do something which might
displease you as being contrary to the good of the Church, but
we desired to treat together with you of a man who was accused
before you (as you yourself wrote), and who came to our See
asserting that he was innocent, not refusing judgment on his
original appeal ;   of his own accord calling for his accusers, and
condemning the things of which he said he was falsely accused
by rumour.

We thought, and indeed we know, that the entire petition
was explained in our former letter ;   and we believe that we
had sufficiently replied to the letters you wrote in answer.
But we have unfolded the whole roll of your letter which was
sent later by the deacon Marcellinus.   You have understood
the entire text of our letter as if we had believed Celestius in

everything and had given our assent, so to speak, to every syllable without discussing the words. Matters which need a long treatment are never rashly postponed, nor without great deliberation must aught be decided on which a final judgment has to be given. Wherefore let your brotherhood know that we have changed nothing either since we wrote to you or you wrote to us ;[1] but that we have left all in the same state in which it was when we informed your holiness of the matter in our letter ; in order that your earnest request might be acceded to. Farewell."

It was not long before St. Zosimus wrote a very different letter, the famous *tractoria* or *tractatoria*, which finally condemned the heretics. Let Marius Mercator tell the story :

"When the bishops of Africa wrote an answer exposing the whole cause which had been threshed out there, sending the acts of their councils which had been held about him whether present or absent, he was then called for a fuller hearing, that he might hasten to fulfil his promise of condemning the aforesaid chapters [of Paulinus], and so be absolved from the excommunication he had undergone from the African bishops.[2] But not only did he not appear, but he fled from Rome, and *for this was condemned by the said Bishop Zosimus, of blessed memory, in a very long and complete document*, in which the chapters of which he was accused are contained, and the whole case of Celestius himself and his yet more depraved master Pelagius is plainly related. Of these writings we note that *similar copies were sent to bishops, to the Churches of the East, to the province of Egypt, to Constantinople and Thessalonica and Jerusalem.*"

After quoting passages of Pelagius' writings, Mercator continues :

"All these chapters are contained in that letter of Bishop Zosimus, of blessed memory, which is called *tractoria*, by which Celestius and Pelagius were condemned."[3]

Here is St. Augustine's account with regard to Celestius :

[1] I read with the Ballerini, l. c., iv, p. 585 (1015) : *Nihil nos post illa quae uobis scripsimus uel litteras uestras quas accepimus.*

[2] In 411. This had never been removed, though Celestius had ignored it for more than five years, till it was confirmed by St. Innocent.

[3] *Commonitorium,* c. 1, P.L., vol. xlviii, p. 78, and in App. St. Aug. vol. x, p. 1687.

"When afterwards the awaited letters from Africa arrived in Rome . . . then when his presence was demanded, that by certain and clear answers it might be brought to light whether it was deceitful or orthodox, he absconded and refused the examination. *Nor was that decision to be delayed any longer which might avail for the good of others,* if not of their own obstinacy and madness."[1]

And of Pelagius he writes :

"He. deceived the judgment of the Palestinians ; therefore he was acquitted there. But the Church of Rome, where you know that he is well known, he could by no means deceive, although he tried his best ; but, as I said, he could not succeed. For the Bl. Pope Zosimus called to mind what his predecessor, worthy of imitation, had thought of his acts. He attended likewise to the opinion felt by that Roman faith which is worthy of being proclaimed in the Lord (*praedicanda in Domino Romanorum fides*) ; he saw their common zeal inflamed in concord against his error on behalf of Catholic truth. Pelagius had long lived amongst them, and his doctrines could not be unknown ; and they well enough knew Celestius to be his disciple, so as to be able to give a most faithful and firm testimony to the fact." [2]

Further on he speaks again of the manner in which Pelagius tried to deceive the " episcopal judgment of the Apostolic See " (*ibid.* xvii. 19) :

" He seemed for a time to say what was in accord with the Catholic faith [viz. in his letter and *libellus*], but he was *unable to deceive that See to the end.* For after the rescripts of the African Council, into which province his pestilent doctrines had crept, but which it had not so widely pervaded, other writings of his were made public by the care of faithful brethren in the city of Rome, where he had lived a very long time, and had first been occupied with these conversations and disputes. *These were attached by Pope Zosimus, to be anathematized, to his letters which he wrote to be carried throughout the Catholic world*" (*ibid.* xxi. 24).

The *tractoria* of Zosimus is lost, and we do not know its date. The trial of Celestius would naturally be as soon as

---

[1] *C. duas Epp. Pel* II, iii. 5, p. 574.
[2] *De pecc. orig.* viii. 9, p. 389.

might be after March 18th or 21st, when the Pope wrote to Africa. This is implied by the passages from Mercator and St. Augustine just quoted. In fact the Pope had been waiting for nothing but the reply of the council, and he had already waited six months instead of two. At all events it took place before April 30th, for on that date a rescript of the Emperor Honorius expelled Celestius and Pelagius and their partisans from Rome ; any summons to attend and any condemnation for non-appearance must have been previous to this, unless they were a mere farce ; while Celestius could just as well be expelled after he had fled as could Pelagius, who had not been there for years.

The brothers Ballerini think that the summons took place within a week after the Pope's letter, for Easter fell on April 7, and Palm Sunday, March 31st, would have been the proper day for absolving Celestius, in order that he might communicate at Easter. In itself this seems most likely. Only one wonders why the Pope should have written to Africa without waiting for the result of the trial a few days later. Perhaps, because he foresaw that the Africans would turn out to be in the right, he preferred to send them at once a rebuke and an excuse, before he was obliged to acknowledge his own mistake.[1]

---

[1] It has been frequently upheld that the decree of April 30th expelling the pilgrims from Italy was obtained from the Emperor by the Africans, and that it was prior to the condemnation by Zosimus. This is most unlikely. That the Emperor would accede to the request of bishops for the extrusion of heretics in their own province is most natural ; that he should expel them from Italy and Rome without asking the local bishops is inconceivable, and above all when the Pope was known to be inclined to take off their excommunication. There are only two arguments brought in its favour, since the imaginary legation of Vindemialis was exploded by the Ballerini. *First*, the MSS. of a *codex canonum* (*Opp. St. Leon.* vol. iii, p. 170 (490)) head the Emperor's rescript : *Incipit sacrum rescriptum, acceptis synodi suprascriptae gestis.* But the preceding synod is that of May 1st, so that the heading is a mistake. It cannot well refer to the acts of the preceding synod, as they are not in the *codex* at all. *Secondly*, the similar rescript of the following year addressed to Aurelius of Carthage, mentions the former rescript thus : *In quo secuta est clementia nostra judicium sanctitatis tuae.* Now this second rescript was sent to all primates, and another copy to St. Augustine as a special compliment. We have only the copy addressed to the primate of Carthage ; and the words quoted are clearly just as applicable if the rescript was a consequence of the Pope's decision, which, as we have seen, followed the opinion of the Africans, while to the *tractoria* were appended the acts of their council to be signed, together with the Papal letter.

We have shown above that the **condemnation of** Celestius and

As a fact, nothing could be more generous than the way in which he repaired the error his kind heart had prompted, for to his *tractoria* he appended the constitutions of the African council, to be signed with it by all the bishops of the world. This subscription was made doubly obligatory by a second decree of the Emperor Honorius in the following year; it already obliged as a Papal demand. No one will suppose that Pope Zosimus considered that the signatures of the bishops would give to his decision an œcumenical force which it would otherwise have lacked. It was to be a notification of a decree, and the subscription to it would be a submission, as well as an episcopal judgment increasing the moral weight of the document. The Gallican view is no more countenanced by other contemporaries than by St. Augustine. All hail the decision as final,[2] and none lays any stress on the consent of Christendom as giving it validity.

On the contrary, St. Prosper says the Pope had " armed all the bishops with the sword of Peter," " *Africanorum conciliorum decretis beatae recordationis Papa Zosimus sententiae suae robur annexuit, et ad impiorum detruncationem gladio Petri dexteras omnium armauit antistitum.*" [2] Again, he says that the approbation of the African council was a condemnation of Pelagianism throughout the world : " *Concilio apud Carthaginem habito ccxiv episcoporum, ad Papam Zosimum synodi decreta perlata sunt, quibus probatis, per totum mundum haeresis Pelagiana damnata est.*" [3] He thus introduces a quotation from the *tractoria :* " *Sacrosancta beati Petri sedes ad uniuersum orbem sic loquitur.*"[4] "The sacred see of Peter thus addresses the whole world."

Pelagius must have been before the issue of the rescript ; and this fact alone shows that it was the cause of it. That the *tractoria* itself was published by the middle of April is highly probable. St. Augustine seems to place it before the Council of May 1st (*Ep.* 215, vol. ii, p. 972), *item quod Papae Zosimo de Africano concilio scriptum est, ejusque rescriptum ad uniuersos totius orbis episcopos missum, et quod* posteriori *concilio plenario totius Africae contra ipsum errorem breuiter constituimus* and in *De pecc. orig.* xvii, 18, p. 394, and in Possidius, *Vita Aug.* 18, it is clearly placed before the rescript of April 30th, (see below).

　[1] e.g., St. Aug. Retract. ii. 50, vol. i, p. 650, *Pelagiana haeresis cum suis auctoribus ab episcopis ecclesiae Romanae, prius Innocentio, deinde Zosimo,* coöperantibus *conciliorum Africanorum litteris damnata est.*

　[2] C. Collat. xxi. (xli), 57, p. 362 (271), or in App. vol. x. St. Aug. p. 1831.

　[3] *Chronicon., ad an.* 418, p. 740 (591) ; St. Aug. *ibid.* p. 1724.

　[4] C. Coll. xv. and *cf. Carmen de Ingratis,* i.

　　　Tu causam fidei flagrantius Africa, nostrae
　　　Exsequeris ; tecumque suum jungente uigorem

Marius Mercator writes :

"(The *tractoria*) was sent to Constantinople and throughout the world, and was strengthened (*roborata*) by the subscriptions of the Holy Fathers. Julian and his accomplices refusing to sign it, and to consent (*consentaneos se facere*) to those Fathers, were deposed not only by imperial laws, but also by ecclesiastical decrees, and banished from all Italy. *Many of them came to their senses, and being corrected of their errors, returned as suppliants to the Apostolic See, and being accepted, received back their sees.*"[5]

The last portion of the passage is sufficient indication that " roborata " in the first portion does not mean a strengthening of the weak, but a reinforcement to the strong.

St. Possidius, who was one of the five bishops who sent to St. Innocent a common letter, writes in his life of St. Augustine :

"And since these heretics were trying to bring the Apostolic See round to their view, African councils of holy bishops also did their best to persuade the holy Pope of the City (first the venerable Innocent, and afterwards his successor, St. Zosimus), that this heresy was to be abhorred and condemned by Catholic faith. *And these bishops of so great a See [tantae sedis] successively branded, them, and cut them off from the members of the Church, giving letters to the African Churches in the West, and to the Churches of the East, and declared that they were to be anathematized and avoided by all Catholics (eos anathemandos et deuitandos ab omnibus Catholicis censuerunt). The judgment pronounced upon them by the Catholic Church of God was heard* and FOLLOWED also by the most pious Emperor Honorius, who condemned them by his laws, and ordered them to be treated as heretics. Wherefore many of them have returned to the

---

Juris apostolici solio, *fera uiscera belli*
Conficis, et lato prosternis limite uictos.
Conuenere tui de cunctis urbibus almi
Pontifices, geminoque senum celeberrima coetu
Decernis quod Roma probet, quod regna sequantur.
Note the careful distinction in the same writer's words, *Ep. de Gr. et Lib.* art. iii (App. l. c., p. 1794), *et orientalium episcoporum judicia, et apostolicae sedis auctoritas, et Africanorum conciliorum uigilantia.* . . .
 [5] *Commonitorium*, vi. 10 and *ib.* P.L. 48, p. 107, and in App. Aug. vol. x, p. 1689. Further on, an equivalent for " returned as suppliants" is *sedi apostolicae se submittentes.* In *Lib. Subn. Jul.* p. 1738, he says : *Conuentus detrectasti cum uniuersa ecclesia per totum orbem Pelagium Coelestiumque damnare.*

bosom of holy Mother Church, whence they had wandered, and are yet returning, as the truth of the right faith becomes known and prevails against that detestable error."[1]

Clearly St. Possidius considers that the Popes had the right which they claimed, of deciding the faith for all Catholics.

In the last month of this year, 418, St. Zosimus died, after a lingering illness. He is numbered among the saints, and the generosity of his character shines through the unfortunate mistakes which fill his short pontificate, and which history is not allowed to pass over. His contemporaries, with the exception of those heretics to whom he was too kind, have nothing but praise for his memory.

Meanwhile in Africa another great council, this time a plenary one, was being held. It was opened on the first of May, the third letter of St. Zosimus, rebuking the Africans, arriving two days earlier. If it be true that Celestius had been condemned before Palm Sunday, the news of this may have already arrived. At all events, we know that the first canons the council drew up were nine canons against the Pelagians, which St. Augustine describes as a *résumé* of the constitutions of the preceding council. Ten more canons concerning discipline were drawn up, and finally a resolution was passed that from each province three delegates should be chosen to continue the council, that the remainder of the bishops might be free to return. It is hardly probable that the *tractoria* had yet arrived, so that the letter in answer was doubtless sent to the Pope by those fifteen deputies,[2] who included the Primates of Africa and Numidia, Aurelius and Donatian, with Augustine and Alypius. A fragment of the letter is preserved by St. Prosper :

The African bishops writing in answer to the same Pope Zosimus, and praising him for the salubrity of this sentence, say : "As you have placed in your letters which you have

[1] Possidius. *Vita Aug.* xviii (vol. i, p. 48). *Cf.* St. Augustine (" De pecc orig." xxi. 24, quoted above. *Quae litteris suis, quas conscripsit per orbem catholicum perferendas, Papa Zosimus exsecranda, sicut legere potestis, attexuit.*

[2] The words of Aurelius, writing to the bishops of Africa, on August 1st, 419, " Sive quorum in synodalibus gestis subscriptio jam tenetur, sive qui non potuistis eidem plenario totius Africae interesse concilio," prove that this same council replied, as it is inconceivable that a second *plenary* council should have been held before September.

caused to be sent to all, saying: 'By the assistance (*instinctu*) of God (for all good things are to be referred to their Author from whom they have their being), we have brought all these things to the knowledge of our brothers and fellow-bishops.' This we understand thus ; that you cut off, as it were in passing, with the drawn sword of truth, those who extol the liberty of human free-will against the assistance of God. For what more free than your bringing all these matters to the know-ledge of our lowliness ? Yet you have faithfully and wisely seen that it was by the assistance of God, and you have truly and confidently said so," etc.

While still at Carthage, St. Augustine addressed to Albina, Pinianus and Melania the two books " De gratia Christi " and " De peccato originali," from which we have had occasion to quote. He explains in the former the fallacies in Pelagius's theory of grace, and in the latter he relates the recent con-demnation of the two heretics, and explains the dogma of original sin. Especially noticeable is the way in which St. Augustine defends the Holy See from the charge of having approved error before condemning it. Celestius " could not deceive *that See* " ; Pelagius " could not deceive *that See* to the end." St. Augustine takes pains to refute Pelagius out of the mouth of St. Ambrose, because Pelagius had given him the highest praise in his book on free-will. The words are : " Beatus, inquit, Ambrosius, in cujus praecipue libris *Romana elucet fides*, qui scriptorum inter Latinos flos quidam speciosus enituit, cujus fidem et purissimum in Scripturis sensum, ne inimicus quidem ausus est reprehendere." [1] St. Augustine continues : *Ecce qualibus et quantis praedicat laudibus*, and in the next book : *Quem tanto praeconio laudauit.* [2] He quotes the whole passage again on two separate occasions, [3] and refers to it at least ten times. [4] The inference is that St. Augustine agreed with Pelagius that *Romana fides* and *integerrima fides* are synonyms.

The council over, St. Augustine went by order of Pope

[1] *De. gr. Chr.* xliii. 47, p. 381.
[2] *De pecc. orig.* xli. 47-8, p. 409-10.
[3] *De nupt. et conc.* I, xxxv. 40, p. 436, and c. Jul. I, vii. 30, p. 661.
[4] *De nupt. etc.* II. xxix. 51, p. 466 ; *C. duas Epp. Pel.* IV, xi. 29 ; c. Jul. I, vii. 35, p. 666, and 44, p. 671. *Ibid.* II, v. 11, p. 681, etc. St. Jerome's pride in Roman faith is continual, see pp. 116 foll. For Africa, *cf.* St. Cyprian (Ed. Hartel), *Ep.* 30, p. 550, *Ep.* 60, p. 692, *Ep.* 59, p. 683.

Zosimus to Caesarea in Mauretania, on an unknown errand.[1] He also had there a conference with the Donatist Bishop Emeritus, and was greatly occupied. He felt obliged, however, to answer the letter of a Bishop Optatus, who consulted him whether " creationism " could be held by a Catholic. He tells him how Pelagius and Celestius, " by the vigilance of Episcopal councils, by the help of the Saviour who guards His Church, *have been condemned in the whole Christian world by two venerable bishops of the Apostolic See*, Pope Innocent and Pope Zosimus, unless they amend and do penance." [2] He quotes a passage from the *tractoria*, and comments : " *In these words of the Apostolic See, so ancient and founded, so certain and clear is the Catholic faith, that it would be a sin for a Christian to doubt it.*" [3] We cannot pass over the expression " words of the Apostolic See " ; they mean " the authoritative words of the successor of Peter," not merely the doctrine of an eminent bishop.

Returning to Hippo, St. Augustine found awaiting him a letter from Marius Mercator, together with a book by him against Pelagianism. He replies warmly, praising his dear son's zeal for their conversion.[4] Doubtless it is to this encouragement that we owe the writings of Marius, so often quoted above.

The innocence of Pelagius had been defended at Rome by the priest Sixtus, afterwards Pope St. Sixtus III, who was to confirm the Council of Ephesus. He had now publicly renounced their championship, and St. Augustine wrote him a letter of congratulation (*Ep.* 191). Sixtus replied, and St. Augustine wrote a long answer, in which he says :

"We must acknowledge to your charity that we were very sad when rumour was that you favoured the enemies of the grace of Christ. But that this sadness might be wiped away from our hearts, a like rumour declared, first, that you had been the first to pronounce anathema against them in a crowded concourse of people. Next, when the *letters of the Apostolic*

[1] Ep. 190, 1 : *Quo nos* injuncta *nobis a uen. P. Zosimo, apostolicae sedis episcopo ecclesiastica necessitas traxerat, cf.* Ep. 193, 1, and Retract. ii. 51. Possidius, *Vita Aug.* 14 : *Quo eum uenire cum aliis ejus coëpiscopis sedis Apostolicae litterae compulerant.*
[2] *Ep.* 190, 22.
[3] *Ibid.* 23. *In his verbis Apostolicae sedis tam antiqua et fundata certa et clara est catholica fides, ut nefas sit de illa dubitare Christiano.* Vol. ii, p. 866.
[4] *Ep.* 193.

See about their condemnation were sent into Africa, your letter to the venerable Aurelius followed also ; and, though short, it indicated sufficiently your vigour against their error. But now, when you write more clearly and fully your opinion of that dogma, it is *the very faith of the Roman Church* itself which speaks—that Church to which the Apostle Paul spoke at such length of the grace of God through Jesus Christ our Lord.''

About the beginning or middle of the year 419, two letters of Pelagian authorship (the one ascribed to Julian, Bishop of Eclanum, and addressed to the new Pope Boniface, the other, by eighteen other dispossessed bishops) were much read.   The vigilance of the Roman faithful brought these to the Pope's notice, and he sent them to St. Augustine by St. Alypius of Tagaste, the famous companion of that saint's conversion, who had been on a voyage to the court at Ravenna, and had stayed a short time at Rome.   St. Augustine at once wrote the four books *Contra duas Epistolas Pelagianorum,* and dedicated them to the Pope in the following words : [1]

"I knew, by the voice of fame, and frequent and trustworthy messengers had brought me word, blessed and venerable Pope Boniface, how full you are of the grace of God.   But after that my brother Alypius had seen you in bodily presence, and (being received so kindly and heartily and having conversations with you full of mutual affection, and dwelling with you, though for so short a time, yet joined to you by great love) since he has poured himself and me also into your heart, and has brought you back to me in his own, my knowledge of your holiness has become as much more intimate, as our friendship has become more sure.   And you do not disdain, you who are not uplifted in mind, though sitting on a prouder seat (*qui non alta sapis, quamuis aliius praesideas*), to be the friend of the lowly, and to return the friendship which is bestowed upon you.   For what but this is friendship, whose name is derived from love (*amicitia,* from *amor*), and which is never fruitful save in Christ, in Whom alone it can also be eternal and happy ?
Therefore, taking greater confidence through my brother, by whom I have learned to know you more familiarly, I have dared to write something to your beatitude of the matters which now excite anew all our episcopal care to vigilance on

[1] l. c. I. i, vol. x, p. 550.

behalf of the Lord's flock. . . . Since the heretics do not cease
to rage against the fold of the Lord's flock, and search all
around for entrance, that they may tear to pieces the sheep
bought at so great a price, and since the pastoral watchtower
is common to all of us who fill the *episcopal office (in which you,
however, are lifted on a loftier pinnacle)*, I do what I am able,
in the little portion of that duty which falls to my lot, in so far
as the Lord gives me power, with the help of your prayers,
to provide antidotes and remedies for their poisonous and
insidious writings. . . . This answer which I am sending to
their two epistles, one of which is said to have been sent by
Julian to Rome, in order, I suppose, to discover or to make
partisans ; the other, which eighteen other self-styled bishops,
who share his errors, dared to write to Thessalonica, to try
and gain by their wiles no less a person than the bishop of that
city ;[1] this answer, then, I have decided to send to your
holiness, not that you may learn from it, *but that you may
examine it, and, wheresoever anything may chance to displease
you, correct it*. For my brother Alypius mentioned to me
that you deigned yourself to give him the letters which could
not have come into your hands but by the great watchfulness
of our brethren your sons. I thank you for your cordial
kindness, in that you did not wish these letters of the enemies
of the grace of God to remain unknown to me, when you found
my name openly calumniated therein."

This long passage, which needs no comment, may close our
series of extracts from St. Augustine, though his labours
against this heresy were to continue for ten years longer, till
the time of his last illness.

The remaining history of the struggles of Pelagianism with
the Holy See calls only for brief summary.

Julian of Eclanum, who had refused to sign the *tractoria*,
sent in a *libellus* to the Pope in the usual form. After a confession of faith, he concludes with submission :

" We have written and sent this to your Holiness, as it appears
to us according to the Catholic rule. *If you think we ought to
hold otherwise, write us a reply*. But if it is impossible to
contradict us, and yet some wish to stir up scandal against us,
we declare to your Holiness that we appeal to a plenary
council."

Thus he does not think of appealing to a general council

---

[1] Metropolitan, and Papal Legate.

from the Pope's decision, but only to enforce the Pope's hypothetical approval of his doctrine. St. Augustine puts down the demand to a desire for notoriety.[1] Julian goes on to explain that his reason for not signing the Pope's letter is his unwillingness to condemn the innocent unheard, who had purged themselves by *libelli*, and declared themselves Catholics. Never will he renounce this zeal for justice ! [2]

The remainder of the lives of Pelagius, Celestius and Julian is obscure and unimportant. Henceforward interest settles on the history of the semi-Pelagians, and this does not enter into our present plan. Celestius was again banished from Rome, by another edict,[3] under St. Boniface. St. Celestine also banished the Pelagians, and confirmed the decrees of his predecessors. He sent St. Germanus to Britain as his legate (*vice sua mittit* [4]), who had been chosen, with Lupus of Troyes, for this mission by a council in Gaul. Thus our island was liberated from the heresy to which it had given birth, and by its acceptance of a Papal delegate its Catholicity is testified. Under the same Pope Celestine, Pelagianism was condemned by the œcumenical Council of Ephesus, which declared in its letter to the Pope that it had confirmed all his decisions on the subject.[5] Besides this, St. Prosper was made his legate in Gaul against the semi-Pelagians,[6] and he wrote a famous letter to the bishops of that country, approving the writings of St. Augustine, which St. Prosper treats as a final judgment which must for ever stop the mouths of those who had been fighting against them : *maleloquentiae est adempta libertas.*[7] Writing his book *contra Collatorem* against Cassian, in the time of Sixtus III., the next Pope, St. Prosper, states his confidence " that what God has worked in Innocent, Zosimus,

[1] *C. duas Epp.*, Pel IV, xii. 33, p. 638.
[2] St. Aug. vol. x, App. p. 1732-6.
[3] St. Prosper, *in Chron.* an. 429.
[4] *Ibid.* p. 1755.
[5] St. Prosper (c. Coll. xxi. 58, l. c. p. 1831) sums up St. Celestine's action : *Adeo et praecessorum suorum statuta et decreta synodalia inuiolabiliter seruanda censebat, ut quod semel meruerat abscidi, nequaquam admitteret retractari. Nec uero segniore cura ab hoc eodem morbo Britannias liberauit . . . et ordinato Scotis episcopo [Palladio], dum Romanam insulam studet seruare Catholicam, fecit etiam barbaram Christianam. Per hunc virum etiam Orientales ecclesiae gemina peste purgatae sunt, quando Cyrillo. . . . Apostolico auxiliatus est gladio*, etc.
[6] Prosper, *Resp. ad cap. Vinc.* I (*Ibid.* p. 1843), and Celestine, *Ep.* xxi. *ad Gallos*, P.L. 50, p. 528.
[7] The continuation of the passage just quoted. The whole should be read.

Boniface, Celestine, he will work also in Sixtus, and that in the guardianship of the Lord's flock there is reserved to this shepherd the special glory of expelling hidden wolves, as they did the open ones."

To the letter of St. Celestine to Gaul is appended in all MSS. and editions a short collection of quotations from recent decisions of the Apostolic See. It seems most likely that this appendix was composed by St. Prosper.[1] It testifies not only to the belief of its author in the infallibility of the Roman See, but to the profession of that same belief in Gaul also, and declares that any who disobeys is a heretic. The work is a defence of St. Augustine's doctrine, by appealing to higher authority ; and no one can suppose that the author did not believe that saint, but lately dead, to have held the same view as himself of the authority of the Holy See in matters of faith, a view in which he supposes all Catholics to agree. The introduction commences thus :

"Since many who boast the Catholic name remain in the condemned opinions of heretics, whether by wickedness or by want of wisdom, and presume to dispute with pious champions of the faith ; and since, while they do not hesitate to anathematize Pelagius and Celestius, they yet reproach our doctors with exceeding the right measure, *and because they profess to follow and approve only what the most sacred See of the blessed Apostle Peter has sanctioned and taught against the enemies of the grace of God by the ministry of its prelates,*[2] it has become needful to inquire diligently what the rulers of the Roman Church have judged concerning the heresy which arose in their time, and what they decided to be held as to the grace of God against the dangerous defenders of free will. At the same time we shall add some decisions of African councils, *which the Apostolic prelates in fact made their own when they approved them.* Therefore, in order that those who doubt as to any point may be instructed, we make the constitutions of the holy fathers plain in a compendious table, so that any who is not over-contentious may recognize

---

[1] So Coustant. The vigorous and epigrammatic style of the few words of introduction is in favour of this view, but perhaps suggests still more that St. Leo, then a Roman deacon, was the author. Anyhow the document was drawn up at Rome. One expression has become famous : *Ut legem credendi lex statuat supplicandi. Ep.* xxi, *Celestini, l. c.*, and St. Aug. x, *App. p.* 1757.

[2] *cf. Videsne quid sapiat per ministrum suum Catholica fides ?* quoted before from St. Augustine, *Op. Imperf.* vi. xi, p. 1520.

that the whole dispute is summed up in the short quotations subjoined, and that *no reason for contradiction remains to him, if he believes and professes as Catholics do.*"

The author gives four short extracts from the letters of St. Innocent to the councils of Carthage and Milevis, and next two from the letter of St. Zosimus " to the bishops of the whole world." He adds to one of these the commentary given by the reply of the African council (which we have quoted above from St. Prosper, *contra Collatorem*). He next gives a quotation from the Carthaginian council of 214 bishops, saying of it : " Quasi proprium Apostolicae Sedis amplecti-mur." After these " inviolable sanctions of the most blessed Apostolic See," *beatissimae et Apostolicae Sedis inviolabiles sanctiones*, he refers to the customary intercession at Mass, and to the law of infant baptism as testifying to the same effect, and concludes, that he leaves aside more subtle ques-tions, for " satis sufficere credimus quicquid secundum praedictas regulas apostolicae sedis nos scripta docuerunt ; ut prorsus non opinemur catholicum, quod apparuerit prae-fixis sententiis esse contrarium " ; " We believe to be amply sufficient whatsoever the writings of the Apostolic See have taught us, according to the aforesaid rules ; so that we absolutely regard as not Catholic anything which is seen to be contrary to the decisions we have just quoted."

With this estimate of the authority of St. Innocent and St. Boniface we may conclude. Those who care to read the documents (given in the appendix to St. Augustine, vol. x.) concerning the semi-Pelagians, will find once more the whole question referred to the successor of Peter by an African bishop, Possessor ; while the famous second council of Orange, the decrees of which are usually accepted by High Church Anglicans, was confirmed by Pope Boniface II. at the request of its president St. Caesarius of Arles, and thus the last ghost of Pelagianism was laid, until modern rationalism should again deny the necessity of the grace of God.

APIARIUS

In the preceding paper it has been related in detail how the supreme authority of Rome in matters of faith was appealed to and proclaimed by St. Augustine and the African Church during the fight against Pelagianism. We could gather from the history of that time that a teacher of heresy could be tried in any diocese or province, but that an appeal always lay to Rome. With Rome rested the final decision and definition of the Faith, to be subscribed by the Bishops of the whole world, and to be enforced by the edicts of the Emperors.

It would not follow as a logical sequence that the same holy Bishops who so confidently appealed to the Faith of Peter, and upheld the finality of Papal judgment upon a question of dogma, would equally recognize and obey the jurisdiction of the Pope in their own provinces when discipline alone was concerned. The two powers are indeed closely connected, but yet in practice a broad line might be drawn between them. Infallibility does not apply to ecclesiastical laws and procedures, which are liable to alteration. They may often result in injustice in their application to particular cases. Besides, an ecclesiastical court may be corrupt or venal. Holy men have felt it their duty to resist or remonstrate with Rome ; though in important matters history has usually recorded its verdict in favour of the central authority. To accept a definition of faith is easy, if one is not already a heretic. To accept a new regulation is hard, and to obey a command or submit to correction is harder still. It has been vehemently and violently taught that the Africans denied and repudiated all superior jurisdiction in the Roman Church, though they venerated it as the Chair of Peter, and the Apostolic See. The story of Apiarius has been the one proof employed.

This story has been treated by the Protestants with their usual contempt of historical accuracy. The Magdeburg

Centuriators declared that by this one incident the whole case of the Roman Pontiff must fall prone. Till this day it remains one of the *pièces de résistance* of controversy. The learned Gallican canonists, usually pillars of truth against Protestant error, incessantly reiterated the history of Apiarius as an instance of the rights of National Churches.[1] So much has been written, that it would seem almost an impertinence to waste paper and ink on so threadbare a subject. And yet a perfectly accurate and unbiased account is hard to find.[2]

The Protestant version of the affair is somewhat as follows : Popes Zosimus, Boniface and Celestine tried to usurp a supreme jurisdiction by the use of pretended Canons of Nicæa. The African Church nobly resisted this wicked intrusion, brilliantly exposed the lying of the Popes, and turned their legates out of doors with insults, declaring that they would never bow their necks to the yoke of Rome. The documents tell a less picturesque tale, and one far less distinct in outline.

It is at best but a fragmentary history. We have little more than three documents : the corrupt and incomplete acts of a Council, its letter to Pope Zosimus, and the letter of another Council to Pope Celestine I.[3] Out of these scanty materials what theories have been framed, what dogmas confirmed and illustrated! In the following paper we will try to keep to facts.

---

[1] I have not consulted Dupin, whose heretical views are well known, nor the more moderate de Marca, whose *Concordia* was written by him when a lawyer and a layman, and retracted later. But I have studied Van Espen's very careful account, as Puller refers to him. (*Comm. in can., Diss, in Syn. Afr.* and *Scholia in Ap. Can.*) His view may be held by any Catholic at the present day, but I need not specify the points on which I disagree with him. I quote his words as to the denial of the right of bishops to appeal to Rome : *Cur enim coercendis malevolorum tergiuersationibus et friuolis appellationibus haec statui non potuit disciplina, sine Episcopi Romani Primatus aut superioritatis laesione, aeque ac sine Regiae auctoritatis violatione ubique pene receptum est a sententia capitali lata a magistratu civili nullam admitti appellationem ad supremum Principis senatum ?* It is evident how far Van Espen is from the Protestant position.

[2] I cannot agree with the account given by the Ballerini. (*Opp. S. Leonis* II, p. 957, *P.L.* LV, p. 565.) Tillemont and Hefele are good. Jungmann is an apologist. It seems to me there are imperfections in both Dr. Bright and Dr. Rivington. Fr. Bottalla and Fr. Puller exaggerate in opposite directions. I have done my best to be careful and fair, I dare say with imperfect success.

[3] These are to be found in any of the great collections of Councils. I do not see any reason to question their authenticity. The late Dr. Rivington told me that he regretted having spoken so strongly on the subject in *The Primitive Church and the Chair of Peter*. A new and

Apiarius was a priest of the town of Sicca in Proconsular Africa, known to Englishmen as the scene of Newman's story *Callista*. The bishop of the See was Urbanus, formerly a priest of Hippo under St. Augustine,[4] in whose house he had doubtless lived. He excommunicated Apiarius for certain grave crimes. Apiarius sailed to Rome, and appealed to Pope St. Zosimus. The kindly Pope, who had been so easily deceived for a time by Pelagius and Celestius, and was duped in a similar way by the lies of Patroclus of Arles, was apparently inclined favourably to listen to the complaint of the African priest. It is true that no canon, and possibly no custom of the Catholic Church, authorized the appeal of a priest to Rome. But two reasons may be given to explain why the Pope did not simply dismiss Apiarius without a hearing. In the first place he was led to believe that Urbanus[5] had committed some fault so gross as to deserve excommunication, if he did not make amends. In the second place we notice the luminous fact, that until that time the only court constituted by African canon law for the trial of a priest, was one consisting of his own bishop with five others, and from their judgement there was no appeal.[6]

Such a rule was undoubtedly very hard. In the great Synod of May 1st, 418, a new canon was made, which gave permission for priests and clerics to appeal, as bishops might already appeal, to the primate of their province, and to a plenary council of Africa.[7]

" It was also decided that if priests, deacons, and the other

very elaborate vindication of the genuineness of the letter " Optaremus " appeared in the third edition of Puller's *Primitive Saints and the See of Rome*, pp. 204-14.

[4] Aug. *Serm. frag.*, I, *P.L.*, vol. 39, p. 1719. Urbanus is also mentioned in 439, Aug. *Ep.* 229. He was a priest at Hippo in 412 (Ep. 143) and went to be made bishop (accompanied by the subdeacon Peregrinus) in 414 (*Ep.* 149). I get these references from Christianus Lupus, whose interminable dissertation, however, no one could read through.

[5] See the letter of the Council of 419 to Boniface, quoted in full further on.

[6] Conc. Carth, in 387 or 390, canon 10 is thus summarized by Bp. Hefele, *E.T.*, vol. II, p. 391 : " A bishop can only be judged by twelve bishops, a priest by six, a deacon by three bishops (besides his own)." The words in parentheses are certainly wrong. They should run : " including his own," as appears by the Synod of Hippo in 393, ca., 8 (Mansi III, pp. 696 or 871 and 920).

[7] Can. 17 (125 of *Codex. Eccl. Afr.* Mansi III, p. 822).

inferior clerics in their cases complain of the judgement of their own bishops, neighbouring bishops, being called in by them with the consent of their own bishop, shall hear them and decide the cause, whatever it may be. And if they think fit to appeal from these, they shall appeal only to African Councils or to the primates of their provinces. But if any should appeal across the sea (*ad transmarina*) he shall be received to communion by no one in Africa."

It is probable that the cause of the composition of this canon was nothing else than the case of Apiarius. But the connexion generally given between the two events is incorrect. For instance, Bishop Hefele,[1] following the Ballerini[2] writes :

" This (appeal) greatly displeased the Africans, and in the seventeenth canon of their General Council of May 1st, 418, they ordered, probably with special reference to this, that no priest, deacon, or inferior cleric should on any account appeal to a Court on the other side of the sea."

Doubtless the Africans were angry. But this canon is not an effect of their anger. As we have seen, it greatly enlarged the rights of priests and clerics. The denial of the right to appeal to Rome in their case was perfectly reasonable, and was undoubtedly approved by the ultra-Papal Nuncio Faustinus, who at the end of the Council of 419 signed not only this very canon, but also another in almost the same wording, at the drawing up of which he was present ; nor is there any evidence that he made any objection to either the one or the other.

The real cause of the composition of this canon may have been the perception that Apiarius had a real grievance in having no court of appeal. It is obvious that the two parts of the canon hang together ; " transmarine " appeals of priests and inferior clerics are forbidden explicitly (no doubt

---

[1] II, p. 463.

[2] The Ballerini (l.c. supra) evolved from this idea a most ingenious explanation of the whole case. They thought that Zosimus sent Faustinus to Africa because he was so much horrified at this canon, and expected that the Africans would next deny the right of appeal to bishops also. He grounded the latter right on the canons of Sardica, and the appeal of priests on custom ; hence the distinction between *constitutiones* and *consuetudo* made by Faustinus. I am sorry to quit such admirable guides, but it seems to me that there is no proof that the Popes objected to the canon of 418.

they were implicitly forbidden before, in the opinion of the Council), after all excuse for them has been removed by the permission of appeals to the Primate and to African Councils. And this permission, as we have seen, was absolutely new. " It was defined by a Council," wrote St. Augustine in 402,[1] " that the cause of a priest is terminated by six bishops." And he had written, in 397, of Caecilian, bishop of Carthage, and his colleagues : " It was not a case of priests, or of inferior clerics, but of colleagues (i.e. of fellow-bishops) who might reserve their case for the judgment of other colleagues, especially of the Apostolic Sees."[2] Clearly, St. Augustine means that bishops could appeal to other Bishops, i.e. a larger Council, or *ad transmarina*, while the lower order of ecclesiastics could do neither.[3]

But it is further possible that this canon was not spontaneous, but was actually suggested or ordered by the Pope himself. It is always assumed that the embassy of Faustinus was received by a Council in the winter of 418. No trace of such a Council exists. The Council of 419 refers to " our letters of last year to Pope Zosimus " and it is natural to suppose that a plenary Council of Africa is referring to letters sent by another plenary Council. Any council called hastily together by Aurelius in the autumn would necessarily have been small, informal, and even of little weight. There is much reason therefore for supposing that the envoys of the Pope arrived before the end of the great Council of May 1st, 418. The nineteenth canon of that Council chose deputies who should stay behind with full powers, because the remainder of the bishops were anxious to get away.[4] But it is not stated

---

[1] St. Augustine is writing to the Primate of Numidia about one of his priests to whom, for his misconduct, he would not commit a church, and who intended to appeal (which had to be done within a year) to the Primate, that he might have a proper trial before six Bishops. *Ep.* 65.

[2] The Ball. (*l.c.*, p. 965) are wrong about the 10th canon of Hippo, 393 (Mansi, iii, p. 921), which only refers to cases (i.e., of Bishops) in which appeals to a higher court were allowed already.

[3] *Ep.* 43, 7. Caecilian had been condemned unjustly by a council of seventy bishops, the authors of the Donatist schism. St. Augustine (n. 14) suggests that the Donatists might object that Pope Melchiades and his assessors had no right to interfere in a cause which had been finally judged by seventy bishops. He answers, *ex abundantia*, that it was the Donatists themselves who appealed to the Emperor, and the latter then appointed the Pope and others to judge. But, as in the text, St. Augustine held that Caecilian had equally a right to appeal, not to Constantine, but to the Apostolic Sees—"*ad transmarina.*"

[4] See above, p. 176.

what business they performed. They do not seem to have drawn up any new canons, though probably they drew up the letter, of which a fragment has come down to us, to Pope Zosimus, in answer to his " Tractoria " against the Pelagians. They may very well have been also engaged on the affair of Apiarius, and have written the letter which was referred to by the Council of 419.[1]

Now in this letter they promised the Pope to observe two points until an inquiry into the Council of Nicæa, viz., " That bishops should be allowed to appeal to Rome, and that the causes of clerics should be finally heard before the Bishops of their own provinces."[2] The former point being simply negative, and never having been actually forbidden in Africa, did not need any canon. The second point is exactly covered by the present canon. It is most natural therefore to suppose that the canon was made after the receipt of the Pope's letter ; while, if we were to suppose that the canon was made in the spring and that the Pope's embassy came in the autumn, we should be surprised that no mention was made by the Africans of the fact that they had already dealt with the matter.

The legation from Rome, whether it arrived in spring or autumn, was a solemn and dignified embassy such as might have been sent to an oecumenical Council, consisting of a bishop, Faustinus of Potentia in the March of Ancona, and of two priests, Philip and Asellus. These latter are mere κωφα πρόσωπα Faustinus, by his arrogance, was the cause of almost all the subsequent troubles.

Zosimus died, after some weeks of illness, on the 28th December, 418. The legates remained in Africa, and awaited

---

[1] After the Council of May, 418, St. Augustine, in accordance with an " ecclesiastical necessity laid on him by Pope Zosimus," went at once to Cæsarea in Mauritania. Van Espen has elaborately argued that this was the Council summoned to meet Faustinus, and Dr. Bright appears to agree with him. But why in Mauritania, of all places ? And why should St. Augustine have had a special summons from the Pope ? (Aug. *Ep.* 190, 1, and 193, 1 ; *Retract*, ii, 51 ; Possidius *Vita Aug. cap.*, 14). The view is impossible, and it would only allow the date of Faustinus's arrival to be put a month later than I have put it or not at all later, as the summons to the Council of Cæsarea would have to be sent out. The view in the text seems to me quite satisfactory. The case to be tried may have been that of one of the Bishops who appealed to Rome, mentioned in St. Aug. *Ep.* 209 (see end of this article). This has been suggested to me by reading Puller, *Prim. Saints*, App., p. 490, 3rd edition. But it was presumably with regard to Donatism that St. Augustine was sent by the Pope.

[2] See the full text of the letter to Pope Boniface given further on.

the next General Council. Before its assembly they seem to have discovered that the Africans were neither schismatical nor·obstinate. They apparently wrote to the new Pope Boniface that they had calmed the threatening tempest, for we find him answering on the 28th April in a short letter which may be paraphrased as follows (it is too corrupt to translate) :

" You will hear by the bearers of this how all the choir of your brethren rejoiced, and the crowd of the saints exulted in the Lord when they heard the long-delayed news of your safety ; and the care of the members for their head (?) was praised with equal joy. [They had doubtless written to congratulate Boniface.] Christ has looked favourably upon your efforts, in that He has deigned to unite the divided and to heal the broken. This must be more fully recounted by you when our brethren and fellow-priests, Dulcitius and Felix, soon arrive."[1]

This letter may have already arrived when the great Council of all Africa was opened at Carthage on May 25th, 419, by Aurelius, the venerable Primate, no less than 217 Bishops being present. Aurelius opened the proceedings by a speech in which he said that much business had been begun[2] since the day fixed for the assembly, whilst the arrival of the legates from the different provinces was awaited. He thanked God for the greatness of their numbers. " The business in hand is to produce the copies of the Nicene Council which we now possess and which were framed by the Fathers, and signed here by our predecessors ; and also all that has been salutarily ordained according to that model with regard to all the grades of clerics, from highest to lowest." And the whole Council said : " Let them be produced."

We see from this why the Bishops were called in such numbers to the synod. It was for the purpose of publicly reading the Nicene decrees as they posssessed them, and of assuring the Pope of their loyal acceptance of them. The Pope probably believed that in Africa, as at Rome, the decrees which we now know to be Sardican were appended to the Acts of the Council of Nicæa. The production of the Africans'

---

[1] First printed by Mansi, and to be found also in Migne among the letters of St. Boniface.

[2] *Multa flagitata sunt.* The meaning seems to be that certain canons, agreed to later, had been suggested and drafted.

original copies would prove to Faustinus that when they
denied all knowledge of decrees, which at Rome were regarded
as part and parcel of the decisions of the 318 Fathers, they
were not (as he may at first have imagined) feigning ignorance
of statutes which they did not wish to observe.

Further, all the subsequent legislation of the African Church
was to be recited in the presence of the Papal legate, who
would see for himself how faithfully that Church had adhered
to Nicene principles, and how ignorant she had been of the
Sardican canons which the Pope was trying to enforce under
the name of Nicæa.

We have no means of knowing whether it was Faustinus
who suggested this course, or whether it was offered by the
Africans themselves. But it seems very likely that the successful negotiations, for which St. Boniface in his letter praised
his envoy, were nothing else than his agreement with the
Africans that this review of African canon law should be made
in a Pan-African Council. The result has been fortunate for
posterity; for the long list of canons read at this famous synod,
and commonly known as the *codex canonum Africanae
Ecclesiae*, has preserved to us the acts of many Councils
of which history would otherwise have known nothing.

Daniel, the notary, then read the canons of Nicæa; he was
interrupted, however, by Faustinus, who rose and spoke words
to the following effect :[1]

" We have received from the Apostolic See some orders in
writing and some in verbal directions to be treated of with your
Blessedness as we remember was the case in the former acts[2]
(viz. the Council of 418, whether spring or autumn), " that is,
as to the Nicene canons that both their command [*constituto*]
and their custom be observed. Let us therefore first treat
of these, if it please your Blessedness (and afterwards all that
has been done [viz. by other councils] or begun [by this
council before all the deputies had arrived, viz. certain canons
read later on] shall be put down in the acts and signed), that

---

[1] The two speeches of Faustinus are evidently much compressed
by the writers of the minutes, and the text is corrupt.

[2] This is usually taken to mean : " Some of our instructions are in
writing in the Pope's *commonitorium*, and some are unwritten." But
it appears that all their business was put down in the *commonitorium*.
It seems to mean simply : " We have been told to put before you some
things which are in writing (viz., two pseudo-Nicene canons), and
other things which are not (viz., certain customs in connection with
them).

you may be able to inform the Apostolic See in your reply,
that it may be plain to the venerable Pope that we have
admonished you ; though, in fact, the minutes (? *capitula
actionum*) have been already put down in the conciliar acts
[ready for signature after they had been read]. About these,
therefore, we must do what your Blessedness pleases, as we
said before. Let the *commonitorium* therefore be produced,
that your Blessedness may know what is contained therein,
so that an answer may be given to each of the [four] points."

Bishop Aurelius said : " Let the *commonitorium* be produced
which our brethren and fellow-priests have lately quoted in
the acts [viz. of the council of last year] and let the rest of
the things which have been done or are to be done follow [viz.
the canons to be reviewed and the new canons to be passed].

Daniel the Notary recited :

" Bishop Zosimus to his brother Faustinus and his sons,
the priests Philip and Asellus—You know the commission we
entrust to you. Do all therefore as though we were present,
as in fact we are in your person, and still more because you
have our mandate and the words of the canons which we have
inserted in this *commonitorium* for fuller security. For thus,
dearest brethren, was it decreed in the council of Nicæa
concerning the appeals of bishops :

' If a bishop be accused, and the bishops of the region
assemble and judge him and degrade him from his dignity,
and if he should have appealed to the most blessed bishop of
Rome and desires to be heard, and claims to have the examination renewed—let him [the Pope] write to the bishops who
are in the neighbouring and adjoining province to make a
complete inquiry, and decide according to the evidence of
truth. But if he who asks for his cause to be heard anew
should move the bishop of Rome by his prayer to send a priest
from his side [*e latere suo*] it will be in the power of the bishop
[of Rome] according as he shall will and judge. And if he
shall decide to send assessors to judge, together with the
bishops, having the authority of him by whom they are sent,
it shall be as he wills. But if he consider that the bishops are
sufficient to put an end to the matter, let him do as he shall
judge by his most wise judgment.' "

This is the 7th canon of Sardica, believed at Rome, as we
have said, to be Nicene. Alypius of Tagaste here interrupted :

" We have already written about this in a letter of our
council [of last year, to the Pope], and we promise to observe
this, which was decreed in the Nicene council. Still I am

moved by the fact that when we examined the Greek copies of this Nicene council, these things, I know not why, were not to be found there."[1]

St. Alypius continues by begging St. Aurelius to send to Constantinople, where the original acts of the council were said to be preserved, and also to the patriarchal Churches of Antioch and Alexandria, for true copies. " We promise, therefore, as I said before, to observe these canons until perfect copies shall arrive." The Pope should be invited to send also.

Faustinus thereupon remarked that the Roman Church suffered no prejudice by Alypius throwing doubt upon the canons. Let them write to the Pope by all means, that he might inquire for perfect copies. But it would be better that he alone should make the inquiry for fear the Easterns should think there were divisions in the West. Aurelius then said that a letter must be composed to the Pope to accompany the acts of the council. Novatus, the legate of Mauretania Sitifensis, asked for a canon to be read which he remembered to have been in the *commonitorium*, concerning priests and deacons, which Daniel thereupon read. It is the 17th canon of Sardica :

" As to the appeals of clerics, i.e. those of lower rank, there is a plain reply of the synod for your guidance. We insert it. It runs thus : ' Bishop Hosius said, What is yet on my mind, I will not keep back. If any bishop being angry (which he ought not to be) should be moved hastily or harshly against one of his priests or deacons, and wishes to expel him from the Church, it must be provided that an innocent man be not condemned nor deprived of communion. Let him who is expelled have the right of appealing to the neighbouring bishops for his cause to be heard and more carefully treated, for it would not be just to refuse him a hearing. And let the bishop who justly or unjustly rejected him suffer patiently that the matter be discussed, and that the sentence be either approved or improved.'"

---

[1] Dr. Bright says Alypius spoke " with fine irony," which Fr. Puller improved into " with a twinkle in his eye." This may or may not be. I have translated exactly : " this which was decreed." It is not simply : " Whatever was decreed." If the Africans had suspected the Pope of wilful deceit, would they have promised to accept the canons for a time ?

St. Augustine then said : " We promise to observe this also, whilst a more diligent investigation of the Nicene council is being made." All then acclaimed the Nicene council.

The speech of Faustinus which follows is quite impossible to understand, except that he repeats that the Pope should be asked to inquire about this canon also.

Aurelius then proposed that the reading of the Nicene acts, and of the other canons, be proceeded with. It was also agreed that letters should be sent to Constantinople, Antioch and Alexandria, and that if in the copies received from thence the canons were not found, another council should be summoned to consider the matter.

After the canons of Nicæa and twenty-seven African canons had been read, six new canons were passed. The first of these is a repetition of the canon of 418 quoted above, about the appeals of clerics but with certain alterations :

418 (*cod. can.* 125).

Item placuit, ut presbyteri, diaconi, uel ceteri inferiores clerici in causis quas habuerint, si de judiciis episcoporum suorum questi fuerint, uicini episcopi eos audiant, et inter eos quicquid est finiant adhibiti ab eis ex consensu episcoporum suorum.

Quod si et ab eis prouocandum putauerint, non prouocent nisi ad Africana concilia, uel ad primates prouinciarum suarum.

Ad transmarina autem qui putaverit appellandum, a nullo intra Africam in communionem suscipiatur.

419 (*cod. can.* 28).

Item placuit, ut presbyteri, diaconi, uel ceteri inferiores clerici in causis quas habuerint, si de judiciis episcoporum suorum questi fuerint, uicini episcopi eos cum consensu sui episcopi audiant, et inter eos definiant adhibiti ab eis episcopi.

Quod si et ab eis prouocandum putauerint, non prouocent ad transmarina judicia, sed ad primates suarum prouinciarum aut ad uniuersale concilium, sicut et de episcopis saepe constitutum est.

Ad transmarina autem qui putauerit appellandum, a nullo intra Africam ad communionem suscipiatur.

If Dr. Bright[1] had consulted the Ballerini or even Hefele,

---

[1] *The Roman See*, p. 136 note : " A clause, probably added later, says that Bishops had often been forbidden to do so." There is no " probably " in the question. The original canon of 418 was read and approved by the present Council as its 125th canon. There is no doubt about the text of either as given above.

he would not have fallen into the old mistake of supposing that the words *sicut et de episcopis* refer to the prohibition of appeals *ad transmarina*. The clerics are being given the same rights which had been often (e.g. by the Councils of Hippo, 393, can. 6 and 7, and Carthage, 397), granted to bishops, to appeal to their primates, and to plenary councils. But not one canon had ever been made to prohibit the appeals of bishops, or it would have been necessarily repeated in the long list read to the present Council. Besides, Faustinus and the two Roman priests would certainly not have signed the canon in this sense. If a last and conclusive proof is needed, we have only to recall the fact that the Council had just inclusively decided to permit episcopal appeals for a few months at least.[1]

In a second session of the 30th May, the process of reading canons was continued and completed, though not all the Bishops were able to remain. The Acts were finally signed by Aurelius of Carthage, Valentinus, Primate of Numidia, Faustinus the legate, Alypius, Augustine, Possidius, and eighteen others, in the name of the whole 217, and by the priests Asellus and Philip.

On the following day the letter to Pope Boniface was written. It must be given in full :

" To the most blessed lord and our honourable brother Boniface, Aurelius, Valentinus, Primate of Numidia, and the rest of the whole Council of Africa who were present to the number of 217.

It has pleased the Lord that, with regard to the matters which our holy brethren, Faustinus our fellow-bishop and our fellow-priests Philip and Asellus, treated of with us, our humility should write an answer not to Bishop Zosimus, of blessed memory, but to your Veneration, who have been appointed by Providence in his room. We must therefore shortly relate what has been concluded with the agreement of both parties, and not all that is contained in the lengthy rolls of acts of the Council, in which, though charity was preserved, we were detained by some trouble of dispute. But we have chosen out of the acts what appertained to the case in hand. Your predecessor, if he were yet in the body, would be pleased that we have arrived at a peaceful conclusion, lord brother.

---

[1] This will answer the add. note to Puller, *Prim. Saints*, 3rd ed., p. 490.

The priest Apiarius, about whose ordination and excommunication and appeal no light scandal had arisen, not only for the Church of Sicca, but for the whole Church of Africa, sought pardon for all his faults and was restored to communion. But before this, our fellow-bishop, Urbanus of Sicca, without any hesitation, corrected what it was thought fit to correct in him. But because we were bound to consider the peace and quiet of the Church not merely for the present, but for the future also, and since many things had occurred of such a sort that it was our duty to guard against the same or even worse in the future, we agreed that the priest Apiarius should be removed from the Church of Sicca, retaining, however, the rank of his office, and that he should be given a letter of recommendation, that he might exercise his priestly functions wherever else he would or could. And this we conceded to him without difficulty, when he requested it, by a letter of our own.[1]

But before the case was thus closed, among other things which we discussed at great length,[2] it was reasonable that in the course of the proceedings we should ask our fellow-bishop Faustinus, and our fellow-priests, Philip and Asellus, to bring forward the business which had been enjoined them. They explained some of it by word of mouth without any writing. But when we inquired rather what they had brought in their letter, they produced a *commonitorium* which was read to us, and which is appended to the acts which they take with them to you.

In this they were ordered to treat with us of four matters : the first, concerning appeals of bishops to the bishop of the Roman See ; the second, that bishops should not make unnecessary voyages to Court ; the third, concerning the hearing by neighbouring bishops of the causes of priests and deacons if improperly excommunicated by their own diocesan ; the fourth, concerning the excommunication of bishop Urbanus, or even summoning him to Rome, if he would not correct what it appeared he ought to correct."

We have already spoken about the fourth point. As to the

---

[1] It would appear that this affair of Apiarius was dealt with in the days intervening between the 25th and 30th of May, for the letter prefaces the account, which immediately follows, of the discussion about the Nicene Council with the words : " Before this case was thus closed."

[2] It is evident that the " acts " which we possess, and which have been already described, are but fragments, probably summarised also, of the " lengthy rolls " sent to the Pope. The *Codex canorum* however, makes them still of some bulk.

second there was no difficulty. The seventh, eighth, and ninth canons of Sardica, which forbade bishops going to Court without reason, were framed especially against the Africans, on the complaint of their own Primate Gratus. The synod of Hippo in 393, decreed that no bishop must " cross the sea " without receiving approval and *formatae* from his primate. This was confirmed by the Council of Carthage of June 26th, 397.[1] However, these rules proved insufficient, and at another Council of Carthage on the 23rd August, 405, a letter was read from Pope Innocent, saying again that bishops should not lightly cross the seas. This was agreed to ;[2] and on the 13th June, 407, a new rule was made[3] that those who wished to go to Court must obtain *literae formatae* (from their primate) to the Pope, and then from him get *formatae* to the Court. The letter continues :

" As to the first and third points (that is, that bishops should be allowed to appeal to Rome, and that the cases of clerics should be finally heard before the bishops of their own provinces), we have already taken care to notify in our letter of last year to Bishop Zosimus of venerable memory, that we would allow their observance for a time without any prejudice to him, until an inquiry into the statutes of the Council of Nicæa. And now we beg of your Holiness that you will cause them to be observed by us just as they were drawn up and decided at Nicæa, and also that you will have the canons which the legates brought in their *commonitorium* put in practice at Rome. They are as follows : "—

Next are quoted the two canons of Sardica, already given in full :

" The above have been inserted in the acts of the most accurate copies of the Nicene Council, until the arrival of authentic copies of that Council. If these canons were only observed at Rome and in Italy by you just as they were decreed and as they are contained in the *commonitorium* which was quoted to us by our colleagues sent by the Apostolic See, and in the same order, then we should neither be compelled to suffer things which we do not now choose to mention, nor to bear the unbearable.

[1] *Conc. Hipp.*, 27, Mansi, p. 923 (*Conc. Carthag.*, 28, *Ibid.*, p. 884), renewed in present council as can. 23 (*Ibid.*, p. 723).
[2] Renewed as can. 94 (p. 709).
[3] Renewed as can. 106 (p. 807).

But we believe that, with the help of the mercy of our Lord God we shall no longer suffer from this insolence, now that your Holiness is at the head of the Roman Church. And such conduct will be observed towards us with paternal charity, as ought to be observed even without our complaining, and such as you also (with the wisdom and justice with which the Most High has endowed you) perceive to be due, unless perchance the canons of the Nicene Council are otherwise (than you think). For although we have read many codices, yet we have never read in Latin codices of the Nicene Council the canons which you have sent us in the *commonitorium*.

However, because we have been unable to find them in any Greek codex here, we desire the more for them to be brought to us from the Churches of the East, where, it is said, these decrees are to be found even in the original copy. For this purpose we beseech your Reverence to be pleased to write in person to the bishops of those parts, that is to say, the Churches of Antioch, of Alexandria and of Constantinople, and to others also, it if should please your Sanctity, that you may obtain from thence these same canons, decreed in the city of Nicæa by the Fathers ; and by this you will, with the help of God, confer a great benefit upon all the Churches of the West. For who can doubt that those are the most accurate copies of the Council of Nicæa held in Greece [in a wide sense] which after being brought together from such diverse and famous Greek Churches and compared, are found to agree ? Until this is done, the rules quoted to us from the *commonitorium* as to appeals of bishops to the bishop of the Roman Church, and concerning the termination of the causes of clerics before the bishops of their own provinces, shall be observed, we promise, until proofs arrive. And we are confident that your Blessedness will assist us in the Will of God.

The remainder of the things which were done or confirmed in our own synod, our fellow-bishop Faustinus and our own fellow-priests Philip and Asellus are taking with them, and they will, if you think fit, make them known to your Holiness." (And in another hand) " Our Lord preserve you to us many years, most blessed brother." There subscribed also Alypius, Augustine, Possidius, Marianus (?) and the other bishops.

This letter was written in considerable irritation, yet in a studiously moderate tone. The Africans declare their willingness to keep the alleged canons of Nicæa for the present, though they have some suspicions as to their being genuine. We must admire this moderation, since the first impulse on such an occasion must always be rather to say : " We will not keep them until they are proved to be genuine." It is difficult to imagine any adequate reason for this conduct, if they did not recognise that it was the office of the bishop of Rome to enforce the canons of the Church and watch over their observance.

At the same time they say very emphatically that they expect the Pope in future to observe his own laws. Apiarius had no right of appeal to the Pope under the very canon quoted. What was more aggravating was the presence of most objectionable legates, sent to see that Apiarius was properly treated, and to sit and judge with the Council. Yet another canon quoted by the Pope suggested that he might send a legate in this manner in the case only of a bishop who appealed. The Pope is setting a bad example if he goes beyond the canons which he himself quotes. How, then, can he expect the Africans to keep exactly within them ?

Of the unbearable and unmentionable conduct of Faustinus we have no details, for that these expressions refer to him is obvious.[1] If it was any action of the Pope himself the Council would have explained.[2] But the assembled bishops thought it beneath their dignity to complain of the behaviour of a man with whom in the end they had made terms, and whom they expected to see no more of. For the next few years St. Augustine is engaged in apologizing for Zosimus's hasty action about the Pelagians, and in praising him to the skies. He

---

[1] The meaning is : " If you had kept to the canons you would not have sent us this unbearable man." Janus, with his wonted insolence, writes (*E.T.*, p. 79) : " The African Bishops wrote to Pope Boniface in 419 : " We are resolved not to admit this arrogant claim." *Non sumus jam istum typhum passuri.*" His rival in shamelessness, Dr. Littledale (in a passage in which he mixes up the letter to Boniface with that to Celestine), has : " They told him that nothing should make them tolerate such insolent conduct on the part of the Papal envoys (*executores*) ; that is to say, in fact, since these were only discharging his commission, on his part " (*Plain Reasons*, p. 120). The latter distinguished controversialist forgot, or did not know, that the letter was to Boniface, but the commission was from Zosimus ! Neither writer is aware that in Latin *non sumus passuri*, even taken alone, does not mean " we won't put up with." The method of quotation reminds one of the preacher against chignons, who took his text from Matt. xxiv. 17, " Top not come down." The sentence, translated as a whole, is a polite speech to Boniface : *Sed credimus . . . quod tua sanctitate Romanae ecclesiae praesidente, non sumus jam istum typhum passuri.*

[2] On further thoughts, I do think it probable that not only Faustinus but the Pope who sent him is complained of. For we know how violent and unreasonable Pope Zosimus could be in other cases.

probably understood thoroughly that Pope's impulsive and excitable character. This very year St. Alypius went to Rome, and was received with the greatest friendliness by St. Boniface, to whom St. Augustine immediately afterwards dedicated his treatise, *Contra duas epistolas Pelagianorum*, giving the Pope among other expressions of respect, praise for his humility and condescension from his high place to those of lower station, such as Augustine himself and Alypius (see p. 179).

" Such was the style in which this great council of more than two hundred bishops, under the guidance of such glorious saints as St. Augustine, St. Aurelius, and St. Alypius, thought it was right and proper for them to address the Pope." Thus Fr. Puller. For my part, I think it a very proper letter.

On the 6th of November, the Africans were able to send to Rome the copies of the Nicene acts which they had received from Constantinople and Alexandria, and which naturally did not include the canons of Sardica.[1] It does not appear that another council was summoned, or any official letter sent, other than probably a communication from Aurelius. From that moment, there can be no doubt, the truce agreed to with regard to the observance of the Sardican canons was at an end. We hear nothing more on the subject except in the famous letter *Optaremus* written by a later Council to Pope St. Celestine, of which the date may be 423 or later.[2] Ferrandus quotes the summary of a canon from the 20th Synod of Carthage, as read in a Council of 525 : *Ut nullus ad transmarina audeat appellare*, which we naturally connect with this letter. Now the 18th Synod was in 421 ; so that if the 19th was in 422, the 20th would be in 423 or later.

We learn from the letter that Apiarius had again been excommunicated, and had again appealed to the Pope, who had restored him to communion, and had sent Faustinus back with him to Africa to have the sentence carried out.

---

[1] The letters from Atticus and St. Cyril have survived. The latter may be genuine in spite of the wrong date of Easter. But the Greek version which we possess I imagine to have been translated back from the Latin by the translator of the canons, etc.

[2] Tillemont, believing the election of Celestine to have been at the beginning of 423, thought the letter must be dated after the tumults which lasted from the death of Honorius (Aug. 423) to July 425. He has been followed by Coustant (s.l.) and the Ballerini (*Opp. S. Leonis*, III, civ. *P.L.*, p. 121). But Celestine was elected about Sept. 10th, 422, so that Tillemont's view falls to the ground. Hefele gives the date 424. I do not know his reasons.

Faustinus did his best, or his worst, but the facts were too much for him :

"To the most beloved lord and our honourable brother Celestine, Aurelius, Palatinus, Antonius, Tutus, Servusdei, Terentius, Fortunatus, Martinus, Januarius, Optatus, Celticus, Donatus, Theasius, Vincentius, Fortunatianus, and the rest who were present in the universal African Council of Carthage. We could wish that even as your Holiness has intimated your joy at the arrival of Apiarius in the letters you have sent us by our fellow-priest Leo, so we in like manner could send these writings with joy at his acquittal. The cheerfulness on both sides would be better founded, and would seem less precipitate if it preceded instead of following the hearing. For upon the arrival of our holy brother and fellow-bishop Faustinus, we gathered a council together, and we believed him to have been sent in order that, as by his assistance Apiarius had been formerly restored to the priesthood, now he might by his labours be acquitted of the grave accusations urged against him by the people of Thabraca. But the course of examination by our Council discovered such enormous crimes of his, that they were too much even for the patronage and pleading which Faustinus substituted for judgment and justice. For how at first he resisted against the whole Council, and cast upon it many insults, under colour of asserting the privileges of the Roman Church, and wishing him to be received into communion by us, on the ground that your Holiness, believing him to have appealed (which he could not prove), had restored him to communion." (This sentence appears to be corrupt.)

Apiarius apparently claimed that he had appealed to a higher court in Africa, and that this ought to have stayed execution of the sentence. The claim that he had appealed to Rome would have been absurd, as the Africans would have paid no attention to it. The Pope must have heard him on this plea of his.

"This, however, was in no wise permissible, as you will understand better by the acts. For after the judgment had been discussed with much labour for three days, while we inquired with great grief into the various accusations, God the Judge, strong and patient, cut short both the obstructions of our fellow-bishop Faustinus and the tergiversations of Apiarius himself by which he tried to hide his unspeakable disorders. For whilst he held fast to the black and shameful obstinacy with which he hoped to hide the filth of his passions by the impudence of his denial, God straitened his conscience, and published even before man the secrets which He had already condemned in his heart as in a mire of crimes, so that in spite of his crafty denial be broke forth into a confession of all the evil deeds of which he was accused. And at length of his own will he convicted himself of all the incredible charges, and converted into groaning the very hope by which we both believed and desired that he might be acquitted of such shameful stains. Only that this our sadness was mitigated by one consolation, that he both absolved us from further labour of inquiry, and provided a medicine, such as it was, for his own wounds, in spite of the unwillingness and rebelliousness against conscience with which he confessed, lord brother.''

So far there has been no complaint of the Pope's action, but only of the disgraceful conduct of Faustinus, even worse probably than at the Council of 418. But now the tragic conclusion of the attempt to acquit the miserable Apiarius is used as an argument to exemplify the absurdity of trying a case in a different province without witnesses or evidence. With much justice the African bishops continue :

" Therefore, after the due salutation, we greatly beseech you that henceforth you will not too readily admit to your ears those who come from hence, nor be willing henceforward to receive into communion those whom we have excommunicated because your Reverence will easily perceive that this has even been defined by the council of Nicæa. For though its rule concerns the lower clerics and lay persons, how much more did it wish the same to be observed with regard to bishops? —lest those who are suspended in their own province should prove to be restored to communion by your Holiness *praepropere uel indebite* hastily or improperly.''

This argument that when the Nicene council forbade bishops to receive to communion priests and clerics excommunicated by another bishop, they wished the same *a fortiori* to be observed with regard to bishops, must be admitted to be somewhat forced ! But the council is evidently anxious at all costs to prevent the recurrence of such scandals as that of Apiarius, and chooses to forget that the council had carefully excepted the case of a cleric excommunicated by an angry or unjust bishop.

No doubt the principle which the council had inherited from St. Cyprian, that a case should be concluded where it is begun, is in itself a sound one.

But it does not seem to have struck them to consider (as the Council of Sardica, consisting mainly of bishops who had been present at Nicæa, was forced by the facts to realize) that an opposite principle must often check the action of this wise theory ; that is, the propriety of the recourse to an un-prejudiced outsider, when those on the spot are determined to condemn an innocent man.

" And let your Holiness, as is worthy of you, reject also the infamous appeals (*improba refugia*) of priests and lower clerics, both because this right has not been taken away from the African Church by any definition of the Fathers, and because the decrees of Nicæa most plainly committed not only clerics of inferior grade, but even bishops to their own Metropolitans. For they most prudently and justly perceived that all business should be finished in the place where it was commenced. Nor would the grace of prudence from the Holy Ghost be wanting to any, by which equity should by the bishops of Christ be both perceived with wisdom and preserved with constancy. Above all, because it is allowed to each, if he is offended with the judgment of the examiners, to appeal to the Councils of his province, or even to an universal Council (of Africa). Unless perchance there is anyone who can believe that our God can inspire justice in examination to a single man,[1] whoever he may be, and deny it to countless bishops assembled in a council. Or how shall even the ' transmarine ' judgment itself be correct since it will be impossible to produce

[1] I think it impossible that Dr. Rivington should be right in thinking that *uni cuilibet*, " a single man whoever he may be," refers to Faustinus, who had not been a judge at all, certainly not a sole judge. Dr. Bright takes it as a disrespectful reference to the Pope himself, " to a single man, however highly placed." I do not see why this should be dis-respectful. But I think that the words are more correctly translated " to any individual." The latter had said above *that the Holy Ghost would inspire prudence and justice to single Bishops* to try their own clerics, and *to single Metropolitans* to judge the bishops of this province. But the Africans allowed appeals not only to primates of provinces, but also the " innumerable bishops " of a Pan-African Synod, who would be *a fortiori* to be trusted. The next sentence seems to speak clearly of the " transmarine " court as higher still, although impossible in practice. It is also remembered that no one supposed Popes to decide important matters without a Council (including many bishops) such as were constantly being held at Rome, and which did some of the work of the modern congregations.

the necessary witnesses on account of infirmity or sex or age, or many other impediments ?

For that any should be sent as from your Holiness's side (*a latere*), we have not found to be ordered in any synod of the Fathers ; since what you sent before by the same Faustinus our fellow-bishop as proceeding from the Council of Nicæa, in the truer councils which are received as Nicene, sent to us from the original by Holy Cyril, our fellow-bishop of the Church of Alexandria, and by the venerable Atticus, Bishop of Constantinople, which even before this were sent on by Innocent the priest, and Marcellus the subdeacon (by whom they had been forwarded to us) to your pre-decessor Bishop Boniface of venerable memory, in these we have not been able to find anything of the sort.

And further, do not send, do not grant your clerical *executores* to any who may ask, lest we should seem to introduce the smoky pride of the world into the Church of Christ, which offers the brightness of simplicity and the daylight of humility to those who desire to see God.

For as to our brother Faustinus (now that the miserable Apiarius is removed from the Church of Christ for his unspeakable disorders) we are certain that with the rectitude and moderation of your holiness, Africa will suffer from him no more."

And in another hand : " Our God keep your Holiness for a longer age praying for us, lord brother."

This letter is a far more angry one than that to Boniface ; but there was certainly some cause for heat.   It is not indeed signed with the famous names of Augustine, of his lifelong friend Alypius, or his biographer and pupil Possidius. Perhaps, when we remember the extreme deference with which a Pope was always in those days addressed by Africans, we may find the present letter too strong in its expressions, as it is certainly one-sided in its arguments.

But the Gallican and Protestant inferences from it are plainly groundless.

The Gallicans imagined that the Africans were bravely upholding the rights of a National Church.   The Protestants claim that the matter and manner of the letter alike reject the Pope's supreme jurisdiction.

A careful examination, however, will assure the reader that the Africans simply refuse (on sufficient grounds) to admit the Pope's version of the Nicene canons, and accuse him of not observing the true Nicene canons himself, which of course he professed to do.

If we suppose that the Africans admitted a superior authority in the Pope, their action is easily explained. If we suppose that they denied him all prerogatives except of honour, it is simply inexplicable.

If they admitted his superior authority, we shall say: The Africans expected the Pope to enforce canons, but not spurious canons; they expected him to hear appeals of Bishops sometimes, but they did not like it; they expected him to reject appeals of priests, but when he did not, they could not ignore his action, or refuse to respect his authority.

But if they denied him all real jurisdiction in Africa, why did they take any notice of his repeated absolution of Apiarius? Why were they not indignant at his threatening to excommunicate, or summon to Rome one of their bishops? Why did they not treat Faustinus, whose embassy was not authorised even by the Sardican canon, as a mere messenger, instead of as the representative of a superior? Why did they not write to the Pope that he had no power to judge cases of appeal from Africa, whether of bishops or clerics? Why did they not add that to send clerical *executores* would be absurd, as they did not recognize their authority?

It is impossible, lastly, that the Africans should have had sentiments concerning those claims and that authority, differing from those of the Pope himself and of the rest of the Church, without our having some knowledge of the ruptures, and even schisms, which must have resulted, besides the imagined rebelliousness of this single letter.

But we must note further that the unwillingness of the Africans to allow episcopal appeals had not prevented these in the past, and did not prevent them in the future. Our information is extremely scanty; but there seem to have been a great many.

In the very year 423 of which we have been speaking, or at the end of 422, St. Augustine wrote his well-known letter to the newly-elected Pope, St. Celestine, about the wicked bishop, Antony of Fussala, who had been condemned in Africa to the loss of his episcopal authority (though retaining his title and dignity) as a punishment for his exactions and oppressions. He had appealed from this decision to the Primate of Numidia, who had believed everything he said, and had sent him to Pope Boniface as wholly innocent of the charges

against him.   The Pope sent him back with a letter, restoring
him, or at least ordering a fresh trial, on condition that it
should be shown that he had correctly related the facts in his
libellus of appeal.

St. Augustine writes to St. Celestine, as St. Boniface had
died during the interval, to assure him that he had been wholly
misled by Antony.   And he answers the culprit's objection
that he ought either to be deprived of his bishopric, or to be
given the full authority due to his rank, by giving precedents
for this arrangement :

" There exist instances (in which the Apostolic See either
itself judged, or confirmed the judgment of others) of bishops
who for certain faults have been neither deprived of episcopal
rank, nor yet left wholly unpunished.   I will not seek for
examples very remote from our time, but I will relate recent
ones.   Let Priscus, a bishop of the province of Caesariensis,
cry out (like Antony) : ' Either I ought to have a right to the
primacy (by seniority) like the rest, or I ought not to have
retained the episcopate.'   Let Victor, another bishop of the
same province, who received the same punishment as Priscus,
and is never communicated with by any bishop save in his
own diocese, let him, I say, cry : ' Either I ought to receive
communion everywhere, or else not even in my own district.'
Let Laurence, a third bishop of the same province, cry in the
very words of Antony : ' Either I ought to sit in the chair to
which I was ordained, or I ought not to be a bishop '."

The Gallicans and Protestants are forced by their thesis to
suppose that the three appeals from Mauretania Caesariensis
had all occurred since the Council of 419, viz., within three
years and a half, and that the period which elapsed between the
council of 419 and the council which wrote to St. Celestine,
was a time of truce, in which the Pope might do what he liked.
As the copies of the Nicene canons which came from the East
were sent on at once to Rome, it is impossible to imagine why
the African bishops should have extended the time.   If
they admitted the Pope's strict right to hear episcopal appeals,
but begged him not to use it, their letter is intelligible and so
is that of St. Augustine.   But if they absolutely denied the
right, it seems absurd to suppose that they would calmly
allow a great many bishops to appeal, and yet raise no protest
at all, and reserve all they had to say until the case of the simple
priest Apiarius happened to turn up again.   When we remem-

ber that, as I have shown conclusively, they did not in 419 forbid bishops to appeal, and had never done so previously, it is obvious they had no ground for objecting to Antony's appeal.

Tillemont had no doubt some reason for imagining this extraordinary and illogical truce, in that he took " *sicut et de episcopis saepe constitutum est* " in the canon of 419, to forbid episcopal appeals. But since the Ballerini showed the utter impossibility of this meaning, and since that Council made no reference whatever to bishops, it is at least unfortunate that modern controversialists should harp on a long discredited theme. As to the Council which wrote to St. Celestine, it could not have brought such a truce to an end with such vague words as those in which it argues that what the Nicene Council said of priests ought to be applied still more to bishops, and begs the Pope to respect this principle.

But even if the three cases of episcopal appeals specified by St. Augustine, and the many other cases which they must imply,[1] had all taken place since 419 there remain the remote cases, *remotissima non requiram, recentia memorabo*. It is absurd to suppose that St. Augustine means cases anywhere but in Africa.

We are simply driven to the conclusion that, much as the Africans had come to dislike appeals of bishops to Rome, these had been by no means unknown in Africa. Further, we must conclude that they had no power to make any canon against them, as their inference from the Council of Nicæa was probably put forward for the first time in this letter to Celestine, and was not even moderately convincing. Lastly, we see plainly that they could not disregard an appeal to the Pope by a bishop, if the Pope chose to allow it. This is proved by the fact of their great deference when two Popes had received the appeal of a simple priest, contrary to the very canons which he himself quoted.[2]

[1] For we cannot suppose that all appeals ended in the same decision. Some bishops may have been acquitted, others have been deposed altogether. Antony could hardly have complained of the half-hearted treatment he had received as unprecedented, if there were actually no Roman precedent for any other, even for acquittal !

[2] The boldness of suggesting that bishops should no longer be allowed to appeal seems to have been the result of the Africans' triumph in the case of the Sardican canons. It has been said above that this council perhaps passed a canon summarised at a council in 525 as *ut nullus ad transmarina audeat appellare*. *Nullus* might, of course, include bishops ; but there is no reason to suppose it refers to anything

Nearly thirty years afterwards, when the African Church had been for many years under the barbarous oppression of the Arian invader, we find St. Leo the Great (*Ep.* xii) sending to Africa directions for the proper selection of bishops, enforcing rules of the Church, and receiving the appeal of the African Bishop Lupicinus, whom he sent back to Africa to be tried over again.

In the face of all these facts, it is impossible to assert that the Pope's jurisdiction was not acknowledged by the Church of North Africa.

It is also interesting to notice that the Africans were entirely in the wrong about Nicæa and Sardica. The latter council was strangely unknown in Africa ; St. Augustine said it was a synod of heretics, confounding it with the *conciliabulum* of Philippopolis.[3] But its decisions were accepted throughout the East, and have always formed part of Eastern canon law. By an unfortunate accident of transcription, the canons (beginning " Hosius said ") were amalgamated with those of Nicæa in early Latin collections of canons ;[4] hence Popes Zosimus and Leo could innocently quote them as Nicene. But the Council had the same president and the same papal legates as Nicæa ; St. Athanasius was present, and many

more than a re-enactment of the former canon about priests and clerics. It should be remarked that the Sardican decrees were eventually received in Africa. How " ultramontane " the African bishops were at the end of the barbarian persecution may be seen from the synodical letter of the African bishops exiled in Sardinia to the Scythian monks A.D. 523, in the appendix to the 10th vol. of St. Augustine, the letters of the great St. Fulgentius of Ruspe, or that of Bp. Possessor to Pope Hormisdas.

[3] It is curious that in the Council of Carthage of 348. the Primate Gratus (himself mentioned at Sardica, and apparently p.esent there) had actually quoted the Council of Sardica by name. It is also curious that in the sixth century the African canonist, Ferrandus, shows knowledge of a canonical collection where the Sardican canons were numbered as Nicene. The ignorance of Aurelius and Augustine and their contemporaries is the more odd. The ignorance at Rome of the distinction between Sardica and Nicaea survived up to St. Leo, five and twenty years later.

[4] A succinct account of the MSS. and families of MSS. which still count the Nicene and the Sardican canons as one series, or show traces of such a reckoning having existed in their parents, will of course be found in Maassen's *Geschichte der Quellen des Canonischen Rechts*, 1870, pp. 50-63. A dissertation on the subject has long been awaited from Prof. C. H. Turner in his great unfinished work on occidental canon law. The earliest quotation of the Sardican canons as Nicene is by St. Jerome, *Ep.* 69, 5, *ad Oceanum*, written about 397. The learned Doctor is using a collection current in Rome.

Eastern as well as Western Sees were represented. It was seldom reckoned as " oecumenical," because it decided nothing as to the faith. But its disciplinary decisions were universally accepted. That they were unknown in Africa is more surprising than that they should have been joined on to those of Nicæa, with no fresh title, in Italian manuscripts. But St. Hilary up to his exile had never seen the creed of Nicæa !¹

The whole story illustrates the peculiar position of the vast African Church. It was regarded by the Easterns as a part of the Roman " Patriarchate " ; it has no official dealings with the East except through Rome. Yet it is not governed by Papal decretals, like Gaul and Spain, nor by a legate, like Illyricum. It has its own councils and its own customs, its own canon law. Yet this canon law is assimilated to that of the West ; and the Popes can examine it and insist upon its being in conformity with the rest of the Church. They would hardly have interfered to this extent within the Patriarchate of Alexandria, or even the more loosely governed Patriarchate of Antioch (except, perhaps, if grave injustice had ever been common). Carthage has therefore no Patriarchate, and never claimed to have one. But the African system of provincial and general councils, developed even before St. Cyprian, enabled these provinces to be self-governing, under a general supervision by the Popes. And we have seen that African councils were very jealous of this relative independence, and had no intention of being governed as Spain and Gaul and Britain were governed. But their autonomy was somewhat less than that of Ephesus or Caesarea of Cappadocia, and their relations with Rome were habitually very close and very cordial.

¹ Hil. *De synodis*, 91.

VIII

THE AGE OF JUSTINIAN

WHEN Justin the first became Emperor in 518, his elevation was shared by his nephew, Justinian. Justin was a capable soldier, but an illiterate Macedonian peasant. Justinian was a highly educated and intellectual man of 36. He was associated in the government by his uncle with successive titles, until he was made a partner in the Empire before Justin's death.

The influence of Justinian begins with the nine years of his uncle ; his autocratic rule, autocratic indeed beyond precedent, lasted 38 years. So that the "age of Justinian" lasts for 47 years, from 518 to the end of 565, when his restless activities ceased at the age of 83.

When Justin with his nephew reached the supreme power, the empire was nominally Roman, but really Byzantine, including the East without the West. The last vestiges of the Western empire had perished miserably 42 years earlier. Gaul was full of Franks, Goths and Germans. The Vandals had committed their vandalisms, and had ruled all North Africa for 100 years. They were Arian heretics, who persecuted the Catholics, or Romans, as they were called, with ferocity, and had reduced the flourishing provinces with their 500 or 600 bishoprics to ruin. The Arian Visigoths occupied Spain. Italy and Sicily nominally belonged to the Emperor, for they were governed, and indeed extremely well governed, by the Arian Gothic king at Ravenna, as a vassal of the Emperor, whose image was on his coins. The Emperor still named one of the consuls ; the Senate still sat in Rome ; the Prefects of Italy and Gaul, and all the great functionaries of State were taken from the great Roman families. But the army and its generals were always Gothic and Arian. The Emperor was a distant name. The Goths were ruled by their own laws, but governed the Romans by Roman law. Theo-

210

deric the Great really hoped they would live happily side by side.

This division of West from East had its ecclesiastical counterpart in the fact that the whole Eastern Empire was officially divided from the Western Church and from Rome at the moment of Justin's accession by the " Acacian schism."

The division arose thus. After the condemnation of the Monophysites by the Council of Chalcedon in 451, the Catholic Emperors Marcian and Leo I. had been unable to force or persuade these heretics to accept the Council and the letters of Pope Leo. Acacius, who became bishop of Constantinople in 471, suggested to the Emperor Zeno the method of " comprehensiveness " ; and the latter issued in 482 a document, known as the Henoticon of Zeno, addressed to the Christians of Egypt, which described the doctrine of the Incarnation without speaking of the Two Natures, asserted the three councils of Nicæa, Constantinople and Ephesus, and condemned anyone at Chalcedon or elsewhere who might have taught any contrary doctrine. The council of Chalcedon is simply dropped, though it remained a law of the Empire.[1]

Though the more extreme Monophysites were not conciliated by this measure, as they refused to communicate with anyone who did not reject the Council, the Patriarchs Peter Mongus of Alexandria and Peter Fullo of Antioch, who were the heads of the heresy, accepted the compromise, and communicated with Acacius. Many orthodox monks and others appealed to Rome, so far as they had the power.[2]

[1] At the end of 515 the Emperor Anastasius can write to Pope Hormisdas (who had asked that the definition of Chalcedon might be observed, *Coll. Avell.* Ep. 115) : " We are surprised that you should have written to us about the holy Fathers who assembled at Chalcedon, since their decisions have frequently been confirmed by the decrees of our predecessors, and since no other council has met by which its dispositions should be weakened, nor have we made any law, the innovations of which might annul the statutes of the aforesaid episcopal council." (*Ib. Ep.* 125). This was true in the letter, however false in the spirit.

[2] A schism of this kind involves the bishops, but not necessarily anyone else. So long as an Eastern bishop was not a Monophysite and had not condemned the Council of Chalcedon, the fact of his being willingly or unwillingly subject to a Patriarch, who was either Acacius himself or in communion with Acacius, was at least a misfortune. The monks, the laity, had no redress, nor had the clergy. Only in extraordinary cases could they write to Rome ; nor could they be bound to do so. They went on as best they could, and remained full members of the Catholic Church, whether they understood the theological or canonical questions involved or not. Even where a bishop

In 484 Pope Felix excommunicated and deposed Acacius, who retorted by removing the Pope's name from the diptychs of Constantinople.

Zeno, who had seen the decay of the Imperial power in the West, and was acknowledging the Gothic rule of Italy, cared little for communion with Rome, provided he could obtain unity of religion in his remaining dominions. The next Emperor, Anastasius, pursued the same policy; but towards the end of his reign a rebel and a rival, Vitalian, took the side of orthodoxy, and threatened Constantinople itself.

Anastasius in terror turned to Rome, and asked for a council on the subject of a new formula of union, proposed by some Scythian monks. This was in 515, after 31 years of schism; and he writes humbly to Pope Hormisdas: " Your high reputation brings back to our memory the goodness of your paternal affection, so that we ask from you what God and our Saviour taught the holy Apostles in His Divine doctrine and especially blessed Peter, in whom He constituted the strength of His Church." (*Coll. Avell. Ep.* 107). Hormisdas thereupon dispatches legates with very careful instructions and a formula of supplication to be signed by any bishops received to communion. The Roman Senate also wrote, supporting the Papal conditions.

But Vitalian was vanquished. Anastasius thrust out the legates by a back door, had them embarked on a rickety ship, with orders that no city should receive them on their return journey. He wrote to Pope Hormisdas a curt sermon on mercy and forgiveness, ending : " We can accept abuse and contempt with patience, but not commands " (*Coll. Avell. Ep.* 138).

A year later he died, July 8th, 518, in the midst of a storm of thunder and lightning. His captain of the guards, Justin, was proclaimed Emperor two days later. He was known to be orthodox; and on the following Sunday, which was Easter day, at the end of Mass in the great Church of Constantinople, the people shouted and demanded that the Patriarch John should go up into the pulpit and proclaim the council of Chalcedon, which at length he was obliged to do. On the

was manifestly a heretic, it would usually be necessary to receive the sacraments from him or his clergy, until he was convicted and deposed by authority. The same would happen in the case of an intruded bishop. In Egypt the laity themselves were ferociously heretical; and there were many heretics in Syria. But the greater part of the Eastern Empire was orthodox.

following day the enormous crowds forced him to anathematize Severus, and on the next Sunday to restore Pope Leo to the diptychs.   The acclamations to the Mother of God, to the council of Chalcedon, to the orthodox Emperor, to the former Patriarchs who had died in exile, fill many columns of print.

John was believed to have condemned the council in order to be appointed Patriarch by Anastasius, three months earlier.[1]   The enormous crowds and the enthusiasm of the populace convinced him that it paid best to be orthodox. The people of Constantinople indeed remained Catholic for centuries under the yoke of many schismatical and heretical Emperors.

A few days later, on August 1st, the Emperor wrote briefly to the Pope to announce his accession.   But on September 7th he understands the situation better, and asks the Pope to send legates for the peace of the Church.   The Patriarch John also writes to the same effect, accepting Chalcedon, and promising to restore the Pope to the diptychs.   A third letter is more to the point ; it is from the Emperor's nephew, the Count Justinian, who alone sees what is important—the faith is safe under Justin, but the name of Acacius is the difficulty.   He begs the Pope to come in person to Constantinople if possible ; for he says he is acquainted with the Pope's recent letters to the deceased Emperor and those of his predecessors.   Justinian is already well up in ecclesiastical affairs, and henceforward his letters to the Pope are more important than the official ones of his uncle.

The Papal legates, St. Germanus, Bishop of Capua, and four others, arrived at Constantinople on March 25th, 519, and were received with the highest honour.   They had very elaborate instructions from the Pope, especially to have no communication with the Patriarch or any other bishop, until he had signed the petition to the Pope which had been previously sent to the Emperor Anastasius.

This famous document, known as the " formula of Hormisdas," runs as follows :

" The first condition of salvation is to keep the rule of the true Faith, and in no way to deviate from the tradition of the

---

[1] So Cyril of Scythopolis in his life of St. Sabbas, *cap.* 56; Cotelier, *Ecclesiae Graeciae monumenta* (1686), vol. ii, p. 310.

Fathers, because the statement of our Lord Jesus Christ cannot be put aside, when He said : ' Thou art Peter, and upon this Rock I will build My Church.' *These words are proved by their result in facts*, for in the Apostolic See the Catholic religion is always preserved inviolate.

' Desiring not to fall from that faith, and following in all things the decisions of the Fathers, we anathematize all heresies, especially that of Nestorius.' [And so forth— including Acacius].

Hence we approve and embrace all the letters of blessed Leo, Pope of the city of Rome, which he wrote concerning the right Faith.

Wherefore, as we have said, following in all things the Apostolic See, we also profess all its decrees ; and for this cause, *I hope that I shall deserve to be in one communion with you*, which the Apostolic See proclaims, *in which*[1] *is the entire and perfect solidity of the Christian religion*, promising in future as to *those who are separated from the communion of the Catholic Church, that is, those who do not agree in all points with the Apostolic See*, that their names shall not be recited during the Holy Mysteries."

Notice especially in this supplication the assertion that our Lord's promise to Peter *is proved by its historical verification :* the true faith always retained without spot in the see of the Apostle, communion with which is the entire solidity—that is, the Rock foundation—of the Christian religion.

Notice, also, that Justinian knew beforehand that the Pope would send this document to be signed. He knew the tremendous claims of Popes Gelasius and Symmachus. But there was nothing in them surprising to Constantinople. It had been accustomed for centuries to accept the Papal claims and to profess the faith of Rome, whenever the emperors allowed it. The appeals from Eastern monks which had lately been forwarded to Rome were in the same strain.

The Emperor gave orders that the bishops of the Empire should obey the Pope and sign the *libellus*. The papal legates journeyed about and met with refusal and violence from the heretics. The only difficulty made by the orthodox was their unwillingness to exclude from the diptychs of their churches the names of deceased bishops, who had unavoidably been in communion with Acacius, though without approving

---

[1] The words " in which," *in qua*, probably refer to " communion " rather than to " See."

his errors: " Let your apostleship show," wrote Justinian to the Pope, " that you have worthily succeeded to the Apostle Peter, since the Lord will work through you, as Supreme Pastor, the salvation of all." The Pope admitted the plea ; but decided that each case should be inquired into by the bishop of Constantinople.[1]

[1] *Coll. Avell. Ep.* 196, July 9th, 520, Justinian to the Pope : " A part of the Easterns cannot be compelled by exiles, sword or flames to condemn the names of those who have died after Acacius ; and this difficulty causes delay to the general concord." And in another letter of September 9th, the Emperor writes very strongly (*Ep.* 232) that there are certain Churches in Pontus and Asia, and especially in the East, whose clergy and people have been threatened and persuaded, but to no purpose, to omit the names of their former bishops, for whom they have a high regard, but regard it as worse than death if they have to condemn the dead. He did not, he says, receive the *libellus*, desiring blood and executions, but for concord. He appeals for some mitigation of the Pope's severity ; " For the matter is not without a previous judgment of the Apostolic See, so that it is not so much to be called an exception as a deliberate decision : since Anastasius of religious memory, the Head of your Church, openly and clearly decided, when he wrote about this matter to our predecessor, that it was enough if those who desired peace should omit the name of Acacius only. Pope Hormisdas was obviously much afraid that toleration should thus be extended to former bishops who had actively co-operated in the schism, *Coll. Avell., Ep.* 138. He thinks it paradoxical that Christians would rather be in schism with the dead, than in unity with the living. Is it not just that those who are not moved by the Emperor's example should be subjected to his command ? Medicine is often unpleasant ; and those who are cured against their will, are benefited thereby. The Emperor must beware lest the difficulties have been raised in order to destroy the agreement. There may be cunning behind. The Pope is evidently of opinion that force should be used, as was the universal view of his age, supposing there was a real opposition to the reunion on the part of those who were secretly heretical. But he concludes with a reasonable moderation. He has been moved, he says, by the envoys, who urged that indulgence must be had to those who were innocent or ignorant of the question. (It seems that the Papal legates had been insisting that the names of all bishops deceased during the schism must be omitted from the diptychs of their Churches ; whereas many of them, perhaps most, must have hated the schism, though they could do nothing against it.) The Pope adds that he is writing to the new Patriarch Epiphanius to receive to communion those whom he thought worthy, or innocent of communion with Acacius, *libelli tamen tenore seruato*. The letter to Epiphanius tells him to " put on our person " to decide these matters, and to inform the Apostolic See of the names of those he has reconciled, giving also the words of their *libellus*, since in every case the profession is to be *eodem tenore conscripta*. (*Ep.* 237, 17). The interposition of Justin and Justinian was justified ; but the Pope knew it was partly due to the riots that the heretics had caused in some places ; and the severity he recommends was made necessary by the same disorders. He was determined that no deceased bishop, who had been wilfully and knowingly in communion with heretics, should be commemorated in the diptychs.

It is well known that Protestant and Gallican writers have represented this formula as imposed by force upon the independent East, and deeply resented. This is pure imagination. The Monophysite bishops, of course, refused the formula, because they were heretics, and not because they objected to dictation from Rome. On the part of the orthodox who signed, *we do not hear of any difficulty whatever being raised on the score of Papal pretensions.* That the Pope must define the faith—that the tradition of Rome was without spot— was the belief of the Easterns before and after. The orthodox had groaned under Zeno and Anastasius, in their forcible separation from the centre of Catholic Communion. Now they rejoiced, prelates and people alike.

The total result was that about two thousand five hundred bishops signed the *libellus, without alteration,* and sent the copies to Rome.[1]

Thus the first use by Justinian of his influential position was to reunite the East to the West by the profession of the faith of Peter, much as Theodosius the Great had done 140 years before. A copy of the *libellus* and the news of its signature was sent by the Pope to the Latin countries, and the bishops wrote him congratulatory letters.

Justinian was already a theologian, and in this same year interested himself in the formula put forward under Anastasius by the Scythian monks : " One of the Trinity suffered." In any orthodox mouth this would mean " suffered in His Human Nature," but a Monophysite would mean " suffered in His One Nature, Divino-Human Nature," or even in a " Theopaschite " sense. It would not do as a formula of union on account of its ambiguity. The persistent monks worried Justinian, as they worried the Popes. He writes to Rome for a decision, " For we believe to be Catholic that which shall have been intimated to us in your religious reply " (*Ep.* 188). At first against the monks, he becomes doubtful, and at length is quite sure the Pope ought to approve it.

In the year 526 King Theoderic obliged Pope John I. to proceed to Constantinople in order to induce the Emperor to reopen the Arian Churches in the East and for other business. He made the journey, though sick and infirm, accompanied by three ex-consuls and a Patricius. The Greeks rejoiced

---

[1] So Rusticus, the deacon and nephew of Pope Vigilius, a few years later, *P.L.* 67. 1251-2 ; Mansi viii. 579.

that " for the first time since the Empire was Christian, now in the days of Justin, the Eastern portion had merited to receive the Vicar of the Apostle Peter." The whole city came as far as the 15th milestone, with candles and crosses in honour of the blessed Apostles Peter and Paul. The Emperor prostrated himself to the earth, and received John " as though he were Peter in person." The Pope was given a throne on the right hand side of the great church, and sang the Mass in Latin, and crowned the Emperor, though he had reigned already eight years.[1] On the return of John to Ravenna, he was imprisoned by Theoderic, who had recently murdered Boethius and Symmachus. John died in a few days and is venerated by the Catholic Church as a saint and a martyr.

About this time Justinian married the famous Theodora, of whom Procopius tells such terrible tales in his Secret History. Was it true that her previous life had been infamous, and that on the throne she was unscrupulous and ruthless ? Was her palace built upon dungeons and oubliettes ? Is this history or pure fiction ? Or is it just the tittle-tattle of the court, having some basis in fact ? For our present purpose this does not matter. We know at least that, though nominally a Catholic, she protected and favoured the Monophysites. Justinian loved her devotedly till her death in 548. He trusted her judgment, and seldom acted without consulting her, even stating this in his laws. Magnificent and luxurious, of small stature but very beautiful, she had the heart and courage of a man ; and in the revolt of the city, when the factions of the Hippodrome, the Blues and the Greens, had united against Justinian, it was her courage which saved the Emperor and the Empire.

On August 1st, 527, Justin died, and Justinian reigned alone. He was now forty-five years of age.

Justinian was of middle height, of good features. His manners were full of graciousness and charm. (We must remember that all who approached the Emperor and Empress prostrated themselves.) He often showed remarkable clemency to opponents. He was kind to the poor and the distressed, though like other autocrats he was sometimes cruel, sometimes over-indulgent to favourites, and necessarily at times suspicious of his most loyal servants. Very dignified,

---

[1] This account is combined from the *Liber Pontificalis*, the so-called *Chronicon Valesii* (probably Maximus, Bishop of Ravenna) and the *Chronicon Marcellini* (in Mommsen's *Chronica Minora*).

he never deigned to show anger. He ate little, chiefly veget-
ables, and drank no wine. On the first two days of Lent he
touched no food, and fasted rigorously the rest of that holy
season. He worked half the night and rose with the dawn.

By this hard work he was able to direct minutely the
administration of an immense empire ; to draw out campaigns
for generals in countries he had never seen, or to issue rules
for the exact observance of monks and nuns ; to reform abuses
down to the smallest detail, or to regulate the etiquette of the
court, or decide on questions of Christian doctrine.

His love for absolute authority in the smallest matters
lasted his life. But towards the end of his reign his energy
slackened, either from old age or from the effects of the plague
from which he suffered in 542, or from the loss of Theodora's
virile influence in 548, or from all these causes ; and the
weakness and indecision which accompanied his intellectual
gifts became apparent.

Soon after his accession he took·in hand the great work by
which his name will always be famous, the codification of
Roman law. Theodosius the second had made a collection
of his own laws in the previous century ; but Justinian was
the first to make a complete code in order of subjects, accompanied by a Digest of all the commentaries of the great jurists
of former times, and by a manual of legal studies called the
" Institute." This tremendous work was hurriedly and
inaccurately performed by a committee under Trebonian.
The code took only a year, the Digest only three years to
compose. But it has saved for us fragments of legal writings
which would otherwise have been totally lost, and it is complete enough to have served as the basis of all European law
for fourteen centuries.

In the Code the first place is naturally given to the ecclesiastical laws. Section 1 of the first book begins with the title :
" Of the Supreme Trinity and the Catholic Faith." The
first law is that of Gratian and Theodosius in 380 which declares
" We will that all the peoples under our sway shall hold the
faith delivered to the Romans by the Apostle Peter, which he
still preserves there."[1] The next three laws are of 381, 448
and 452, enforcing the councils of Nicæa, Ephesus and
Chalcedon respectively. Then follow three laws of Justinian
himself as to the faith ; the eighth and last law of this section

[1] See above p. 15.

is a letter of Pope John II., embodying and approving a letter from the Emperor.

This alone is an extraordinary fact. No other laws are known to Imperial days than edicts of Emperors. Every other law in the codex of Justinian is an edict of his own, or of some former Emperor. The only exception is this letter of a Pope.

This epistle concerned the monks of Constantinople known as ἀκοίμητοί Acoemetenses, whose monastery had been faithful to Rome throughout the Acacian schism, and had been able to send valuable information to previous Popes. The Monophysites now accused them of secret Nestorianism. They angered Justinian especially by refusing to accept the formula of the Scythian monks, which he had been persuading the Pope to approve.

Hence the Emperor took it upon himself to denounce them as heretics (without naming them) in an edict to the people of Constantinople on March 15th, 533, adding an explanation of the true faith. The monks sent two of their number to Rome to appeal to John II. The Emperor, eleven days later, addressed to the Patriarch Euphemius another condemnation with a similar definition of faith, and assertion of the four General Councils. The commencement of this letter is important, as it became a law of the state, the seventh in the codex. After explaining the state of affairs, the Emperor says :

" We have issued an imperial edict, with which you are acquainted, refuting the madness of the heretics, having altered and altering nothing of the state of the Church as it exists by God's grace up till now, as your Blessedness is aware, but in all things preserving the union of the Holy Churches with the most blessed Pope and Patriarch of elder Rome, to whom we are writing to the same effect. For we do not suffer that anything concerning the condition of the Church should not be brought before his Blessedness, *as being the Head of all the most holy Priests of God,* and because as often as in these parts heretics have arisen, it is by the sentence and just judgment of that venerable See that they have been brought to naught."

To the Pope he wrote on June 6th :

"Ascribing to the Apostolic See and to your Holiness that honour which has always been, and is, our desire, honouring your Blessedness as a Father, *we hasten to bring all that concerns the state of the Church to the knowledge of your Holiness ;* for we have always had a great desire that unity with your Apostolic See and the state of the Churches may be preserved as it is at present without any impediment ; and for this reason we hastened both *to subject* and to unite all the bishops of the whole East to the See of your Holiness. And at the present time, therefore, though the matters in question here are plain and undoubted, and are firmly held and taught by all the bishops according to the teaching of your Apostolic See, we have thought it necessary that they should be brought to the knowledge of your Holiness. *For we do not permit any question which is raised in ecclesiastical matters, however manifest and certain, not to be made known to your Holiness, the Head of all the Churches.* For in all things, as we have said, we are in haste that the honour and authority of your See shall increase."

Justinian then exposes the case as in his edicts, and concludes :

" We therefore beg of your Fatherly affection, to send letters to us, and to the most holy bishop of this City, the Patriarch, your brother (since he also has written by the same messengers to your Holiness, hastening to follow in all things the Apostolic See of your Blessedness), and to inform us that your Holiness receives all those who rightly confess what we have written, and condemns the unfaith of those who have dared Judaically to deny the right faith.

For thus the love of all for you and the authority of your See will grow (*reading* crescet), and the union of the holy Churches with you will be preserved undisturbed, when all the most blessed bishops have learnt from you the pure doctrine of your Holiness with regard to these matters."

The letter was carried by the bishops of Ephesus and Philippi.

The Pope writes back praising the Emperor's devotion to the Apostolic See, to whose author the Lord said : " Feed my sheep," since the regulations of the fathers, the statutes of princes, declared it to be the head of all the churches. John has interrogated the monks ; they have refused to submit, and he has excommunicated them. He confirms the edict of Justinian. This is the Papal letter which is unique as having become an edict of the code, including, as it does, the Emperor's letter to which it replies.

Unfortunately under Justinian the administration was not so good as the laws. Trebonian himself, John the Cappadocian still more, and many others, were rapacious and cruel. Justinian himself, always in want of money for his enormous enterprises, is said to have sold places in his government against his own strict laws.

But his plans were amazing in their breadth. He intended nothing less than the reconquest of the whole Roman Empire; Italy and Sicily he took by the brilliant victories of Belisarius; he lost then again by the vigour of the Gothic Totila, and again reconquered them by the genius of Narses. A great part of Roman Africa, though not the two Mauretanias, was subdued by Belisarius from the Vandals, lost in a revolt, and reconquered. A part only of Spain was recovered, and no expeditions to Gaul and Germany and Britain ever became possible. The defensive wars in the East were frequently disastrous. Antioch was lost, for a time, in 540. These wars were cut short by unsuccessful treaties, in order that the Western wars might be prosecuted. The Huns and Slavs from the North were again and again not far from threatening Constantinople itself.

Thus the accomplishment was not equal to the immensity of the plan. But it was astonishing in itself. Justinian had begun as Emperor of the East, he died Emperor of the West as well. Yet Rome had been emptied by Totila, and had lain 40 days without an inhabitant ; and after Justinian's death the Lombards overran the Italian peninsula and wiped out his work.

But his idea was yet more grandiose than all this. For Justinian, his Empire meant Christianity and the faith of St. Peter. It was above all from Arian domination, in his view, that he was freeing Italy and Africa and Spain. Far better than these wars, were his engagements and treaties with many barbarian tribes, who had settled round the Black Sea, or threatened the north of Thrace ; in these cases he attained by fighting or diplomacy their conversion to the Christian religion.[1] I think it can hardly be doubted that his piety was the mainspring of his actions and his policy. He felt himself to be the Vicegerent of the Almighty to rule the

[1] Such as the Tzaunes, Abasges, some of the Heruli and of the Huns. Also in Africa some Berber tribes behind Tripoli.

world and bring it all to the service of Christ.   His wars were holy wars.   In later centuries a Byzantine battle began like a church ceremony.   Even in the sixth century every enterprise was consecrated by religion.

He was well aware that judicious persecution is a great help towards conversion !   He had, however, witnessed the unsuccessful attempts of Anastasius for conciliation.   He strengthened the existing laws against pagans, Jews and heretics.   After two years of reign he closed the famous University of Athens, and the heathen professors fled to Persia ; but the Persian king obliged Justinian to receive them back.   Pagans are all to go to church with their families, and to be instructed.   On their refusal they will lose all right of possessing, and suffer penury, as well as due punishment.   To offer a heathen sacrifice is a capital crime.   The Manichaeans or Borbonitae are to be put to death.   Many were burnt at Constantinople after the Emperor had made vain attempts to convince them.   John of Ephesus, though a Monophysite, was employed in this apostolate.   He boasts that in 546 he gained 70,000 pagans in Asia Minor, including nobles and rhetoricians and physicians, and many at Constantinople. Tortures discovered these men, and scourgings and imprisonment induced them to accept instruction and baptism.   A Patricius, named Phocas, hearing that he had been denounced, took poison.   The Emperor ordered that he should be buried as an ass is buried.   The pious Emperor paid all the expenses of this Christian mission, and gave to each of the 70,000 Asiatics the white garments for their baptism and a piece of money.

Jews were tolerated, but they could not hold magistracies, nor possess Christian slaves, nor go to law against a Christian. The Samaritans, however, could not inherit nor bequeath, nor have synagogues.   Many of them were in reality pagans or Manichaeans.   In 529 they revolted and devastated Palestine. An army repressed them, massacred them, or sold them as slaves, unless they submitted to baptism.   But they still remained Samaritans, and the laws against them were twenty years later reduced.

In 551 John of Asia burnt the chief church of the Montanists in Phrygia, together with the bones of the prophets Montanus, Maximilla and Priscilla.   The Montanists, in 529, had burnt themselves in their own churches.   Other heretics were given three months' grace.   All magistrates and soldiers had to swear that they were Catholics.

Arians had to be spared at first for fear of reprisals by the Goths. But in 533 Justinian attacked the Vandals in Africa, and in 535 the Ostrogoths of Italy. After victory their churches were taken away ; they were forbidden to hold any public offices. Services were forbidden them, and baptism. Their importance as conquerors disappeared and their sects faded away.

The severity of these measures was not equal in all places ; and in the latter part of Justinian's reign more tolerance was allowed, by weakness, not on principle.

One heresy, however, had a special position. Monophysitism had been practically on a level with the orthodox faith under Zeno and Anastasius. It occupied all Egypt. Its chief leader, Severus of Antioch, was the ablest and most voluminous controversialist of his day. Historians like Zacharias and John ; learned Aristotelians like the Tritheists ; men of energy like Jacob Baradai ; these were but a few of its eminent men. Its strength was in the countries where Coptic and Syriac were spoken. Justin did not at first venture to persecute, only to dethrone the heretical bishops. In 533 Justinian held at Constantinople a conference between six orthodox and six Monophysite bishops. He must have enjoyed the discussions, and the flattery which accompanied them.

In 535 a new Patriarch of Constantinople, Anthimus, showed himself to be a Monophysite, and was found to have sent secret letters of communion to heretical leaders. His appointment was said to be due to the Empress Theodora. The deposed Patriarch of Antioch, Severus, actually visited Constantinople. Riots by the Catholic people ensued. Appeal was made by the monks of the city to Pope Agapetus.

It so happened that the Gothic king Theodatus was sending the Pope as his envoy to the Emperor as his only hope of inducing Justinian to make peace. For Belisarius was now destroying the Gothic rule, and accused Theodatus of having murdered Queen Amalasuntha, daughter of Theoderic the Great.

Pope Agapetus was received by Justinian " *cum gloria.*" He was a man of learning and sanctity, of the same great Roman family as Felix III. and St. Gregory later. The *Liber Pontificalis* relates an interview with the Emperor. The Pope refused to communicate with the Patriarch. Justinian exclaims : " Either you consent to us, or I shall have you carried into exile." The Pope replied with joy : " I,

sinner that I am, desired to come to the most Christian
Emperor Justinian ; and I find Diocletian. But I do not
fear your threats." He added : " That you may know that
you are not a Christian, let your bishop confess two Natures
in Christ." The Patriarch Anthimus is sent for ; and in
answer to all the Pope's questions refused always to admit
the two Natures. Thereupon we are told, " Justinian
Augustus, filled with joy, humbled himself before the Apostolic See, and adored the blessed Pope Agapetus."

But something more was needed. Justinian had supported
this heretic ; and he had to sign the same *libellus* which under
Pope Hormisdas he had ordered all the bishops of the East to
accept and send to Rome. A great humiliation for the
Emperor. The Pope was taken ill a few days later, and died.
His body was taken back to Rome in a leaden coffin and
buried in St. Peter's.

Agapetus had summarily deposed Anthimus as having been
translated from the See of Trapezus contrary to the canons.
The new patriarch, Menas, held a great council after the
Pope's death, to try the question of heresy. At this council
the bishops who had accompanied the Pope were present ;
and also the famous deacon Pelagius, afterwards Pope
Pelagius I., whom Agapitus had appointed his nuncio for
Constantinople. The acts of the council are extant, and
supply many interesting points of evidence as to the devotion
of the East to the Roman See.

The rage of Theodora at this triumph of Roman orthodoxy
over her conspiracy to restore heresy and the Henoticon may
easily be imagined. The death of Pope Agapetus was
regarded by her party as a judgment of God. She continued
to protect Anthimus in secret, and determined to engineer
the election of a Pope who would restore the heretical
Patriarch, and depose Menas. The Roman deacon Vigilius
was at Constantinople with Pope Agapetus when the latter
died. Theodora gained him by promising her influence to
elect him Pope, while he on his part led her to believe that he
entered into her views. He cannot have intended in reality
to restore Anthimus and communicate with Severus or
approve the Henoticon ; for no Pope could possibly thus
reverse the decisions of his predecessors or run counter to the
unanimity of the whole West and half the East. But Theodora was a woman, and believed all was possible to her
autocratic will.

At any rate, on the return of Vigilius to Rome, he found a
new Pope had been already installed in June, Silverius, a
subdeacon only, of the Roman Church, but eminent as the
son of the great Pope Hormisdas. The *Liber Pontificalis*
declares that the Gothic king Theodatus forced this election
upon the Romans by corruption and threats ; but this is not
supported by any other authorities, and is probably exaggerated.

It was at this moment that Justinian began his wars for
the recovery of Italy. Belisarius entered Rome in December
and Silverius advised the Romans to make no useless resistance. Antonina, the wife of the great general, was the friend
and the tool of the Empress Theodora. The story told by
the *Liber Pontificalis*, supplemented by Liberatus of Carthage,
is as follows :

Theodora wrote to the new Pope that he must come in
person to Constantinople to restore Anthimus. Silverius, on
receipt of the letter, groaned and exclaimed : " Now I know
that this matter has brought an end to my life." He wrote
back : " Never will I do such a thing as restore a heretic who
has been condemned in his wickedness." Theodora sent
letters by Vigilius to Belisarius, saying : " Find some occasion
against Silverius and depose him ; or at least send him to us.
Herewith you have our most dear deacon Vigilius, who has
promised to recall the Patriarch Anthimus."

Belisarius said : " I will obey the mandate ; but whoever
is concerned in the murder of Pope Silverius will have to give
an account to our Lord Jesus Christ."

False witnesses were suborned. Silverius was said to have
written to the king of the Goths to come to the Asinarian
gate, and the Pope would deliver to him the city and Belisarius. Silverius took refuge at the Church of St. Sabina.
He was induced to visit Belisarius, whose stepson, Photius,
son of Antonina, swore that he would be safe. On the second
visit to the general's palace on the Pincian, the clergy who
accompanied him were kept back at the first or the second
curtain. Silverius and Vigilius went within alone, and found
Antonina in bed, and Belisarius sitting at her feet. When
Antonina saw him she cried out : " What have we done to
you, Pope Silverius, that you should wish to betray us to the
Goths ? " As she spoke, the subdeacon John entered and
stripped off the Pope's pallium, and taking him into a bed-
room, undressed him and put on him the habit of a monk.

The subdeacon Xystus, seeing him thus, went out and announced to the crowd : " The Lord Pope is deposed and has become a monk " ; and all those who heard this fled.   So far the tales which have come down to us.

Silverius appeared no more ; but was secretly conveyed out of the city and banished to Patara in Lycia.

But the bishop of that city was horrified, and repaired without delay to the Emperor, appealing to the judgment of God at the expulsion of the bishop of this great See, saying that " *in the world there are many kings, but there is none like that Pope who is over the Church of the whole world,* but is now expelled from his See."

This declaration of a bishop of Asia Minor in 537 astonishes us to-day, because we have been so long fed with Protestant and Gallican fables about the anti-papalism of the Eastern Church.   But in the sixth century it was normal.   Justinian listened.   Till then he had believed the reports from Rome, and the lies of his wife.   He now ordered the Pope to be taken back to Rome, and a trial to be held.   If he was proved to have written the traitorous letters he should live as a bishop in any city, but if they were shown to be forgeries he must be restored to his See.

Silverius had been deposed on May 11th, 537, after a year of reign.   He had not even reached his place of exile, when on the 29th of the same month, Vigilius attained his ambition and was elected Pope by order of Belisarius, who cowed the Roman clergy, Silverius being regarded as deposed by his imprisonment.

The Romans were shocked, believing Vigilius to be answerable for the accusations against Silverius.   They appealed to the Emperor, alleging that Vigilius in a fury had aimed a blow at a notary, who fell down and expired at his feet ; that having given his niece in marriage to the consul Asterius, he had caused him to be beaten to death.

Meanwhile Silverius had been brought back to Italy, and Vigilius in terror appealed to Belisarius, " Give up Silverius to me, or I cannot fulfil my promises."   The unfortunate Pope was seized by the servants of Vigilius and carried to the island of Palmaria, where he died, as it was believed, of starvation, in June of the year (as it seems) 538.

Now all this history is told us by contemporaries biased against Vigilius.   The events related were largely secret and unlikely to be divulged.   What Vigilius promised to Theodora we can never know ; nor how far he was personally responsible for the death of Silverius. We hear that miracles took place at the tomb of the unfortunate son of St. Hormisdas. Since the 11th century his name has been in the list of Saints, and he is commemorated each year in the Missal and Breviary as a martyr.

As for Vigilius, the letter which Liberatus says he sent secretly to communicate with Anthimus, Severus and Theodosius, and to condemn the two Natures and the Council of Chalcedon, is an unblushing forgery. It may also be untrue that Belisarius asked him for 200 pieces of gold which he had promised, and that he refused. It is certain that during the seventeen years of his shameful pontificate he was perfectly orthodox. Theodora had gained nothing.

While the Empress was thus attempting to get Papal authority to tolerate the Monophysites, her husband was beginning severe measures. From the moment of the deposition of Anthimus in 536 he concerted with the Roman deacon Pelagius the substitution of orthodox bishops for heretics, even in Egypt, where the people were all fanatical against the Council of Chalcedon. According to the exaggerated story of John of Ephesus, the Patriarch of Antioch, Ephrem, expelled all Monophysite monks in Armenia and Mesopotamia, and ordained a death penalty against any who gave them shelter ; the heretics were publicly scourged, tortured or burnt. John of Tella, who boasted of making 170,000 converts to heresy, was killed in 538. An Egyptian monk called Paul of Tabenna was chosen by the nuncio Pelagius as orthodox Patriarch of Alexandria. But after three years, about 541-2, Pelagius had to sit with the Patriarchs of Antioch and Jerusalem and others in a council at Gaza to depose him as privy to the murder of a deacon ; they substituted Zoilus to his lofty position.

All this time Theodora was harbouring the exiled bishops secretly in her palace, whence apostles went to Nubia and Mesopotamia, and whence she supplied consecrators to renew the Monophysite hierarchy which was dying out. In 545, nine years after the death of Agapetus, the Monophysites had but three sees in their possession. But James Baradai consecrated in various provinces twenty-seven bishops and more than 100,000 priests and deacons, and gave his name to the sect.

About the year 543 Justinian made another incursion into

theology. It was unfortunately a recognized custom that emperors should make laws against heretics, and describe the heresy in the law. Justinian went further. He issued an edict describing and refuting at length the errors of Origen, appending a series of canons under anathema, with an anathema to Origen himself, though he had died a member of the Catholic Church.

But the decree was apparently prompted by the Papal nuncio, Pelagius. It was subsequently—not previously—accepted by a local council, and sent to Pope Vigilius, who approved it.

The growth of Caesaro-papism is apparent, and danger was coming.

Two Origenist monks had been favourites at court and had received two of the greatest sees : Domitian that of Ancyra, Theodore Askidas that of Caesarea in Cappodocia. As a counterblast to the condemnation of Origen they urged that of Theodore, bishop of Mopsuestia, who had been the precursor of Nestorius, having died before the condemnation of Nestorianism by the council of Ephesus in 431. To his name were joined those of Ibas of Edessa, whose somewhat Nestorianizing letter to Maris had been read at the council of Chalcedon without disapproval, and of Theodoret, bishop of Cyrus, the great commentator and historian, who had been received by that council and by Pope Leo as orthodox. It was urged that one of the chief grievances against Chalcedon at the conference in 533 had been its approval of Ibas and Theodoret. Extracts were made from Theodore, Ibas and Theodoret—all clearly Nestorian as they stood without explanation. These became famous as the " Three Chapters."

Justinian wrote a letter, now lost, to the five Patriarchs, condemning the Three Chapters, in 544, adding an anathema to anyone who should say this condemnation showed any disrespect for the council of Chalcedon.

The Patriarch Menas at first refused to sign this edict. He did so under pressure ; and the Emperor promised to restore him his signature if the Pope should refuse to sign ; the bishops present then consented with difficulty to sign also. The Patriarch of Jerusalem signed, after a public protest. The Patriarch of Antioch refused, and then signed to avoid being deposed. The Patriarch of Alexandria signed, and sent a message to the Pope to say that he had been forced to sign though he disapproved.

These four Patriarchs were cowards; but they were orthodox; for the Three Chapters as they stood deserved condemnation. It was the obvious disrespect to Chalcedon and the agreement with the heretics which rightly alarmed them, besides the condemnation of bishops who had died in Catholic Communion—more especially of Theodoret, who had repented his first attacks on St. Cyril, had accepted the council of Ephesus, and had been accepted by that of Chalcedon.

The whole of the Western episcopate was solid against the Emperor. Italy, in spite of the war with Totila, was nominally his, and so was the greater part of Africa. Vigilius thus supported, refused to sign. Justinian ordered him to be brought to Constantinople. He was seized in the Church of St. Cecilia and put on board a ship. The crowd asked his blessing, to which they cried " Amen." Then they pelted him with stones and sticks and crockery, shouting : " Thy famine be with thee : thy plague be with thee : thou hast done evil to the Romans. Mayest thou find evil where thou goest."

Vigilius was delayed in Sicily for a great part of a year. Thence he sent a fleet laden with corn to alleviate the sufferings of the Romans, with a bishop, Valentinus; but the Goths seized the ships at Ostia and Totila cut off the hands of the bishop. Pelagius arrived from Constantinople with great wealth and distributed his riches with generosity. He attempted in person to gain an armistice from Totila, but failed, and the siege of Rome began. Totila later sent Pelagius as ambassador to Constantinople, where we shall meet him again.

Vigilius arrived at Constantinople on January 25th, 547. The Emperor came to meet him ; " they kissed with tears." The people sang before the Pope " *Ecce uenit Dominator Dominus* " as he proceeded to the new Church of St. Sophia. Vigilius had already disapproved the signature of Menas and had commended Dacius, bishop of Milan, who was residing in the capital, for having broken off communion with the Patriarch.

After a year and four months of resistance the Pope had changed his mind, whether, as was reported, owing to threats, or violence, or bribes, or, as he himself said, because of further study. He issued a decision, the *Judicatum*, now lost. He would not degrade his office by approving the Emperor's definition of faith ; but he condemned the Three Chapters in moderate terms. The Emperor is delighted. But the Pope finds himself in union with the Easterns, whose reluctant signatures he had condemned, and forsaken by his own Western Church, and even by his own deacons.

The deacon Pelagius appealed to the opinion of the famous canonist, Ferrandus of Carthage, disciple of the great St. Fulgentius. Ferrandus, before his death, made a reply which expresses the common view of the Westerns :

He takes for granted that the condemnation of the Three Chapters involves a partial revision of the Council of Chalcedon : " Respect," he thinks, " will be lost for the venerable Council confirmed without any doubt in all the Churches of East and West for so very many years." Every part of the Council is true : " There, by its legates, was present the Apostolic See, which holds the Primacy over the universal Church. There were the pontiffs of venerable Sees, wise as serpents, simple as doves, and innumerable shepherds of lesser cities." He argues " If the decrees of the council of Chalcedon are reconsidered, let us ponder whether those of Nicæa will not be in the same danger. Universal councils, especially those which have received the assent of the Roman Church, have authority next after the canonical Scriptures."

The Illyrian and Dalmatian Churches refused with Africa to accept the *Judicatum*. Vigilius wrote a long letter to Gaul to defend it.

Two years after the *Judicatum*, the Pope, still in detention at Constantinople, feared a division of the Church. He withdrew this solemn decision. The many bishops present in the city and the local clergy came to him in the Palace of Placidia, and he forbade, under pain of excommunication, any action to be taken as to the Three Chapters, until a General Council should meet. After this, on August 14th, 550, he fled to the Church of St. Peter in Hormisda, and there renewed his order. The Praetor came with armed men in battle array to the Church and dragged the Pope by his legs from the altar, which would have fallen upon him had not his clergy held it up.

The Pope returned to the Palace of Placidia rather than be dragged thither by force ; and he made the Emperor swear to do him no further harm. But he suffered intolerable things, he says, and was in continual danger. He managed to escape at night on December 23rd, and crossing the Bosphorus, took sanctuary opposite in the famous pilgrimage Church of St. Euphemia, in which the Council of Chalcedon had been held just a hundred years before. Here the Emperor could not touch him without seeming to the world to be intentionally violating that Council, as he was accused by East and West of doing.

The Patriarchs of Alexandria and Antioch, on hearing of the Pope's change of mind, withdrew the signatures they had given to the Emperor's edict. Justinian deposed them. The chief focus of opposition was in newly reconquered Africa. The primate of Carthage was therefore accused of treason and a new one created.

Justinian now justified himself by a new edict, called a " Confession of Faith," at the end of which the Three Chapters are again condemned. Vigilius thereupon retaliated by excommunicating any bishop who should accept it. The bishop of Milan denounced it, in the name of his own province, and of Gaul, Spain and North Italy.

The Pope was ill but safe. On February 5th, 552, he issued an encyclical : " Vigilius, bishop of the Catholic Church, to all the people of God," describing bitterly the ill-treatment he had undergone, and explaining the excommunication against any who should touch the question of the Three Chapters until a common deliberation. This public complaint was a grave blow to Justinian. But the Pope at the same time published the excommunication of Theodore Askidas, which he had held over for nearly six months. He recited the repeated delinquencies of Theodore, his frequent promises of reform, declaring him the author of the condemnation of the Three Chapters, which was a matter only for bishops, to whom our Lord gave the power of binding and loosing. Together with Theodore, the Patriarch Menas is also excommunicated ; " *with all his metropolitans and micropolitans and any other* bishops of the East who have joined in the prevarication of Theodore," " *in the person of and by the authority of St. Peter the Apostle, whose place we hold, though unworthy,*" Dacius of Milan and twelve other bishops of the West joined in signing this document, which was actually posted up in the churches and public places of Constantinople.

The effect of the Pope's belated boldness was electric ; Justinian was nonplussed. The Pope would not quit the sanctuary nor trust his oaths. The Patriarch Menas, together with the metropolitans of Ephesus, Cæsarea (that is Theodore himself), and many others, having incurred excommunication, came across the Bosphorus and presented to the Pope a petition more searching and humiliating than the *formula* of Hormisdas. They begin by accepting the four general councils, especially Ephesus and Chalcedon, at which the Popes had presided by their legates.

" And we promise that we will follow throughout and in detail whatever is contained in all the acts of the Council of Chalcedon and of the other aforesaid synods, *according as it is written in the four synods, in common consent with the legates and Vicars of the Apostolic See (in whom on each respective occasion the blessed Popes of Elder Rome, your Holiness's predecessors presided), defined, or judged or constituted or disposed, whether as to faith or to any other cases, judgments, constitutions, or dispositions, immovably, inviolably, irreprehensibly, irreformably, without addition or imminution* . . . and so forth. . . .

Whatever things were there said by common consent with the legates and Vicars of the Apostolic orthodox See, these we venerate and receive as orthodox.

Whatever they anathematized or condemned, that we anathematize and we condemn ; and we preserve all irreformably and unchangeably as, by the aforesaid councils in common consent with the Vicars of the Apostolic See, they are read to have been judged or defined or constituted or disposed.

And we promise that we will in all things follow and observe also the letters of Pope Leo of blessed memory, *and the constitutions of the Apostolic See which have been published whether as to the faith or the confirmation of the aforesaid councils.*

Against the constitution of the pious Emperor and of your Holiness, in the recent case of the Three Chapters, I have made no *libellus* ; but I will and I consent that any such documents should be restored to your Blessedness.

With regard to the insults inflicted on your Blessedness and to your See, I did not commit them ; but because it is right to hasten for peace in all ways, I ask pardon, as though I had committed them."

Thus each of the chief bishops of the East has to lick the very dust, before a Pope who has been insulted by the civil power, is in sanctuary for safety, has personally no good character, is not obviously in the right, and has already twice contradicted himself. Such is still the prestige in the East of the See of Peter, even in an unworthy representative.

Menas died almost immediately. His successor, Epiphanius, and the new Patriarchs of Alexandria and Antioch and the

Metropolitan and Papal Vicar of Thessalonica, and other bishops who had not sent in the former *libellus*, gave in another, less legal in form, but equally humble, in which they " accept and embrace the letters of the Apostolic See of Rome." They beg for a conference under the presidency of the Pope.

The Pope then demanded to be allowed to go to Italy, or at least return to Sicily, in order to consult, "according to custom," the bishops of the West before the council. Justinian refused. He then demanded that at any rate as many Westerns as Easterns should sit in the council. Again Justinian was obdurate. So, when the council assembled at last on May 5th, 553, the Pope refused to come, and sent no legates.

In the eight and a half years since Vigilius had left Italy, many bishops had died there, and none had been appointed in his absence. Gaul and Spain could send no representatives to the council. The Illyrian bishops refused to appear, regarding Vigilius as an antipope. From Africa only those could come whom the Emperor approved as on his side. The Western bishops who were with the Pope at Constantinople stayed away.

The council contained in consequence only 25 Latin bishops, against 131 Easterns. Eutychius of Constantinople presided, in the absence of legates.

The Emperor sent a letter in which he posed as a defender of the Faith, like Constantine, Theodosius, Marcian and Leo ; he boasted of the reunion he had accomplished after the Acacian schism, and demanded the condemnation of the Three Chapters, which Pope Vigilius had, he said, repeatedly condemned since he came to Constantinople. The bishops, however, began by reading aloud the humble petitions they had sent to the Pope, and the reply of Vigilius to the Patriarchs, agreeing to a conference about the Three Chapters.

The Patriarchs and principal bishops thereupon made a solemn procession to the Pope, to beg him to come and preside. He replied that he was too ill, but would give an answer next day. But even then he declared that the Eastern bishops outnumbered the Western, and proposed a conference of the patriarchs only, each bringing one bishop. Finally he promised to issue a writing within twenty days ; if he failed to do this, he would agree to whatever the Council decided.

The Council therefore met in several sessions, in which a great quantity of documents were read.

Meanwhile Vigilius, in spite of illness, had drawn up a decree, or *Constitutum*, a very fine piece of theology. He refused to condemn the persons of Ibas, Theodoret or Theodore of Mopsuestia, but he does condemn 60 propositions taken from the writings of the latter.

By the authority of the Apostolic See, he forbids anyone to speak, write or publish anything contrary to this Constitution, but threatens no penalty. Sixteen Western bishops, who abstained from the Council, signed the document.

The Pope asked three bishops and four great functionaries to inform the Emperor that his answer was ready. They replied that, if it was addressed to the council, they would treat him as Head, Father and Primate : " But if it is to the Emperor, you have your own messengers."

The Emperor refused to look at the document, saying : " If it condemns the Three Chapters, it is useless, as the Pope has already condemned them. If it defends them, then he is contradicting himself." Thus the Pope's decision never came before the Council at all.

The Emperor sent to the Council three letters of Vigilius in which he had defended his original *Judicatum*, and two confessions of faith in which he had anathematized Theodore, Ibas and Theodoret, and a written oath, signed by Theodore Askidas and the patrician Cethegus, that he would condemn them. This last was doubtless believed in by Justinian ; but it had evidently been invented by Askidas and the patrician, as they carelessly dated their signature on the day after Vigilius had taken refuge in the Church of St. Peter in Hormisda. The Emperor also sent a dissertation proving that the Pope, by changing his mind, had now excommunicated himself.[1] The Council, of course, could not have done so.

This is at least amusing. The Pope had excommunicated

---

[1] *Mansi*, vol. ix, col. 366. But this addition to the seventh session was not printed before Hardouin. It is not in the ordinary MSS., but is given by Hardouin and Mansi from the longer Paris MS., which seems to give an unabridged form of the Acts. But this particular document is dated July 14th, whereas the seventh session was on June 3rd (!) and the eighth and last on June 2nd according to the same MS. The real dates appear to be the seventh session on May (26th or) 30th, and the eighth on June 2nd. The date of the Emperor's communication can hardly be the date of its subsequent publication as an edict, as has been suggested. There is no reason to reject the whole addition as an invention ; it is probably merely a mistake of a scribe, like " June 3rd " for the seventh session. But we must await Schwartz's forthcoming edition.

all who agreed with Justinian ; they had begged for pardon. Now the Emperor appeals to the Pope's earlier decisions from this later recantation. Yet nothing could be more absurd ; since when the Pope was free in Italy he had held the view to which he had returned when in sanctuary at Chalcedon.

The Emperor has concluded in his rage, however : " We have decided that it is not proper for Christians to recite his name in the diptychs, lest we should be found thus to be in communion with Nestorius and Theodore. . . . *But we pre-serve unity with the Apostolic See*, and we are sure that you will preserve it."

This was nonsense. Many of the bishops were the recent nominees of the Emperor. But probably most of them pre-ferred the Pope's policy. Hence their brief reply jumped at the last phrase, and ignored the rest. They said : " The Emperor's view is in harmony with the labours he has under-gone for the unity of the holy Churches. Let us therefore preserve unity with the Apostolic See of the holy Church of Rome according to his letter." The Emperor could take this as agreement or not, as he chose.

This was the seventh session. The Pope had given no directions to the Council, which was officially, at least, in ignorance of his present mind. They were in communion with him, and had apparently no intention of removing his name from the diptychs. Their course was therefore clear : the Emperor had ordered what was perfectly orthodox ; as the Pope gave no lead, they would obey the Emperor, and escape deposition, exile or imprisonment.

Hence, on June 2nd, the eighth and last session of the Council condemned the Three Chapters just as the Emperor had condemned them. Without the Pope's support what else could they do ? Deposition to bishops and clergy who should not accept the decree was enacted as usual.

The assembly was known to be partly packed, partly terror-ized. Would the Pope simply annul it ? The Emperor had no intention of permitting this.

He followed up the decision of the Council by exiling the Pope, the Roman Clergy, and the Western Bishops, im-prisoning two deacons. Some were sent to the mines. Dacius of Milan submitted and agreed to the Council.

Where Vigilius was sent is uncertain. Alone, seriously ill, after six years of banishment and coercion, all his attempts at compromise had failed. Was it best to placate the Emperor

and stop the persecution ?   After six months he had found a
way of explanation.   He had already condemned Theodore
of Mopsuestia, but had refused to condemn Ibas and Theodoret.
He issues a long document on February 23rd, 554, condemning
the extracts from Theodoret and not his person, and arguing
diffusely, but not convincingly, that the letter of Ibas was a
forgery, and was neither written by him nor approved at
Chalcedon.   By this ingenuity he is finally able to condemn
the Three Chapters and satisfy the Emperor.

No official confirmation of the Council by Vigilius is extant.
Evagrius states that he did confirm it.   Not till a year later
was he allowed to return to Italy ; but he never reached Rome,
dying at Syracuse on the 7th June, 555.

Persecutions and imprisonments had followed the Council
in Africa.   Many bishops held out there for years against the
Council.   The Illyrians remained in schism even under
St. Gregory the Great.   They repudiated Vigilius and his
successors as heretical intruders, declaring illogically that
they obeyed St. Leo and the former Popes, and " must ever
hold with the Apostolic Church of the Romans."

For the successor of Vigilius upheld the council.   He was
Pelagius, the deacon who had strengthened Vigilius against
the Emperor.   The Romans refused to accept him at first,
believing him guilty of the death of Vigilius.   With the
countenance of the great general Narses, he organized a
procession with litanies from the Church of St. Pancras to
St. Peter's, where, holding the Gospels and the Cross above
his head, he swore to his own innocence before the assembled
multitude.

His change of front was acceptable to his old friend the
Emperor, but in the West he said nothing about the Council.
The Illyrian schism obliged his successors to defend it, and it
came to be counted as the Fifth General Council.

Justinian had been successful in imposing his policy on the
Church, by coercion and terrorism.   The benevolent legislator
had developed into a tyrant.   At the death of Vigilius he
was seventy-three years old.   His theological vagaries had
turned the Church upside down for ten years, and he had ten
more years of reign.   During that time he saw the schisms
he had caused ; but not a Monophysite was gained to the
Church as a result of all the evil he had done.

His old vigour was now gone ; but still he delighted in his
last ten years to discuss with bishops.   Once again he tried

defining the faith.   Julian, bishop of Halicarnassus, a leading
Monophysite, had long before taught that our Lord's Body was
connaturally incorruptible, and was capable of suffering only
by a special dispensation ; he had been vigorously attacked
by Severus of Antioch, and the heretics were divided in
Aphthartodocetae or Julianists, and Severians or Phtharto-
latrae, or in Latin *Incorrupticolae* and *Corrupticolae*.   Justinian
hoped to gain over the Julianists, and issued an edict that all
Catholics were to hold the Julianist doctrine.   The Patriarch
Eutychius refused ;   he was seized in the church and exiled.
The Patriarch of Alexandria refused, and was threatened with
the same fate.   The Patriarch of Antioch assembled a council of
200 bishops, and sent a respectful remonstrance to the
Emperor, who fortunately died before he could do more
violence, or bring the Pope into the affair.

The fame of Justinian rests partly upon his buildings.
His policy against barbarian incursions was to build a series
of huge fortresses, into which the inhabitants could flock.
There were more than 80 of these across the Balkan peninsula
to the north ; further south there were 150 !   In Thessaly
and Greece were yet more.   Similarly around the Euxine ;
across Mesopotamia ; along the hinterland of Africa, where
many of the ruins of these enormous castles remain.   Walls
were sometimes 15 feet thick, 40 feet high—curtains inter-
spersed with towers.

But the pious Emperor was above all a builder of churches.
Everyone knows St. Vitale at Ravenna, with the portraits
in mosaic of Justinian and Theodora.   Great churches were
founded at Antioch, when it was superbly rebuilt after being
retaken from the Persians.   Theodora built the five-domed
Church of the Apostles at Constantinople.   But the master-
piece was the rebuilding of the Church of Constantine, St.
Sophia, after it had been burnt in the revolt of 332.   Its size
and magnificence and extravagant cost were equalled or
surpassed by its extreme beauty.   Its building became a focus
of legends, for the immense Church was finished in five years.
The genius of the architect, Anthemius, could not explain that
sublime dome.   An angel had made the plan ;   an angel
suggested the triple apse.   One day, the workmen had gone
to rest, and there was only a child of fourteen, son of a foreman,
to guard the building.   A white-robed figure asked the child
why the workmen would not finish the work of God and why
all went off to their food.   The boy replied that they would

soon come back. " Fetch them," said the stranger, " and I will stand guard till you return. I swear it by the Holy Wisdom in whose honour the Church is being built." The child's father informed Justinian, who sent the boy away to a distant land, so that the angel, as he believed him to be, should be bound by his oath to guard St. Sophia's for ever.

Justinian was above all proud of his theology. He would have been horrified to foresee that future ages would regard the Fifth Council as his disgrace, and would find his immortal glory not in wars carried on for him by Belisarius, Germanus and Narses, but in the code he had made by Trebonian and the Church he had built by Anthemius of Tralles.